Village London

Primrose Hill

Village London

The Observer's guide to the real London

Edited by
PETER CROOKSTON

Illustrated by
PAUL SHARP

THAMES AND HUDSON

The illustration on the first page of the book is of Sir William Powell's Almshouses
near All Saints', Fulham.

First published in book form 1978 by Arrow Books Ltd, London
© *The Observer* 1977, 1978

Illustrations © Arrow Books 1978

First Published in the United States by Thames and Hudson, Inc., 1979

Set in Monotype Times New Roman
Printed in the United States of America
by The Murray Printing
Westford, Mass.

ISBN 0-500-29150-X

Contents

Introduction

London is more than just a huge city, it is a collection of villages each with a distinct personality. If you know where these villages are, and what you can find in them, then you have the key to London's cornucopia of pleasures. This book gives you that key by providing detailed information and a character sketch of the most attractive and interesting villages in the capital.

They range from the quiet and rural – like Barnes and Richmond – to the bustling and cosmopolitan – like Bayswater and Soho. These villages give some idea of how big London is and what infinite variety it can provide. If Dr Johnson was never tired of London in the eighteenth century, imagine how much more it would delight him now. London in his day had an eastwards bias, towards the City, with its coffee houses, merchants' emporiums, lawyers' chambers and the docks. In the west it ended at Tyburn, which is now Marble Arch; Bayswater, as we know it today, crammed with Chinese restaurants and French *salons de thé*, did not exist. In the north, the line of Tottenham Court Road ran through fields, and Islington, now rich in Turkish restaurants and Italian delicatessens, was remarkable to him only as the home of his friend, Dr Oliver Goldsmith.

In addition to the huge expansion of London that has taken place since the eighteenth century, it is the immigrants to the capital who have given it such an exciting variety of ambience and taste. They came here in the wake of Britain's Empire-building and Hitler's European depredations, and stitched their own little patches of culture on to the great quilt of London, making Gerrard Street in Soho tinkle like a Kung-Fu movie, Bayswater cafés murmur with Austro-Hungarian melancholy, Islington delicatessens vibrate with vehement Italian.

Casual visitors could miss all this if they were unable to find the villages that give London its multiple fascination. Millions of people come to the capital every year and see very little of its real character. But if only they moved to the right or left of those well-beaten tracks through the West End and the usual tourist attractions, what delights they would discover, what oases to linger by.

In the past seventeen years I have lived in four London villages, and each has brought me different joys. In Barnes, the Thames gleamed from every street corner; in Highgate, kites danced above Parliament Hill Fields; in Islington, street markets blazed with vegetables; and in Fulham, where I live now, restaurants breathe hot garlic on the night.

The aim of this guide is to describe the quintessential character of each village and then to tell you how to get the best out of it – the best shops, restaurants, places of amusement and sights to see. The introductory character sketches are by famous residents of each village who have lived there long enough to appreciate the pleasures and the idiosyncracies of their neighbourhoods. The detailed information that follows the introduction is by journalists who specialize in consumer information – people like Lindsey Bareham, Sell Out and Food Editor of *Time Out* magazine, and Susan Campbell, co-author of *Cheap Eats in London*.

'Village London' was originally a highly successful series in the *Observer Magazine*. Here in book form it has been expanded and brought up to date. We have tried to ensure total accuracy, and at the time of going to press all the places mentioned were alive and thriving.

It's important to remember that this guide was put together by a group of people who enjoy living in London. As I wrote when I introduced the idea to *Observer Magazine* readers: imagine that you have come to London and fallen in with good company – a congenial set of companions who will show you the real London, the one that Londoners know and love.

Peter Crookston

Barnes

The nicest thing about Barnes is that people pass it by. It lies en-folded in a bend in the river, just off the main road south and, having no tube station, retains a village atmosphere which is both precious and soothing to those who live here.

It's a bit bland. Not many New Movements start over pints in the local pubs – but then its beer, London beer, is bad enough to render even Trotsky temperate. And yet the pubs themselves are very nice – provided you only drink shorts.

There are a lot of actors about – but plenty of *real* people as well – people who have lived and worked here for generations. Mr Mudd hangs our wallpaper, Mr Money plumbs, Mr Christmas put the fireplace in, and John Skipper combines carpentry with rowing for the Thames tradesmen. And Hornshaw and Son, electricians, *means* that. He really brings the lad along to help. Barnes is a family place – kids chat to the local coppers – there's a nice common and a pond to feed the ducks by. But avoid Sunday lunchtimes. Then the hearty hordes arrive with open-topped cars and heads to match – choking the place. Those in the know drink behind the locked garden gates of home.

Eating out's nice, too, but then if you're like us, 'out' really means out – so we rarely eat local. But we do spend a fortune on the best Chinese food in London – cooked and served by a friendly family at the Wei Hai Wei.

Some don't like the planes – we love them – hardly hear them now. Anyway, it's nice to look up and feel in touch with what's going on. And we see majestic Concorde at least twice a week. What fools those New Yorkers have been. We *like* Barnes, and after thirteen years we think it likes us. If it had a decent chip shop and Northern ale it would be heaven. But then I'd be twenty stone – so I will settle for how it is.

Colin Welland

WHAT TO SEE

BARNES POND Large, with an island, ducks, moorhens, a pair of swans and a goose called George. Surrounded by willows and cherries, pleasant old houses and with a nice pub.

BARNES TERRACE Fine eighteenth-century houses with ironwork and bow windows, Nos 3 and 7 especially handsome. Once overlooked the river, but GLC built a flood wall blocking downstairs views and marring a pretty stretch of riverside. Gustav Holst lived at No. 10.

BARNES COMMON Flat and scrubby, gorse bushes, blackberries, some fine trees, though the elms have suffered recently. (See Good for Kids.)

CASTELNAU Road of stately nineteenth-century villas, some very elegant ones near Hammersmith Bridge with arched windows and sweeping drives. TOMB OF SIR RICHARD BURTON St Mary Magdalen's RC church, North Worple Way. He was a dashing Victorian traveller and translator of *The Arabian Nights*. His doting wife commissioned this exotic tomb, shaped like an Arab tent, after Westminster Abbey had turned him down.

THE COACH HOUSE Fitzgerald Ave. Folly incorporating a seventeenth-century door and Ionic columns, it looks most peculiar in an ordinary street. Also in Mortlake is Thames Bank, a group of eighteenth-century houses overlooking the river. The Mortlake Brewery, of Boat Race fame, dominates the scene here.

ALL SAINTS CHURCH Lower Common South. Worth looking at for the many windows by Burne-Jones. Often locked, but key in the verger's house nearby.

WHERE TO EAT

A keen student of mid-twentieth-century fashions in eating places can find samples of all of them, each one fossilized in the year of its conception. Barnes High St, Church Rd and the river end of White Hart Lane are where most of Barnes's restaurants are to be found. Sample prices are for average three-course meal for two with wine. Open for lunch and dinner seven days unless otherwise indicated.

THE RIVER BISTRO 15 Barnes High St. T 876 1471. Most popular place for serious eating. Very good French bistro food (southern rather than northern). Informal, sixties atmosphere, run entirely by women, evenings only. Closed Sun. £10–£12.

MACARTHURS 147 Church Rd. T 748 3630. Early-seventies American style Hamburger place, extremely and deservedly successful, much favoured by families. £4–£5.

TETTHERS AT BARNES 5 White Hart Lane. T 876 3335. Done up in early-seventies plush, romantically situated near the river. The sort of food one might find in an old-fashioned, well-run country mansion. £12. Much admired for Sun lunch, £3·50 for four courses, excluding drink, children half-price, babies catered for; need to book, Closed Sat lunch, Sun dinner.

WEI HAI WEI 7 The Broadway, White Hart Lane. T 876 1165. Barnes's only Chinese restaurant advertising Peking cuisine. Well, SW13 is a long way from Peking, but there are devotees, £5–£6. Lunch Fri, Sat, Sun, dinner seven days a week.

THE OLD FISH SHOP (TOFS) 94 Church Rd. T 748 1038. Really was once the fish shop, now *the latest thing* in Barnes, beautifully decorated and fashionable with pop stars from Olympic Sound Studios opposite. Staider customers are not so sure that food and service are good enough for the money. £5–£6.

SAN MARCO 123 Church Rd. T 748 7374. Run-of-the-mill Italian food, including pizzas and breakfast. £4–£15. Closed Sun.

COPPERS 63 Barnes High St. T 876 4299. Tiny, friendly coffee shop and salad place, keeping shop hours. A restorative haven for local traders and shoppers. £2.

LE PETIT BEDON 8–9 Rocks Lane. T 876 2554. 'Too expensive and done up for Barnes' is current local opinion, but it is as good as, if not better, than anything in the West End. £14. Dinner only, closed Sun.

Picnics

Pepys found picnicking in Barnes 'mighty pleasant': it still is, and there are many nice secluded spots on the Common and along the towpath to the east of the village.

WHERE TO DRINK

Both Young's and Watney's have breweries in the area, but as Young's is real ale, our preferences are naturally in the direction of that company's several tied houses. The best pubs seem to be near the river and there's plenty of contrast for those who like entertainment or mixing with the locals.

RED LION Castelnau/Church Rd. Large free house with lawn at rear and cavernous functions room. Pool tables, busy atmosphere, affable staff. Mainly young crowd.

SUN INN Church Rd. Well-run pub opposite Barnes Pond, where you can sit outside and watch the ducks. Ind Coope beers. Good buffet.

COACH & HORSES 27 High St. Excellent drop of Young's real bitter served in a cosy room with access to a cobbled yard where you can drink in the open air. Local clientele loud and chatty.

BULL'S HEAD 373 Lonsdale Rd. Famous jazz pub with live modern or trad groups every night, plus Young's real ales to adequately quench their audiences' thirsts. Hot and cold food, three bars.

WATERMAN'S ARMS Lonsdale Rd/High St. Now selling Watney's fined bitter to compete with Young's brews next door at the Bull's Head. Interesting architecture and less crowded than the Bull.

WHITE HART The Terrace, Riverside. Large, comfortable, old-fashioned Victorian place overlooking the Thames. Young's house.

ALEXANDERS Castelnau/Church Rd. A newish wine bar with house wines from 35p a glass and a fairly wide choice of cheeses, pâtés, salads, etc., as well as hot meals. Tinny muzak but congenial atmosphere.

PICK OF THE BUNCH White Hart Lane. Wine bar recommended for unusually full catalogue of good French wines. The best vintages are pricey, but there are excellent lesser vintages at a moderate price and a fair selection of homemade food, mainly cold.

WHERE TO SHOP

Church Rd: HILLIER AND HILTON, No. 61. T 748 1810. Canopied flower shop always has a selection of flowers rarely seen in cities, often from private gardens. Arrangements to order.

P. J. RICE, PICTURE FRAMERS, No. 57. T 741 3813. Offer less traditional picture frames, and put special finishes on plain wood mouldings.

GORE AND PLAYER, No. 49. T 748 8850. Large corner antique shop, functional and decorative furniture and objects of no particular period.

Barnes High St: CACHET, No. 1. T 876 5048. Middle-price young fashionable clothes for women, much from French Connection; cotton, practical and pretty. Also espadrilles, accessories, handmade underwear.

YVONNE PETERS, No. 17. T 876 3775. Wide range of functional and decorative kitchen items: Le Creuset, Elizabeth David, stoneware by Pearson of Chesterfield and lots of whitewood. Copies of Victorian plate-racks made to order by local joiner.

REMEMBER WHEN 7 Rocks Lane. T 878 2817. Two floors of pine country furniture; large mirrors, tables, cupboards.

GOTHIC COTTAGE ANTIQUES 70 Station Road. T 876 2026. Mainly handstripped pine and country furniture.

White Hart Lane: TWO BITS, No. 1a. T 878 2868. Spacious and light, sells macramé and rope hanging baskets; handmade pottery by London potters; baskets from Hong Kong, Bangladesh and the Philippines; glassware.

RECYCLE, No. 43. T 876 8999. 'We find cast-ons for your cast-offs.' High quality, preferably designer label, secondhand clothes for men and women.

WHITE HART ANTIQUES, No. 71. T 876 6480. Specializes in four-poster beds, copies of antique design or to order, made by Welsh craftsmen of pine or mahogany; plus antique furniture.

REVIVAL, No. 76. T 876 3955. Victoriana, bric-à-brac and antiques piled high; lots of clocks, glass, jugs and china.

THE LUMBER ROOM 39 Lower Richmond Rd. T 876 2223. Shack-like shop specializes in dolls and Victorian toys, books and anything unusual. Lots of pretty and quaint items.

MORTLAKE ANTIQUES 69 Lower Richmond Rd. T 876 8715. Brother and sister do all buying and restoration. Specialize in longcase and wall clocks and old stripped pine furniture. Choice of items practical rather than decorative. Like most antique shops in the area, they are open Sat.

BUYING FOOD

No large supermarkets or street markets; local food shopping is provided by small, often family-run shops.

Church Rd: A. G. TAYLOR & SON, No. 129. T 748 1339. Mr Taylor has been a greengrocer for twenty years and staffs his shop with his family. Exotics in season, also bedding plants and flowers.

WALTONS, No. 125. T 748 1746. Minisupermarket providing English cheddars, a few Italian and French cheeses, cold meats, freshly ground coffee.

W. H. EDWARD, No. 86. T 748 1772. Delicatessen and grocery known for wide range of honeys. Also cold meats and pies, refrigerated French, English, Swiss, Italian and Dutch cheeses and Loseley yoghourt, sorbets, ice-cream and cream.

Barnes High St: G. C. JONES, No. 36a. T 876 8771. Mrs Jones provides a very efficient corner shop where she sells everything: newspapers; sweets, cigarettes, tinned, packaged and frozen foods; light bulbs and fuses. Open till 7.30pm.

LEONARD PARISH, No. 13. T 876 9441. One of three branches of family bakery. Bread handmade; plain buns to cream gateaux.

VILLA FERN, No. 16a. T 878 2468. Aroma of freshly ground coffee is overwhelming when you enter tiny branch of Ferns of Rathbone Place. Sell ten types of coffee beans, filter papers and all methods of brewing coffee. Also Jackson's-style groceries: smoked oysters; Gentleman's Relish; health foods; herbs, foreign biscuits and sweets.

KEEPING AMUSED

GALLERY 86 Castelnau. T 748 8123. 'The only male nude art gallery in Europe!' Drawings, slides, sculpture and engravings. Wed–Sat 2–6pm.

BARN ELMS RESERVOIR Contact 837 3300 for details and fishing permits. Lush vegetation and several forms of wildlife. Serious bird-watchers granted permits if member of recognized ornithological society. (See Good for Kids.)

ALTON GALLERY 72 Church Rd. T 748 0606/8244. 10am–5pm, closed Wed. Two-floor gallery, workshop downstairs. Specialists in all kinds of handfinished picture frames.

AMALGAM GALLERY 3 Barnes High St. T 878 1279. Pottery by famous names, jewellery, crafts and watercolours, prints. Most items under £100. Tue–Sat 10am–1pm, 2.15–6pm.

GOOD FOR KIDS

BARNES COMMON AND BARN ELMS (See What to See.) Good places to run wild, play Cowboys and Indians and hide-and-seek; flat grassland for football. Newts in the pond and streams for catching tiddlers.

MUDLARKING Footpath along the river from Hammersmith Bridge towards Putney is a good base for mudlarking and poking about at low tide – you might find among the old bottles and junk, a Victorian clay pipe or even a Roman coin.

PADDLING AND SWIMMING Paddling pool in the recreation ground off Vine Rd. Putney Swimming Pool, Upper Richmond Rd, T 789 1124, has a newish, L-shaped indoor bath plus a teaching pool. Children 10p, adults 35p.

FISHING (See Keeping Amused.) Serious fishermen with plenty of pocket money could catch delicious six-pound trout in Barn Elms Reservoir. No one under eight allowed, up to fifteen must be accompanied by an adult. Permits from gate house, Merthyr Terrace, T 748 3423; from £2·20 for fly fishing, 25p coarse fishing.

HOW TO GET THERE

BUSES 9, 9A, 22, 30, 33, 37, 72, 73.
BR Barnes, Barnes Bridge, Mortlake, from Waterloo.

Bayswater

Bayswater is a place of no fixed abode, ready at a moment's notice to pack its suitcases and move. Hidden away in Bayswater's bed-sitters and crumbling mansions are sad, seedy, secret agents, prineipessas in reduced circumstances, a deposed king or so, chirpy old whores, hypnotherapists, émigrés reminiscing in unison over coffee and sachermasochtorte, retired singers teaching the ungifted – 'Ah, *ma petite*, you have talent, but first you must work!'

Shouldn't one see it immediately, before it slips across the frontier? I stare at the street-guide, amazed. I *live* there, and didn't even know it. Bayswater, this slippery customer, this versatile *artiste*, the-voice-of-them-all, bounded by Edgware Road, Sussex Gardens, Queensway and Bayswater Road, sashays cheerily up and down the social thermometer. It has Praed Street, Hyde Park Gardens; Westbourne Grove, Orme Square; it has Lancaster Gate, innumerable mewses, it also has Paddington Station. None of these places knows each other, and as for Bayswater, you could ask the people next door.

I live on the edge of the Connaught sprawl, which elegant quarter has suddenly taken to calling itself Connaught Village – a most immodest alias. This 'village' is Connaught Street, where all in one go you can gather up a rare book, rare delicatessen, fruit, flowers, exquisite coffee beans, a chandelier, a lobster; visit a visagiste, get sung at in a French restaurant, or not in an Italian one, and find, wedged between puppies and antique shops, a simple launderette, where shepherds watch their smocks spin-dry while they read the *Financial Times*.

But where is Bayswater skulking? Taxi to Moscow Road, please. I sit in Maison Bouquillon, not really eating cakes. I can see it all. Any minute, now, a hand on the shoulder. 'I'm sorry, sir, I'm afraid I must ask you to accompany me to the Station.'

Fenella Fielding

WHAT TO SEE

AGHIA SOPHIA Moscow Rd. Greek Orthodox Cathedral in Byzantine style. Exterior depressingly grimy, but interesting interior of marble and mosaic. Entrance through Vicarage gate, Mon–Sat 10 am–5pm.

ST JAMES'S PARISH CHURCH Sussex Gdns. Damaged in the war, but one surviving window shows Queen Victoria's coronation. Post-war windows show people and events connected with the area's history: Fleming's discovery of penicillin, Paddington Station, Peter Pan.

10 HYDE PARK PLACE, Bayswater Rd. About four feet wide, said to be smallest house in London, lacking all basic amenities and so usually uninhabited and rather tatty.

PLAQUES on houses include J. M. Barrie, 100 Bayswater Rd; postal pioneer Sir Rowland Hill, 1 Orme Sq.; Lord Randolph Churchill, 2 Connaught Place; Marconi, 71 Hereford Rd. Only way to see Tyburn gallows plaque, and live to tell the tale, is by taking a bus past the traffic island at the beginning of Edgware Rd.

KENSINGTON PALACE T 734 6010. Refreshingly modest palace, bought by William III. Queen Victoria lived here from birth to accession. Her daughter Louise was responsible for the statue by the entrance (may she be forgiven). Attractive sunken garden, and Queen Anne's orangery newly restored to its original splendour. State apartments open March–Sept Mon–Sat 10am–6pm, Oct and Feb 10am–5pm, Nov–Jan 10am–4pm, Sun from 2pm. 20p, children 5p. KENSINGTON GARDENS AND HYDE PARK. More than 600 glorious acres in which to stroll, bask or meditate. Culture in the Serpentine Gallery, physical exertion in or on the Serpentine, ornate Italian gardens by Lancaster Gate and a megalith in the Dell. Temple designed for Queen Caroline by William Kent to complement her curving lake, and converted by the Victorians into a park-keeper's lodge, has recently been restored.

WHERE TO EAT

It is possible to take a brisk walk down Queensway and pass no fewer than thirty restaurants of ten different nationalities in four minutes. More restaurants up side streets, along Westbourne Grove, and along Craven Rd, which links the cheaper end of the trade to a cluster of dearer eating places close to Marble Arch. However there are a few places which are good enough (and reasonable enough) to make Bayswater worth a special visit. These are at the top of our list. Sample prices are for average three-course meal for two with wine. Open for lunch and dinner seven days unless otherwise indicated.

KALAMARAS 76–78 and 66 Inverness Mews. T 727 9122, 2564. Where all true Greek patriots and poets eat when in London. First restaurant has a wider menu plus live Greek music second is unlicensed and cheaper, but both have delicious, authentic Greek food and are happy places. Evenings only, £14 posh one, £8 other. Closed Sun.

ROMANTICA TAVERNA Moscow Rd. T 727 7112. This small candlelit restaurant serves the most delicious kleftikon (roast shoulder of lamb) and souvla (charcoal-grilled lamb fillet) in all Bayswater, according to local residents who have tried them all. £10. Open till 1.30 am seven days.

LE CHEF 41 Connaught St. T 262 5945. Small, so booking essential. Truly and eccentrically French. Snails, anchoïade, couscous. Closed Sat lunch, all Sun, Mon. £10–£12.

KAM TONG 59–61 Queensway. T 229 6065. Best of the many good Chinese restaurants in Queensway, especially for a lunch of tim sum (steamed dumplings). £3·50, drinking tea.

LEE HO FOOK 48 Queensway. T 229 8624. Kam Tong's more expensive brother. £7.

MAISON BOUQUILLON 41 and 45 Moscow Rd. T 229 8684.

LE RELAIS BASQUE 28 Westbourne Grove. T 229 2107. Both run by same organization. Former supplies charcuterie and delicious patisserie with a few hot dishes, including light breakfasts, latter more of a *salon de thé* but menu and hours similar to Moscow Rd. Both will do exquisite meals to take away, from a dinner for two in a bed-sit to an embassy banquet for 600 people. 45–75p for sandwiches. £1–£2 for tea, depending on how many cakes you succumb to. Moscow Rd premises now has *Salon de Thé* annexe. Westbourne Grove is open Sun afternoon and is great for a late lunch.

SUZETTE'S 34 Sussex Place. T 723 1199. Evenings only. Interesting menu includes roast piglet and duck with black cherries. Waiters exceptionally friendly. £10.

STANDARD INDIAN RESTAURANT 21–23 Westbourne Grove. T 727 4818. Old favourite with lovers of tandoori cooking. £9.

MAHARANI INDIAN TANDOORI 27 Westbourne Grove W2. T 727 5154. Discovered by those who can't get into the Standard to be almost as good, less claustrophobic and easier to read in. £8.

SATAY HOUSE 13 Sale Place. T 723 6763. Handy for Paddington station and St Mary's Hospital, and much the cleanest and prettiest place in this corner of Bayswater. Family from Penang serve authentic Malaysian food. £5–£6 (cheaper for a large group). Closed Mon lunch.

CONCORDIA NOTTE 29–31 Craven Rd. T 723 3725. *The* place for late dining and dancing. Ground floor CONCORDIA restaurant for lunch or dinner and a quieter life. Italian menu. £10 without dancing, £16 with. Closed Sun.

CORFU TAVERNA 84 Westbourne Grove. T 229 3773. Crowded at weekends. Really Greek, dinner and dancing place with live music. Downstairs is quite cosy. Usual Greek menu (the boss comes from Corfu). Evenings only. £10. Upstairs take-away; also restaurant, open all day and evening, £7.

SAN MARINO 26 Sussex Pl. T 723 8395. A fine example of Bayswater Italian restaurant style. Noisy, busy; food, waiters and decor indistinguishable from any of a half dozen similar restaurants in the area, but nevertheless good. £13. Closed Sun.

WHERE TO DRINK

VICTORIA TAVERN Strathearn Place. A genuine Victorian building this time, and decorated in an appropriate manner with open fires in colder weather. Real ale from hand pumps and friendly service.

SWAN TAVERN 66 Bayswater Rd (Lancaster Gate). Popular in the summer when the large forecourt overflows with young tourists and local residents. Excellent pub food and wide selection of UK and Continental beers.

BLACK LION 123 Bayswater Rd. Real ale, hot and cold food served all day in this popular Watney's house. Jukebox.

THE CHAMPION Wellington Ter. Large gay pub on Bayswater Rd serving Charrington's ales including the 'real' stuff.

RAILWAY TAP Porchester Rd/Bishops Bridge Rd. Large, rather brassy pub catering mainly for a young crowd. Truman's beers and food served at all times.

KING'S HEAD Moscow Rd. Just off Queensway, an oasis from the madding tourist crowd, serving Truman's ales and bar food. Large saloon with plenty of tables for a quiet tête-à-tête.

THE LEINSTER Ossington St/Moscow Rd. Small but very friendly pub with one large bar and one large landlord. Food all day and what appear to be the only indigenous locals!

WHERE TO SHOP

Bayswater Rd is one of London's great tourist attractions. Artists and craftsmen collect on Sundays and sell their wares from the railings outside the park. Most work sold is 'cheap and cheerful'.

Queensway Bustling street with shops open late at night even on Sunday. Bayswater end is peppered with *bureaux de change*, jean shops and newsagents who stock the world's newsprint. Westbourne Grove end dominated by Whiteley's department store, otherwise few shops of outstanding interest.

WORDS AND MUSIC, No. 21. T 229 0500. Large bookshop specializes in remainders chaotically ordered into a myriad of subjects. Also current paper and hardbacks, some children's titles.

UNITEX, No. 52. T 229 4394. Selling cut-price women's fashion clothes for over ten years. Buy out of season from designers and wholesalers; end of ranges, sample collections, seconds; supplement stock with cheap non-seconds lines. This branch specializes in Scottish clothes: Shetland jerseys, kilts, etc.

WHITELEY'S. T 727 6636. Began trading in 1863. In 1912 completed enormous premises in Queensway, established as a leading department store. Over 100 departments covering furnishing, clothing and accessories, emphasis on value for money. Good electrical department for radios, cassette players, etc.

Westbourne Grove Once busy and flourishing shopping centre now known as Westbourne Grave. Half the street's shops are empty because increased rents forced out the locals.

AFRICAN TRADING CENTRE, No. 59. T 229 8835/6. Vast macramé plant holders hang from ceiling in spacious shop. Clothes, beads, copperware primitive pictures, carvings, stoneware, ivory, ebony and entire snake and crocodile skins imported from Africa.

CENTRAL BAZAAR, No. 70. T 229 3388. Mr Nyman runs the shop his grandfather started over eighty years ago. Long bare-wood floored shop specializes in English china and pottery and can match some patterns over fifty years old. Displays on walls.

S. LINDSEY & SON, No. 10. T 229 1794. Old-established silverware and jewellery shop in a Tudor cottage, offering wide range of vanishing services including replating of old silver, pearl restringing. Watchmaker and jeweller on premises. Knock for admission.

FRENCH KITCHEN & TABLEWARE SUPPLY CO., No. 60. T 229 5530. Showroom that doesn't encourage, but doesn't mind, retail trade. French cooking utensils, porcelain, earthenware, glass, cutlery.

Praed St: BRODIES SPORTS, No. 107. T 262 5130. Specializes in adult and children's clothes; equipment for golf, tennis, squash, cricket, rugby, table tennis, and boxing. Range of firearms and shotguns.

WAREHOUSE, No. 129. T 723 8033. Lively colourful shop, bulk-buys men's and women's high-fashion clothes. Jeans, T-shirts, dresses, separates from France, Italy, Hong Kong. Fast-changing stock, regular bargains.

VIRGIN RECORDS Marble Arch/Edgware Rd. T 402 9748. All albums on British catalogue sold at discount prices. Weekly top fifty (compiled in conjunction with music papers) sold at £1–£2 off. Strong on imports from America, Japan, Ireland, Jamaica, France, Germany and Holland. Stock most punk labels!

Connaught St Strong village feel to this clutch of shops tucked between Edgware Rd, Bayswater Rd and Paddington. Inhabitants are among wealthiest in London, so shops are high class and specialist offering a personal service. CERAMIC CONSULTANTS, No. 12. T 723 7278. Hundreds of designs, many with Design Centre awards, of hand-painted, silkscreened and hand-glazed tiles and plates can be viewed, ordered and bought. All designs by Tarquin Cole and sister Tina, work done in their father's Rye pottery.

DUKE STREET KENNELS, No. 14. T 262 0299. Dogs of all breeds can be ordered for export. Grooming, shampooing and clipping service; doggy toys and foods.

WILLIAM MANSELL, No. 24. T 723 4154. Frederick Charles Salisbury has been repairing and restoring old and modern clocks since 1946, also jewellery and silver repairs. Sells old silverware, other items.

BLUE AND WHITE HOUSE, No. 25. T 262 7900. Seventeenth-century to late-Georgian furniture, rugs and rare books – mostly first editions, also large collection of WW II intelligence and escape stories.

IAN HODGKINS, No. 37. T 723 1623. Antiquarian bookseller, specializes in pre-Raphaelite, art nouveau and 1860s illustrated books. Used to specialize in Victorian children's books so still has good selection. Also book-related ephemera: elaborate book marks, trade cards and pre-1900 letter-headings.

VANESSA LEE, No. 59. T 262 0200. Women's day, evening and cruise-wear clothes, classic style, mostly Continental. Gowns at up to £400.

MAGGIE 4 Porchester Place. T 402 9977. Pretty, simple and casual clothes to suit women of all ages and sizes. Lots of co-ordinates from France, Sweden, Italy, England, Casablanca and Bali. Excellent range of swimwear all year round.

The Unexpected

PHILLIPS WEST 2 Salem Rd. T 221 5303. Company established in 1796 as a fine art auctioneer, rather grand building holds regular auctions of nineteenth-century, Edwardian and good quality reproduction furniture. Viewing every Wed 9 am–7 pm, sale every Thurs from 10 am. Average 400 lots.

BUYING FOOD

Very wide range of shops, often open late, catering for cosmopolitan, rather transient community.

Queensway: KAM YUEN, No. 35. T 221 5713. Rather stark small supermarket. Tinned and dried Chinese foods, sauces and cooking implements; Chinese cookery books.

PATISSERIE FRANCAISE, MAISON PECHON, No. 127. T 229 0746. Pierre Georges Pechon maintains high standards set by his grandfather in 1925. Rotation of 116 different pastries (made on premises) and twenty-nine breads, including excellent French loaf (baked daily nearby) and melt-in-the-mouth croissants.

Moscow Rd: ATHENIAN GROCERY, No. 16a. T 229 6280. John Joannides and his family run Greek/Arabic/Middle-Eastern food shop. Fetta from Bulgaria and Cyprus, honey from Greece, wide range of Greek and Arabic breads (fresh daily), excellent range of spices for Arab cooking. Also delicious fat olives, own taramasalata and humous; Greek wines, olive oil, tinned groceries.

OLYMPIC FOOD CENTRE, No. 21. T 727 3008. International delicatessen, grocery and mini supermarket/off-licence. Fresh-ground coffee, fair selection of cheeses, Continental sausage, cold meats.

MAISON BOUQUILLON, No. 45. T 229 8684. Top quality French patisseries, brioches, croissants, cakes, tarts and biscuits.

Westbourne Grove: LE RELAIS BASQUE, No. 28. T 229 2107. Branch of Maison Bouquillon selling same mouth-watering selection.

TWENTY-FOUR-HOUR SUPERMARKET, No. 68. T 229 3198. One of London's few twenty-four-hour supermarkets; tinned, frozen and packet foods, tobaccos, milk, cheese, fresh vegetables, etc.

D. MORGAN, No. 80. T 229 5239. Fish displayed on a marble slab in the middle of the open and canopied shop. Daily specials chalked up on board.

ASIAN STORES, No. 58. T 727 5033. Reminiscent of an Arab shop. Keep a lot of Asian spices, meat, groceries and a range of Asian and Oriental magazines.

CORFUTRADE, No. 97. T 221 5972. Large spacious delicatessen sells cold meats, smoked fish, Continental sausage, pâtés, olives, Greek pastries, Greek cheeses and own taramasalata; French bread, spices, tinned and bottled groceries. Also off-licence with wines from most countries.

Connaught St: MARKUS, No. 13. T 723 4020/262 4630. Delicious aroma of coffee, sell thirty-two types of beans, all roasted on premises. Also sell all methods for making, and small selection of teas and biscuits.

TROPICAL FRUITS, No. 63. T 402 5770. No. 29. T 262 5887. Tropical fruits in season along with more usual fruit and veg and fresh farm eggs.

JOHN GOW, No. 55. T 723 1612. Excellent selection of fresh fish displayed on the slab. Always have live and cooked crab and lobster.

ANDREANOFF'S DELICATESSEN, No. 65. T 723 9728. Sells fresh bread from Floris on Sunday. Corner shop always has cooked chicken and piece of beef, a whole brie and a selection of salads. Also off-licence and grocery.

Kendal Street: LA RESERVE, No. 47. T 402 6920. Robert Rolls runs very attractive off-licence with vintage clarets, burgundies, champagne and port. Will send current price list.

CRISPINS, No. 24. T 262 9122. Very best in groceries and delicatessen; French and English cheeses cut from the whole cheese, excellent selection cold meats and saucissons, specially made pies, pâtés from France, several different cheesecakes and patisseries made fresh daily. Also Loseley ice-creams, French frozen produce, tinned and bottled groceries, fresh coffee, salads.

Picnics

Almost anywhere in Hyde Park or Kensington Gardens, but remember the £100 litter fine. Sit by the fountains on Marble Arch island, and watch buses whizz by.

KEEPING AMUSED

OFF-BEAT TOURS OF LONDON 66 St Michael's St. T 262 9572. Discover architectural, historical and sociological quirks of the capital. Usually 60p, students 50p and children under 14 free. Lasts about 1½ hours.

PORCHESTER BATHS Porchester Hall, Porchester Rd. T 229 3226. 'The most luxurious Turkish and Russian bath suites in West London.' Gaudy but nice. Refreshments available inside. Ladies: Tue, Thur, Fri. Gentlemen: Mon, Wed, Sat. 9am–9pm (last ticket issued at 7pm). Bath with shampoo about £4. Swimming, private baths also available.

QUEEN'S ICE SKATING CLUB Queensway. T 229 0172. 65 by 220 foot well-lit rink, refreshment area at one end, glassed-in bar upstairs overlooking activities. Mon–Fri 10am–12 noon, 2–5pm, 7–10pm; Sat same, but 7.30–10.30pm. Price 50p–£1 depending on time of day. Membership 25p, skate hire 25p, spectators 25p.

FANGS DISCO Praed St. T 262 7952. Mock-Dracula decor, basket meals. Live music Wed. Mon–Sat 8.30pm–2am. Non-members welcome. Entrance fee from 60p–£1·70.

JOAN PRICE'S FACE PLACE 31 Connaught Street. T 723 6671. Set up by former beauty editor of *Harpers and Queen*. Complete body make-over. Manicure, electrolysis, facials, sun-lamp treatment, lessons in cosmetic application. Mon–Fri 10am–6pm.

Hyde Park: SERPENTINE GALLERY T 402 6075. Exhibitions of contemporary art. 10am–5, 6 or 8pm summer, 4pm winter. Free. Music (brass, jazz, folk) and dance (experimental, mime) most weekends throughout summer. 3–4pm. Contact Annette Morreau, Arts Council of Great Britain, T 629 9495.

BOATING T 262 3751. 10am–7pm (last ticket). Rowing boats 90p, single outrigger 90p, sailing dinghies £1·25, cycle craft 90p, kayak 90p, £1 returnable deposit.

SWIMMING 10am–6pm. Adults Mon–Fri 20p, weekends 30p: children Mon–Fri 10p, weekends 15p. Lifeguards on duty. Winter months, swimming for adults only 6–10am.

OLYMPIC CASINO CLUB 79 Queensway. T 727 3505. By membership under normal gaming regulations (48 hours must elapse before playing commences) Membership £5 per year. 5pm–4am, seven days a week, Sat until 2am. Elegant and subdued, collar and tie for men. French and American roulette, blackjack, punto banco, baccarat. Restaurant, predominantly French cuisine.

GOOD FOR KIDS
BIRD-WATCHING Nuthatches, grey wagtails, teal, wigeon, red-breasted mergansers, golden plovers, lapwings, woodcock, tree pipits, redstarts, pied flycatchers and lesser spotted woodpeckers were among the ninety-one species recently recorded in the two parks.

WILDLIFE If the birds pall, there are squirrels, hedgehogs, rabbits, bats, woodmice and butterflies. Best place to start is the sanctuary by the Hudson Memorial, north of the Serpentine.

ELFIN OAK Gnarled oak stump from Richmond Park transformed in 1930 by sculptor Ivor Innes into an elvish fantasy which has delighted generations of children in Kensington Gardens.

PETER PAN Every old-fashioned child's favourite statue, on the spot where Peter lands when visiting Kensington Gardens. The model was Nina Boucicault, the first actress to play the part.

PLAYGROUNDS Swings, slides and roundabouts beside the Elfin Oak at the north-west corner of Broad Walk, and a smaller collection near Lancaster Gate. Round Pond for model boat enthusiasts.

SERPENTINE (See Keeping Amused.)

HOW TO GET THERE
UNDERGROUND Paddington, Marble Arch, Lancaster Gate, Queensway, Bayswater.
BUSES 2, 2B, 6, 7, 8, 12, 15, 16, 16A, 26, 27, 30, 36, 36A, 36B, 73, 74, 74B, 88, 137, 500, 616.

Bloomsbury

The sociology of where people choose to live in London is quite a complex one. There are theories about it which sound silly, but which experienced estate agents say are constantly upheld. There is the theory, for example, that upward-mobility people like to live on hills (Hampstead, Highgate, Kingston), and the theory that you'll never get a City businessman to live anywhere in central London – he has to feel that he is in some way in touch with 'the country'.

There is the north–south hypothesis, which is quite simply that people from the north of England prefer north London, while people from the south-east like south and west London. There is also the point-of-entry idea; this one says that you tend to live in an area vaguely served by the station or terminal where you first arrived in London. Thus Australians, arriving at Heathrow, discovered Earl's Court, the Continentals like the purlieus of Victoria, and the Irish quarters of London are defined as being however far you can walk from Euston carrying two suitcases – Islington, Camden Town, and for the strong ones, Kilburn.

Bloomsbury can certainly be reached from Euston on foot – even carrying two suitcases – which might explain some of its attraction for me. Part of its attraction, too, is pure (though initially unconscious) nostalgia. A friend seeing Doughty Street for the first time revealed it to me: 'It is so Dublinesque. You could not have chosen a part of London that looks more like Dublin.' And that indeed is true; the Georgian shapes of houses and squares in Bloomsbury give me a constant pleasure that is not unmixed with an echo from my native city.

Bloomsbury is like Dublin in other respects, too; it is curiously classless, being neither associated with upward-mobility nor with urban decay, and it has a character rooted in tradition. In Lamb's Conduit Street, there are people whose grandparents were born in the same street. You don't often get that sense of continuity in London. The Italian community, which is the ethnic mark of Bloomsbury, has been living in this part of London since the seventeenth century, when the Italians first came as fencing masters.

The neighbourhood also has the kind of little shops that are disappearing in big cities – cobblers, haberdashers – and with all that it's so near the *centre* of everything; the West End and Oxford Street and the British Museum and Fleet Street and the City and big stations. That makes me feel cosy, somehow. It's nicely served by pubs, too – the Lamb in Lamb's Conduit Street is the most famous one – though poor on restaurants; the Mille Pini, a tiny but wonderful and amazingly cheap restaurant just off Queen Square is the only really good one that comes to mind (some of the wine bars are OK). It also has special unexpected bonuses – such as one of the best nursery schools in the country; and of course the whole place is a hypochondriac's paradise, being quite stuffed with hospitals.

Mary Kenny

WHAT TO SEE

BRITISH MUSEUM Gt Russell St. Overwhelming national collection of antiquities – Egyptian, Western Asiatic, Greek and Roman, Medieval, Oriental, Prehistoric and Romano-British, plus coins and medals, prints and drawings, manuscripts. Public films and lectures held in the Lecture Theatre, Assyrian Basement. Additional films relating to special exhibitions may be included periodically. The Museum Society also offers tours, lectures and social activities for its members. Contact British Museum Information Booth for details. Mon–Sat 10am–5pm, Sun 2.30–6pm. Closed New Year's Day, Good Fri, Christmas Eve and Day, Boxing Day. Free.

DICKENS HOUSE 48 Doughty Street. Dickensiana for addicts in his only surviving London home. Mon–Sat 10am–5pm. 50p, 40p students, 20p children.

THOMAS CORAM FOUNDATION 40 Brunswick Sq. Offices of old Foundling Hospital, with Court Room and Picture Gallery exactly as they were in original building. Marvellous collection of paintings by Hogarth, Gainsborough, Rysbrack and others; a fair copy of the score and parts of 'The Messiah' bequeathed by Handel, one of the earliest governors; and a most poignant display of tokens left with abandoned children. Mon–Fri 10am–4pm. Closed Bank Holidays and during conferences. 30p, 15p children.

WOBURN WALK AND DUKE'S RD Attractive rows of bow-windowed shop-fronts, *c.* 1822.

JEWISH MUSEUM Woburn House, Upper Woburn Place. Display of ritual art and antiquities. Mon–Thur 2.30–5pm, Fri and Sun 10.30am–12.45pm. Closed Sat and Jewish holidays. Free.

WELLCOME INSTITUTE 183 Euston Rd. Most of fascinating collection illustrating history of medicine has been withdrawn in preparation for move to Science Museum (see South Kensington), but small displays of primitive and non-Western medicine remain, with historical pharmacies. Mon–Fri 10am–5pm. Free.

PERCIVAL DAVID FOUNDATION 53 Gordon Sq. Superb collection of Chinese ceramics. Mon 2–5pm, Tue–Fri 10.30am–5pm, Sat 10.30am–1pm. Closed Bank Holidays and Sat preceding Bank Holiday Mon. Free.

COURTAULD INSTITUTE GALLERIES Woburn Sq. Monet, Renoir, Cézanne, Gauguin, Van Gogh and many more – an unbelievable range of French Impressionist and Post-Impressionist masterpieces. Roger Fry's Bloomsbury collection is among the other bequests to London University displayed here. Mon–Sat 10am–5pm, Sun 2–5pm. Closed New Year's Day, Good Fri, Christmas Eve and Day, Boxing Day. Free.

IRAQI CULTURAL CENTRE 177 Tottenham Court Rd. Frequent exhibitions, lectures, concerts, poetry readings. Ring 637 5831 for details and to check summer holiday closing. Reference library open Mon–Fri 10am–4pm.

BUILDING CENTRE 26 Store St. Bricks to door knobs, kitchens to saunas, in permanent displays and special exhibitions. Bookshop and information service. Mon–Fri 9.30am–5.30pm.

WHERE TO EAT

Most of Bloomsbury's potential restaurant customers, especially those who want to lash out a bit, are to be found eating in Soho. Even in its literary and artistic heyday 'Bloomsbury' ate more in Charlotte Street than it did in its own village. Sample prices are for average three-course meal for two, with drink. Open for lunch and dinner seven days unless otherwise indicated.

MILLE PINI 33 Boswell St. T 242 2434. Only restaurant that comes to *any* of the local inhabitant's minds when asked to say where they'd most like to eat. Excellent pasta, particularly lasagne. Very crowded, but deservedly so. £5. Closed Sun.

CONCA-D'ORO 54 Red Lion St. T 242 6964. COSMOBA 9 Cosmo Place. T 837 0904. Both Italian, good food, possibly less lively and lovable than the Mille Pini. £6–£8. Closed Sat lunch and all day Sun.

SPAGHETTI HOUSE 11a Sicilian Ave. T 405 5215. All this chain are reliable and good value. Extra nice because it has tables outside in traffic-free precinct. £6.

LA TAVOLA CALDA 3–4 Liverpool Victoria House, Southampton Row. T 405 6658. Another in Spaghetti House chain, an enormous range of hot and cold Italian food on a long self-service counter. £4. Closed Sun.

FRYER'S DELIGHT 19 Theobald's Rd. Open Mon–Sat, 12 noon–11pm. NORTH SEA FISH BAR 8 Leigh St. Open Mon–Sat 11.30am–2pm and 5–11pm. Closed Sun. Both first class and spotlessly clean, serve freshest fish available, as well as other food like chicken and pasties, with tea of coffee. 90p per head.

MOTIJHEEL 53 Marchmont St. T 837 1038. SHABAG 52 Tavistock Pl. T 837 8552. Both cheap Indian restaurants, popular with students and local office people. Motijheel £6, Shabag £5.

SHARUNA HOTEL 107 Gt Russell St. T 636 5922. Unusual and delicious Indian vegetarian food served in rather sombre hotel dining room near British Museum. £6.

RUSSELL HOTEL Russell Sq. T 837 6470. KINGSLEY HOTEL Bloomsbury Way. T 242 5881. Two places under Trust House Forte management give glimpse of grandeur of Bloomsbury's oldest hotels. Carvery at former is chef-assisted, latter is DIY, both paradise for carnivores with unlimited helpings from choice of four roasts. £9, drink extra at both.

SALVATION ARMY CANTEEN Judd St. T 387 1656. Very institutional, but three-course lunch for about £1·25 a head. Mon–Fri lunch only.

YWCA CENTRAL CLUB 16 Gt Russell St. T 636 7512. Cafeteria prides itself on home cooking. Roast turkey 66p, semolina pudding 16p. Mon–Fri breakfast, lunch, tea and supper. Sat–Sun lunch only.

Picnics

Most squares are open to public, the largest being Russell Square with a small sand-pit in which to dump toddlers. Quietest is graveyard behind Regent Sq. Statue of Mahatma Gandhi in Tavistock Square might discourage gluttony in slimmers.

WHERE TO DRINK

THE LAMB 94 Lamb's Conduit St. Possibly the nicest pub in central London, serving Young's real ale, a huge selection of malt whiskies and excellent bar food at lunchtime. Lovely tiles and windows. Small backyard for summer drinking.

PINDAR OF WAKEFIELD 328 Grays Inn Rd. A Courage house with interesting curved windows and Victorian decor. Three bars and jazz, music hall and theatre throughout the week. Four minutes from King's Cross station.

MUSEUM TAVERN 49 Gt Russell St. Bang opposite British Museum, crowded lunchtime, but worth a visit in the evening when an excellent drop of Watney's fined bitter can be savoured. Mock but tasteful Victorian decor.

THE ENTERPRISE 38 Red Lion St. Small but comfortable bar with Charrington's real ale.

ONE TUN Goodge St. Just a step across Tottenham Court Rd finds this congenial Finch's pub with central bar, Platform 280 fruit machine, jukebox (often too loud!) and trad jazz on Wed, Sat, Sun. A bit pricey.

LORD WELLINGTON 31 University St. Watney's fined bitter available in this cosy little pub. Surfeit of hospital staff at lunchtime in case you should be taken ill!

WHERE TO SHOP

Narrow streets surrounding the British Museum and Faculties of London University house more specialist and academic bookshops than anywhere else in London. Many date back to the early nineteenth century and retain their original character. Bloomsbury is also rich in old-established and family-run specialist shops.

Gt Russell St: THEOSOPHICAL BOOK-SHOP, No. 68. T 405 2309. Books related to Eastern and Western religions and mysticism, psychology, metaphysics, astrology and yoga.

CLOVER PRESS, No. 66. T 405 9091. Old established commercial stationers supplying local university students, academics, hotels and offices.

WESTAWAY AND WESTAWAY, No. 65. T 405 4479. Cheapest Scottish knitwear particularly cashmere and Shetlands, blankets, wool shirts, gloves, scarves.

COLLET'S CHINESE GALLERY, No. 40. T 580 7538. Apart from Mao's Red Book in various languages, Chinese counting beads, books, beautiful painted paper kites, modern and antique jewellery, small antiques, modern and antique paintings and many small decorative items.

Museum St: M. AYRES, No. 31. T 636 2844. Books, prints and antiquities. Antiquarian book dealer stocking some of earliest titles and specializing in Incunabula (pre-sixteenth century), sixteenth-, seventeenth- and eighteenth-century illustrated books. Also art reference and classical titles. Print dealers, earliest eighteenth century, English up to 1940. Egyptian, Roman and Greek antiquities.

CAMEO CORNER, No. 26. T 637 0981. Established in 1903. Cameos, antique jewellery dating back to Roman times, but mostly Victorian, art deco and art nouveau, also modern jewellery by designers leaving college. Will do complicated repairs and alterations.

ATLANTIS, No. 49a. T 405 2120. New, secondhand and out of print books on microscopy and all aspects of the occult, from astrology to Zen, alchemy and magic.

TIBET SHOP, 10 Coptic St. Everything made by Tibetan refugees. Stock includes embroidered felt boots, cotton shirts, various wool jackets, a range of shoulder bags, some jewellery, religious cards, posters, books and buddhas.

New Oxford St: VIRGIN RECORDS, No. 108. T 580 6177. Largest branch, whole floor devoted to deletions and sale stock. All albums in British catalogue at discount, large discount on albums in their weekly top 50. Imports from America, Japan, Ireland, Jamaica, France, Germany and Holland plus all the punk labels.

SMITHS, No. 53. T 836 4731. Established in 1830, this shop, still with original signs intact is the place for umbrellas, walking and shooting sticks.

WESTAWAY AND WESTAWAY, 29 Bloomsbury Way. T 405 2128. Largest branch (see Gt Russell St).

Southampton Row Full of hotels, booking offices, restaurants and souvenir shops.

MORGANS STATIONERY, No. 102. T 405 0027. Supermarket style, buy in bulk, always have special offers on commercial stationery. Also souvenirs and gift items.

UNITEX, No. 82. T 405 6565. Selling cut-price women's fashion clothes for over ten years. Buy out of season from designers and wholesalers: end of ranges, sample collections, seconds and supplement the stock with cheap non-seconds lines.

J. I. HORWIT, No. 94. T 405 0749. Very fine selection of antique jewellery can be viewed at Mr Faber's old-fashioned jewellers. Specialize in jewels and silver.

A. LYNES & SON, No. 86. T 405 8912. Established in 1844, this bespoke tailor sells men's suiting and cloth by the metre. For export they can fit in three hours and complete in four days.

ATHENA, No. 76. T 405 2742. Athena manufacture everything they sell and provide good quality art reproduction at a price that everyone can afford. A choice of cards, posters and prints either block-mounted, aluminium-framed, in a classical wooden frame or without a frame.

Sicilian Ave Pretty paved-over arcade that houses several unusual shops.

ADEPTUS, No. 9. T 405 5603. Showroom for adaptable, convertible and cheap solid foam furniture with removable covers. Free delivery, leaflets and fabric samples on request.

E.H.W. & CO., No. 12. T 405 5509. Stamps and coins bought and sold. General stock of coins but 'one of the world's best collections' of George VI and Elizabeth II stamps.

Judd Street: T. V. ANTONI, No. 101. T 387 1348. Handmake high-fashion boots, sandals and shoes for women on the premises. All the designs are on display, and Mr Antoni will make to order or may be able to fit you from stock. Supplies London's leading stores and shoe shops.

RON BROWN, No. 100. T 837 3806. Bespoke framer does all work on premises and restores oil paintings. Also sells Medici and Royle greeting cards, odd pieces of pottery and cheap oil paintings.

KNOBS AND KNOCKERS, No. 61–65. T 387 3991. Use some original moulds for reproduction Georgian, Victorian early Elizabethan and modern door furniture. Everything displayed and priced to make choosing easier. Next door external, louvre and wardrobe doors.

Brunswick Shopping Centre, designed by Patrick Hodgkinson, has flats above it. Many entrances, shops form series of courtyards where the wind whistles round your legs. Shops of interest include: MODELSPORTS for modelling kits, sports equipment, replica guns, toys and soft toys: HENRY MARCHANT decorative glassware; GEMROCKS for gemstones and tumbling equipment; and ZODIAC RECORDS.

Lamb's Conduit St: WORKSHOP, No. 83. T 242 5335. Small gallery run by cartoonist Mel Calman holds three-weekly changing exhibitions varying from cartoons to original artwork for commercial illustration. Enormous stock of original cartoons by all leading cartoonists, also prints, lithographs and collectors' items such as Heath Robinsons.

GALLERY 57, No. 70 T 405 1408. Well-chosen mix of fine art reproduction; wrapping papers, cards, children's books and novelty items, basketware, T-shirts and gifty items. Also framing and block mounting service. Weekdays 9am–6.30pm, Sat 9am–6pm.

COPPERFIELD, No. 68. T 405 6016. Plenty of time needed to sort through packed rails of women's clothes. Factory outlet selling many leading fashion names at half the normal price. Tends to be slightly out of harmony with the seasons but great bargains.

ARIES, No. 57. T 405 0855. For over six years Patsy and Susanne have been selling 'everything that a man needs' in their boutique. Smart fashionable French and Italian suits, trousers, shirts, sweaters and accessories.

HOLBORN VILLAGE CRAFT SHOP, 7 Rugby St. T 405 4281. Terrific bargains in beautiful handmade knitwear. Shawls, Arran jerseys, mohairs, jerseys decorated with beads and embroidery, some with matching skull caps. Anything can be knitted to order. Handmade pottery, jewellery, prints, cards, small gift items. Mon–Sat 10am–6pm.

The Unexpected

BLOOMSBURY BOOKSHOP, 31 Gt Ormond St. T 242 6780. Secondhand bookshop specializing in jazz literature. Owned by John Chilton, jazz trumpeter of Feetwarmers and George Melly fame, but run by his wife. American jazz fans make pilgrimages there when visiting London.

KING'S BOOKSHOP, 17a Rugby St. T 405 4551. A new bookshop run by Gerald King in the street where both Dylan Thomas and Sylvia Plath lived.

DAVENPORTS, 51 Gt Russell St. T 405 8524. Huge metal painted sign of a rabbit being pulled out of a top hat, window displays a fraction of stock of jokes, tricks, smoke bombs, funny and terrifying masks. This is where conjurers and magicians buy the tricks of their trade, half of which are not on display. Also fireworks all year round.

LOUIS BONDY, 16 Little Russell St. T 405 2733. Miniature books all under $3\frac{1}{2}$ in. high and as tiny as $\frac{1}{2}$ in. A lot nineteenth-century, but some much earlier, and some modern – usually Hungarian. A few are still sold with original magnifying glass. Good range of old children's books, sixteenth- and seventeenth-century mystical emblem books and art books, including caricatures.

E. H. RANN, 21 Sicilian Ave. T 405 4759. Tie and heraldic shield specialists for over forty years. Over 1000 ties in stock – public schools, university, regimental and services, medical and professional – and will make up ties to specifications. Main business is hand-painted shields.

BUYING FOOD

SHARUNA, 107 Gt Russell St. Delicatessen and grocery part of the Indian-run hotel and excellent vegetarian restaurant next door. Delicious hot and cold snacks to take away, pickles, spices, popadoms, Indian groceries.

CARWARDINES 5 Victoria House, Southampton Row. T 405 4115. Fifteen blends of coffee roasted on premises. Also equipment for all methods for coffee making.

Tavistock Place, Marchmont St Until the arrival of enormous concrete Brunswick Centre, food shopping centred around these two streets. Despite excellent and enormous branch of Safeway, parade of old-established food shops still very popular.

Tavistock Place: ROLANDO'S PATISSERIE, No. 33. T 387 3876. Delicious French loaves and rolls can be bought hot from the oven at this Swiss patisserie. Florentines, fresh cream gateaux; experts at decorating cakes with flaked and piped chocolate.

CONTINENTAL STORES, No. 54. T 837 6616. All sorts of delicious surprises in small well-stocked grocery/delicatessen. Belgian pâtés, ham on the bone, French and Italian sausage and cheeses. Nuts, spices, dried herbs sold loose; three blends of fresh coffee beans sold whole but not ground. Frozen and tinned groceries and Continental delicacies like marrons glacés.

SAMUEL GORDON, 76 Marchmont St. T 387 2271. Displays fresh fish on a large central slab; smoked fish, shellfish, live eels.

SAFEWAY Brunswick Shopping Centre. Bit of a treat because large branch never seems very busy. Weigh your own fruit and vegetables; refrigerated meat and fish; off-licence and delicatessen counter which regularly has a whole brie; good range groceries and hardwares.

KEEPING AMUSED

CENTRAL SCHOOL OF ART AND DESIGN Southampton Row. T 405 1825. Student degree exhibitions open to the public end June/beginning July – ceramics, textiles, graphics, photography. Also regular exhibitions for students throughout academic year frequently open to public.

JEANNETTA COCHRANE THEATRE. T

242 7040. Attached to Central School, it provides space both for student activities and occasional professional performances.

CENTRAL SCHOOL OF ART FILM SOCIETY Room G9, Jeannetta Cochrane Theatre. Guests 30p, members 20p. Screenings of 'classic' or little-shown films Wed 5.45pm during academic year. For further information contact Students Union Office, T 405 3898.

BOOK FAIR Imperial Hotel, Russell Sq. T 837 3655. Over fifty provincial booksellers monthly displaying between 18 000 and 20 000 volumes. Held in the hotel ballroom where turquoise, purple and gilt decor provides an outlandish setting for books ranging in price from 50p to £5000. Every third Mon and Tue: Mon noon–8pm, Tue 10am–3.30pm.

BRUNSWICK GALLERY 102 Judd St. T 837 0604. Mon, Tue, Thur, Fri 10.30am–5pm, Sat 10am–1pm, Wed 10am–7pm. Ron Field organizes one-man exhibitions of contemporary art in front gallery, representative work of previously-shown artists in back.

TONBRIDGE CLUB Judd St. T 837 4406. (National College of Karate) classes held every day, beginners to black belt. Visitors/observers welcome. 11am–10pm. Also public squash court on premises.

EMI INTERNATIONAL (formerly ABC Bloomsbury) Brunswick Sq. T 837 1177. Modern cinema screening 'quality' films and providing showcase for new British cinematic talent. Tickets £1·20, nurses and students 70p.

RAVELLE'S MEN'S HEALTH CENTRE Brunswick Centre, Brunswick Sq. T 837 3819. Full range of exercise and keep-fit activities. Mon–Fri 10.30am–9pm, Sat 10.30am–6pm.

RAVELLE'S LONDON LADY, Clare Court, Judd St. T 278 2754. As men's health centre, plus beauty treatments.

HEALTH EDUCATION COUNCIL 78 New Oxford St. T 637 1881. Infor-mation centre utilizing audio-visual aids and teaching kits in the promotion of good health. Reference library and showroom with free leaflets on many aspects of health education.

COLLEGIATE THEATRE Gordon St. T 387 9629. Drama and musical performances by both professionals and amateurs. Administered by University College, also showing student productions.

VANBURGH THEATRE CLUB Malet St. LITTLE THEATRE Gower St. T 636 7076. Twenty-four-hour membership necessary for these affiliated clubs. £1·05 per year, 50p for students. Performances by the Royal Academy of Dramatic Art spanning whole range of dramatic literature.

ENGLISH TRADITIONAL DANCE Mary Ward Centre, 9 Tavistock Place. Contact Mrs M. Howe, 8 Tayler Court, Alexandra Rd, NW8. T 722 4930. Offering one-day workshops and short courses on traditional English dances, including sociological and psychological implications.

RADHA KRISHNA TEMPLE 7 Bury Place. T 405 1463. Real-life Vedic temple, open twenty-four hours a day. Devotees practising essence of Vedic culture ('God-centred society') beginning at 4.30am, lasting throughout the day. Sunday festival 4–9pm with feast, drama, lectures and chanting. Visitors welcome to taste free vegetarian food (lunch at 1pm), read literature, and find out more about the community.

BHARATIYA VIDYA BHAVAN 37 New Oxford St. T 240 0815/836 0808. Institute of Indian Culture with a shop, Batik paintings, reading room, record library concentrating on all aspects of Indian culture. Also classes in Sanskrit, sitar, hatha yoga and tabla.

THE BRAMPTONS 70 Marchmont St. T 837 5584. Home of one of the largest stocks of original prints in London, seventeenth to nineteenth centuries.

Various subjects such as architecture, natural history, fashion. Work by the engravers for Charles Dickens, Hogarth and Turner.

GOOD FOR KIDS

CORAM'S FIELDS, Guildford St. T 837 6138. Marvellous seven-acre playground on the site of the original Foundling Hospital, from which adults are strictly barred unless accompanied by children (under 18). Swings and other fixed play equipment divided into two areas, one for the under-tens, lawns for rounders and similar games, netball and tennis courts, skateboard ramp, newly resurfaced football pitches (coaching provided during the holidays), sand-pits and a paddling pool. Snacks available in summer. The ILEA organize additional activities and a meals centre in the holidays. Playground Mon–Fri 8am–dusk, Sat and Sun 9am–dusk; supervised activities Mon–Fri 9am–5.30pm in school holidays, 3.30–6pm in termtime. Youth Club Mon–Fri 6–10pm, welcome visitors.

POLLOCK'S TOY MUSEUM 1 Scala St. Hidden behind Goodge St station on the west side of Tottenham Court Rd is this tiny building stacked with ancient dolls, toys, shadow-puppets and Pollock's famous toy theatres. Open Mon–Sat 10am–5pm. 20p (10p students, pensioners and children). The shop on ground floor overflows with doll's furniture, scraps, all kinds of dolls except the nasty modern plastic ones.

HOW TO GET THERE

UNDERGROUND Tottenham Court Road, Goodge Street, Warren Street, Euston Square, Russell Square, Holborn, Chancery Lane, King's Cross. BUSES 5, 7, 8, 14, 17, 18, 19, 22, 24, 25, 29, 30, 38, 45, 46, 55, 68, 73, 77, 77A, 77C, 134, 170, 172, 176, 188, 239, 259.

Camden Town

Owing to the self-inflicted mockery of its media-orientated fringe, Camden Town , or NW1 as it came to be known, is believed to be the habitat of trendy careers and history men. While there is some truth in that image, it was always incomplete and has become largely obsolete. The point of Camden Town lies in its diversity.

Stretching from the creamy grandeur of Nash's Regent's Park terraces to the crumbling squalor of Kentish Town; from the tail-end of self-conscious Hampstead to the anonymity of the great railway termini, it offers an almost confusing range of experiences, people, and atmospheres.

The pubs are largely Irish, voluble but usually pacific. The juke-boxes offer Irish ballads instead of rock 'n' roll, but an exception is The Black Cap, a drag pub featuring such fine artistes as Mrs Shufflewick and Auntie Flo, that aggressive sharp-witted mountain of diamanté and fishnet. It's a pity the pub's become increasingly exclusive. You used to be able to take girls. Now the atmosphere is hostile to anyone in skirts who isn't on stage.

The street markets of the area, while no longer the treasure trove of the early sixties, still contain junk barrows worth picking over.

At Camden Lock there's a real antique market, touchingly old fashioned in its hippy ambience. Here, too, is Dingwall's Dance Hall, a mecca for hopeful rock groups, and Le Routier, a very reasonable restaurant in a deprived gastronomic area. Indeed Camden Lock offers not only one of the few spontaneous complexes in London, but a unique setting of cobbled yard and glittering water.

There are excellent bookshops – Compendium is especially enterprising; antique shops in profusion; a marvellous fish shop with live eels. There's the Round House; a polyglot of racial communities, especially Greek – most of the possible restaurants tend to be theirs. There's a lively opposition to bulldozing bureaucracy. It's an area full of surprises – a shabby Baghdad.

George Melly

WHAT TO SEE

CAMDEN LOCK On the Regent's Canal near top end of Camden High St is a picturesque, unexpected corner. Early Victorian stabling beside the canal turned into craft studios and shops, an antique market Sat–Sun, Dingwall's Dancehall for rock music and a restaurant. Can walk miles along the towpath past hump-backed bridges, old warehouses, back gardens, as far as Maida Hill tunnel one way, Islington tunnel the other. (See Where to Eat, Shopping.)

ST PANCRAS OLD CHURCH Mostly nineteenth century in the Norman manner, crooked and sinister. In churchyard, monuments stand about desolately, including Sir John Soane's eccentric family vault and the grave of the last survivor of the Black Hole of Calcutta.

PRIMROSE HILL Favourite spot for footpads and duels in the eighteenth century. Gives a marvellous view over London.

REGENT'S PARK Everything a city park should be. Magnificent tree-lined avenues, rolling grassland and formal flowerbeds, bandstands, rose garden, a lake with wild little islands, a canal, the London mosque with golden dome and minarets. The Holm and Grove House, best of remaining mansions, both designed by Decimus Burton. (See Keeping Amused.)

NASH TERRACES Cumberland, Chester, Cambridge, and Gloucester Gate – a splendid sight, they line the east side of Regent's Park and look from the Broadwalk more like stuccoed palaces.

DANISH CHURCH Gloucester Gate/ Cumberland Ter. Odd mixture of Strawberry Hill and King's College Cambridge.

PARK VILLAGE WEST Nash in a playful mood – charming villas.

CHRIST CHURCH Albany St. Yellow brick, Grecian style church with a thin spire by Sir James Pennethorne, stained glass window by Rossetti.

LONDON ZOO Needs a whole day to explore – it's worth it. Some buildings, like the giraffe house, original from 1826, while the lion terraces opened a couple of years ago. (See Good for Kids.)

WHERE TO EAT

The change from industrial to cultural at the Round House and Camden Lock has resulted in a few more good eating places in this area. NB for motorists: wide empty streets to west of busy Camden High St one-way system provide plenty of parking spaces. Sample prices are for average three-course meal for two with drink. Open for lunch and dinner seven days a week unless otherwise indicated.

MODITI'S 83 Bayham St. T 485 7890. ANDY'S 81a Bayham St T 485 9718. Two of the oldest kebab houses, well-tested and reliable. Moditi's £7, closed Sun. Andy's £8.

KORITSAS 10 Kentish Town Rd. T 485 5743. Much same menu as above, plus choice of tableclothes and music, or formica and telly. £5–£6. Closed Sun.

ARARAT 249 Camden High St. T 267 0319. Armenian specialities as well as Greek, excellent mezes. £8–£9.

RETSINA 83 Regent's Park Rd. T 722 3194. Newer and very popular kebab house. Moussaka speciality. £8.

MUSTOE'S BISTRO 73 Regent's Park Rd. T 586 0901. Still amazingly cheap, £6 for dinner, £4 for lunch (weekends only), closed Mon.

SESAME 128 Regent's Park Rd. T 586 3779. Not really a restaurant but does good vegetarian and wholefood take-away things and is near Primrose Hill. Under £2. Mon–Sat 10am–6pm.

MANNA 4 Erskine Rd. T 722 8028. More of the same sort of food, filling and wholesome. £5·50. Evenings only. Closed Mon.

CHALCOT'S BISTRO 49 Chalcot Rd, Primrose Hill. T 722 1956. Newish back-street bistro run by couple who live locally. Cooking good, prices very fair. Book, especially for dinner. Closed Sat lunch, all Sun and Mon. Lunch £4, dinner £8–£10.

FROOPS 17 Princess Rd. T 722 9663. Older, far smarter bistro, now felt to be rather expensive by locals. Dinners only, closed Sun. £14.

BARQUE AND BITE Cumberland Basin, Prince Albert Rd. T 485 8137. Near Zoo, and in a boat, hence jokey name. Dine nose to bill with the ducks on the canal below decks or take leafier view from upper saloon. Menu impressive, standards high; so is the bill. Closed Sat lunch, all Sun. £15.

MARINE ICES 8 Haverstock Hill. T 485 8898. Near Round House, popular for Italian food and excellent, pure fruit sorbets. Ideal for children. Open 10am–11pm., last orders 10.30p.m. £6. Ices only on Sun, 13–80p each.

ROUND HOUSE Chalk Farm Rd. Open to general public. Stage bar, salad and snacks. Restaurant proper, now run by Jam (of King's Road fame). Theatre cabaret or live music after performances. £7. Closed Sun.

LE ROUTIER Camden Lock, Commercial Place, Chalk Farm Rd. T 485 0360. Portions are huge, service friendly. Need to specify table by windows overlooking canal when booking. Nice for outdoor eating, too. Lunch about £7, dinner (posher menu) £9. Closed Mon.

DINGWALL'S, Camden Lock. T 267 4967. Restaurant clientele mostly very young. Eating to accompaniment of *very* loud rock, punk, funk or whatever. Hamburgers, steaks, kebabs, chile con carne, etc. A good night out with music, food, drink, dancing – even on occasion George Melly. £12, cheaper early in the week. 8pm–2am. Closed Sun.

OSLO COURT Prince Albert Rd. T 722 8795. For a really good meal, some say the best food in London, Camden Towners nip over the border to NW8. Yugoslav-Welsh management. £18. Closed Mon, Sun evening and Sat lunch, plus two weeks at Easter and three in summer.

Picnics

No problem, with Primrose Hill and the whole of Regent's Park to choose from!

WHERE TO DRINK

BLACK CAP 171 Camden High St. Drag artists appear most every night, but its gay reputation has created an atmosphere somewhat hostile to women. Cocktails to order, Charrington's beers, bar food. Cosy, but chintzy, ambience.

THE QUEEN'S 49 Regent's Park Rd. No connection with The Black Cap despite its name – this Queen was Edward VII's Alexandra. Lovely old stained glass windows, Edwardian decor. Hand-pumped Charrington's draught beers; lagers and Guinness. Wide range of hot and cold snacks and main dishes; also upstairs restaurant. Right by Primrose Hill.

THE BELMONT Belmont St, Chalk Farm Rd. Recently transformed from rather nondescript boozer into smart but comfortable Victorian-style showpiece, conveniently across from Round House. Watney's fined bitter, hot and cold pub food, all usual trappings of up-marketing.

SPREAD EAGLE Albert St/Parkway. Large, comfortable oasis serving Young's real ales in the midst of kegland. Food available, wide cross-section of regulars including Camden Irish and 'serious' art students.

YORK & ALBANY 129 Parkway. Spacious Watney Mann house overlooking Regent's Park. Decent hot and cold food. Useful refreshment stop for early evening joggers, though.

DUBLIN CASTLE 94 Parkway. One of

the pioneers of 'pub food' in London, offers fantastic salads as well as a lunchtime restaurant. Oldish building with warm atmosphere marred only by high prices for Watney's ale.

GRAPELINE 85 Parkway. Pleasant basement wine bar. Food not bad but a little pricey, the selection of vintages commendable.

CARNARVON CASTLE 7 Chalk Farm Rd. Opposite Camden Lock, large Ind Coope house patronized by Dingwall's market traders as well as musicians fleeing from the high prices of Dingwall's Dancehall. Enlightened jukebox, too. Hot and cold snacks and main dishes.

WHERE TO SHOP

Series of busy one-ways lined with shops providing everything. Regent's Park Rd/Gloucester Ave have nice mixture of shops. Parkway is a flourishing little centre with several shops of interest. Chalk Farm Rd rapidly becoming antiques centre, lively to visit on Sat or Sun.

Camden High St: FRANK ROMANY LTD, No. 52–6. T 387 2579. Virtually every tool imaginable – all leading brands, electrically powered and hand operated. Door and window fittings, etc. Don't cover plumbing.

BAGS AND TATTERS, No. 80. T 387 5395. Shoulder and short handle baskets from China, canvas satchels, leather, synthetic, formal and informal bags; women's fashion, costume jewellery of all types.

COMPENDIUM, Nos 234 & 240. T 485 8944. Wide selection of books and papers including politics, feminist literature, anthropology, music in first shop; alternative psychology, drugs, mysticism in second.

Camden Rd: MONTAGUE SAXBY, No. 24. T 485 1302. Established 1903, still sell unbeatable collection of suitcases, trunks, travel bags, vanity cases, wallets, belts, dog collars.

SWANKY MODES, No. 106. T 485 3569. Rail of designs by four ex-dress design students. Crazy and extrovert clothes include skin-tight jeans, slinky sexy dresses and *trompe l'oeil* bikinis. Also fashion accessories.

THE WHIZZER, 72 Crowndale Rd. T 387 8813. Two brothers run this new and secondhand bicycle shop. Unmistakable with brightly painted murals. Repairs and spares.

EAST ASIA BOOKS AND ARTS, 277 Eversholt St. T 387 3531. Over 30 000 books on all aspects of Far East. Texts printed in Chinese, Japanese and English cover acupuncture to economics. Also Eastern works of art and handicrafts.

BARTLETTS, 13 Pratt St. T 485 1429. Large stock of sports clothes and equipment, children and adults. Judo, karate, cricket, football, squash, tennis, badminton; not yachting or skiing.

Dingwall's Market Camden Lock. Sat–Sun. Approximately 100 stalls, manned mainly by young people, sell period clothes, old buttons, home-knitted clothes, clothes imported from China, Mexico and Guatemala, home-made produce, flowers and plants, antiques, bric-à-brac, leatherware, musical instruments.

Camden Lock Workshops Behind market, open all week, visitors welcome to call, watch, buy. Include BLIND ALLEY for silk-screened and individually commissioned window blinds; FIVE JEWELLERS; THREE POTTERS; THE GILT STUDIO, gilding and glass fibre reproductions; and MARC GERSTEIN – stained glass workshop.

Chalk Farm Rd: THIS AND THAT, No. 50–51. T 267 5433. Three floors of late Victorian country furniture mostly stripped pine, some oak. No. 51 specializes in turn-of-the-century inlaid mahogany furniture.

AFTER DARK, No. 20. T 267 3300. Wired and unwired pre-thirties light fittings: standard lamps, ceiling and wall fittings and many table lamps. Repairs to order, sell brass door knobs. **Parkway:** CANDLE SHOP, No. 89. T 485 3232. Candles, holders, candle making materials. More unusual candles include faces, a mug of Guinness and scented candles.

DU DU, No. 95. T 267 1097. Two floors of women's clothes and accessories. Big variety – clogs, boots, exotic dresses, fishermen's smocks – all reasonably priced.

IRONSWARE, No. 46. T 485 7248. Seconds in most kitchen equipment, including farmhouse pottery, casseroles, linen. All sizes clay and terracotta pots, also plants, plant holders.

KLONG, No. 44. T 485 6846. Delightful but tiny, crammed with assortment of fabrics, clothes, jewellery and arts and crafts from Thailand and South East Asia. Stephan will show his prized collection of batiks hidden in the back to those interested.

REGENT PET STORES (PALMERS) LTD, No. 33–37. T 485 5163. Tiny kittens and puppies attract passers-by.

Regent's Park Rd Cut off from Adelaide Rd by the closure to traffic of Bridge Approach, pretty and peaceful street. Many up-market and old-fashioned shops.

PRIMROSE HILL BOOKS, No. 134. T 586 2022. Secondhand and antiquarian books and prints.

ARTS AND FLOWERS, No. 164. T 722 7186. Unusual selection of cut flowers and bedding plants.

LIVING DAYLIGHTS, No. 119. T 586 3911. Gilliam Keightley and Ian Harris paint roller blinds in spacious airy workshop. Stock a range of plain and patterned blinds or work to commission. Also murals.

RON WELDON, No. 109. T 722 0997. Upstairs, eighteenth- and nineteenth-century bulky furniture, wall and grandfather clocks, mirrors. Down perilous stairs for pine chairs and tables. Friendly haphazard shop.

RICHARD DARE, No. 93. T 722 9428. Quality kitchen utensils. Richard Dare chooses all the stock, largely from France. Chunky baskets and a lot of items unavailable elsewhere including the beautiful Quimper pottery.

BOOKSHOP 85, No. 85. T 586 0512. Opened by Tom Maschler, now run by Terry Dougherty. Wide and good selection of paperback fiction, reference, cookery, politics, books by local authors, and poetry (speciality). Fast ordering system. Also left-wing and literary magazines.

SWAN, No. 71. T 722 9268. Charming collection of mainly Victorian prints, drawings, antiques, curios, old carpentry tools, chosen by Mrs MacGregor. Currently selling inexpensive jewellery and old embroidery and lace tablecloths. Generally closed Mon and Tue.

FORMULA, No. 126. T 722 7955. French, Italian and English clothes, bags, belts, sandals and scarves for women. Styles smart and classic, everything colour co-ordinated. Wide price range.

FONTHILL POTTERY, 38 Chalcot Rd. T 722 9090. Practical stoneware pottery by Emmanuel Cooper. Whole dinner services or individual pieces, most items glazed in an oatmeal colour. Lots of half-price seconds.

The Unexpected

CAROLINE BOSLY 13 Princess Rd. T 722 7608. The only woman broker in London's Oriental rug market. Huge warehouse, deals in all types of new or old handmade carpets. Ring for appointment to view.

MARKSONS 8 Chester Court, Albany St. T 935 8682. Reconditioned and new pianos, £270–£4000.

BUYING FOOD

Camden High St: OLYMPIC BAKER AND PATISSERIE, No. 261. T 267 0160. Greek and French loaves baked on premises. Also most Greek cakes and pastries plus some English traditional cakes.

LA BOULANGERIE, No. 89. T 387 0248. Greek, English and Continental patisseries and breads baked at Finchley Rd branch fresh daily.

TOKYO YA, No. 241. T 485 2533. Neatly laid out supermarket: spices, sauces, dried and tinned foods from India, China, Japan, Cyprus, Hungary and Poland. Also some health foods and pulses in bulk.

R. ROWE AND SON LTD, No. 243. T 485 4676. Excellent example of the traditional open-fronted fishmonger. Fresh fish daily includes usual range as well as the less popular octopus, snappers, conger eel, live and boiled crabs, Oriental and Continental fish. Also range of smoked fish.

TALBYS, No. 263. T 485 5000. Do all own fish smoking, sells most fresh fish in season along with live and boiled crabs. Specialize in fish from South Coast.

Inverness St Becomes market during normal weekday trading hours, positively overflows on Sat. Speciality fruit and vegetables.

Plender St Camden High St end has small fruit and vegetable market.

CORNER GREEK SHOP 19 Pratt St. T 267 0864. One of many family-run Greek grocery/delicatessens.

MARINE ICES 8 Haverstock Hill. T 485 8898. (See Where to Eat.)

Regent's Park Rd: CHARCUTERIE, No. 107. T 586 0521. Small basement delicatessen. Fresh salads, quiches, pâtés, tarts, etc. French and English cheeses, wines.

HERMITAGE WINE CELLAR, No. 67. T 722 8576. One of several off-licences in the street but they also sell wine and sherry from the cask – take jug. Italian wines in large quantities.

SESAME, No. 128. T 586 3779. Delightful shop with a delicious smell of food. Bake own breads and pastries, sell pulses, nuts and flour loose from large wooden casks. Also corn germ and sunflower oil, honey in large containers herbs and teas.

GODFREYS 27 Parkway. T 485 1808. Pretty canopied bakery where all breads and pastries baked on premises daily. Very good French bread.

KEEPING AMUSED

CAMDEN LOCK Dingwall's Basin, Chalk Farm Rd. T 485 7963. During summer every Sun and Wed night a series of 'events' with different themes, i.e., 'Cockney Night', 'Jazz Night'. (See also Where to Shop.)

DINGWALL'S DANCEHALL. T 267 4967. Possibly the best rock venue in London. Live music six nights a week (not Sun), lunchtime jazz Sat. Long, well-stocked bar, food, relaxed atmosphere. Entrance £1–£3. (See Where to Eat.)

JORDAN GALLERY. T 267 2437. Small, pleasant gallery tucked alongside right-hand side of basin (facing canal). Different exhibition of modern artists every four weeks, large selection of graphics and postcards for sale. Tue–Sun, 10am–5.30pm.

CAROUSEL 184 Camden High St. T 485 9006. Club/restaurant, on two floors. Dance floor with bar and snack bar offering country'n'western, rock, £1 cover charge. Upstairs restaurant with complete menu. 9.30pm–2am.

ATMOSPHERE GALLERY 148 Regent's Park Rd. T 722 6058. British crafts and graphics. Peaceful two-floor gallery changes exhibitions monthly.

WOMEN'S ARTS ALLIANCE 10 Cambridge Terrace Mews (off Chester Gate), Albany St. T 935 1841. Arts Council-sponsored collective providing exhibition space for women artists. Design, photography, crafts. Workshops, occasional theatre.

MUSIC MACHINE 1 Camden High St (opp. Mornington Crescent tube). T 387 0428/9. Beautiful variety theatre (Charlie Chaplin played there, and

Goons broadcast their shows from here, now rock music venue.) Dance amid cherubs, gilt and pictures of Jagger beneath ten-foot high elevated stage. Two bands nightly, six days a week. 8pm–2am. Four bars and restaurant serving food at pub prices. Ticket prices vary according to bands.

ROUND HOUSE Chalk Farm Rd. T 267 2564. Converted Victorian engine shed housing large and small theatres, shop, restaurant, bar and snack bar. Good venue for unusual or experimental (downstairs) performances. Rock concerts in the bar area on Sun. Prices vary.

MINSKY'S GALLERY Regent's Park Rd. T 586 3533. Tue–Fri 1pm–6pm, Sat 11am–3pm. Monthly one-man shows, specializing in limited edition prints. Picture framing service.

PARKWAY FOCUS GALLERY 76 Parkway. T 267 5119. Non-commercial husband/wife concern, exhibitions according to their personal taste, 'pro-artist'. All exhibits moderately priced, small sculpture courtyard in back. 11am–5pm. Ring bell.

GOOD FOR KIDS

THE ROUND HOUSE puts on special kids' shows most Sat and some weekdays in the holidays, T 267 2541.

PARTYMAD 67 Gloucester Ave. T 586 0169. All the ingredients for marvellous children's parties: candles and cake decorations, squeakers, balloons, masks, thousands of different small toys. Selections of fifty toys for fêtes, etc., by post – from £4·70 (inc. postage). Everything for doll's houses. Closed all day Mon, and Aug.

LONDON ZOO (See What to See.) For 9–18 XYZ Club, £1·50 p.a. sub brings you six free visits a year, plus film shows, lectures, information. Otherwise adults £1·75, children 5–16 85p, under-fives free. Children's Zoo has goats, sheep, ponies, etc., to pet and feed. Camel rides 10p, or see the sights from a llama cart 10p. Elephants' bath time is 11.30am daily. Don't miss Guy the gorilla and the two giant pandas, or forget to check feeding times.

EXTRAS Sail model boats on Regent's Park pond near Hanover Gate and watch for herons nesting on the islands in the lake. Primrose Hill is great for kite-flying.

HOW TO GET THERE

BR Primrose Hill, Camden Rd.
UNDERGROUND Camden Town, Mornington Crescent.
BUSES 3, 24, 27, 29, 31, 46, 53, 68, 74B, 74X, 134, 137, 214, 253.

Chelsea

From its beginnings Chelsea has been a conservative borough, but no one would ever know. It is true that it is the home of an almost extinct tribe of silver-haired ladies who go to the Academy's summer exhibition as though visiting a shrine, but it also seethes with the sad restlessness of bed-sitting room life.

Neither its population nor its architecture is any longer all of a piece. The district is bounded on the south side by that stretch of the Thames whose drabness has been immortalized in the paintings of Mr Whistler, and on the north by the contrasting hurly-burly of Fulham Road. At its eastern extremity, with its back literally and symbolically turned on Belgravia, stands the Royal Court Theatre, the home of plays whose incomprehensibility is thought to be a guarantee of cultural worth. Starting here, with the dizzy, dazzling temptations of Peter Jones department store, the King's Road runs the entire length of the territory, playing on the way every note in the social scale until it reaches the unmapped swamps of Parson's Green.

This thoroughfare has become (especially on Saturday mornings) a conveyor belt of the most eccentrically dressed young people in

England. They come to stare at the antique shops, to sit in the excruciatingly expensive restaurants and to be stared at by one another.

Off this carnival of a main road run smaller streets, many of them pretty and still surprisingly quiet. Here lived men like Mr Rossetti, Mr Wilde, and Mr Sargent. They haunt the place less waspishly now than they did in life, guarding forever what is left of *la vie de bohème*.

I can think of no other area of the metropolis in which you can behave so badly with so little risk.

Quentin Crisp

WHAT TO SEE

HOLY TRINITY, Sloane St. Splendid late-nineteenth-century church by Sedding, details by leading members of the arts and crafts movement.

ROYAL HOSPITAL, Royal Hospital Rd. Founded by Charles II for war veterans, designed by Wren. Great Hall and Chapel Mon–Sat 10am–noon, 2–4pm, Sun 2–4pm. Museum same hours, 5pm in summer. Free.

CHEYNE WALK Beautiful early Georgian houses, including Nos 19–26 on the site of Henry VIII's manor house. Many attractive streets both sides of the King's Rd, liberally sprinkled with plaques.

CHELSEA OLD CHURCH (All Saints), Old Church St. Sir Thomas More's chapel and most of the monuments survived heavy bombing, earliest surviving part early sixteenth century. Delightful interior beautifully restored. Statue of Thomas More outside.

CARLYLE'S HOUSE, Cheyne Row. Perfectly preserved nineteenth-century interior in early eighteenth-century house. His old felt hat hangs on a peg by the garden door, and famous attic study, made as a refuge from 'dogs, cocks, pianofortes and insipid men', is almost exactly as he knew it. Wed–Sat 11am–1pm, 2–6pm or dusk (3.30pm Nov, Jan, Feb), Sun 2–6pm or dusk (3.30pm Nov, Jan, Feb). Closed Dec. 50p (students and accompanied children 25p).

CROSBY HALL, Cheyne Walk. Incorporates the Great Hall of a fifteenth-century wool merchant's City home, moved to Chelsea in 1910. Magnificent arched roof, oriel window and medieval fireplace, Jacobean and Cromwellian furniture. Daily 10am–noon, 2.15–5 pm, or dusk if earlier. Closed some Bank Holidays and for functions. Free.

CHELSEA PHYSIC GARDEN, Swan Walk. America's cotton plantations owe their existence to seed from this garden, begun in 1673 by the Society of Apothecaries and maintained principally for teaching and research. Permission to visit is given only on written application to City Parochial Foundation, 10 Fleet Street EC4, but one can get tantalizing glimpses through Embankment railings.

SLOANE SQ. UNDERGROUND STATION. One of the few with a pub on the platform, but must be unique in having a river overhead. The iron conduit above the track contains the River Westbourne, on its way from the Serpentine to the Thames. The river is joined by Ranelagh Sewer just before it reaches the station.

WHERE TO EAT

To be successful a Chelsea restaurant has to have terrific style and aplomb, like the people who get noticed walking down the King's Rd. There are an enormous number of restaurants in Chelsea – in fact it never stops eating. You can order lunch at 4pm at Le Casserole and eat dinner till 6am at Up All Night. Most restaurants are situated in the King's Rd or Fulham Rd, with more intimate ones in side streets. Sample prices are for a three-course meal for two with drink. Open for lunch and dinner seven days unless otherwise indicated.

AU PERE DE NICO, 10 Lincoln St. T 584 4704. The place to take anyone who still thinks 'Chelsea' means 'intellectual and artistic'. Famous for its way with quails and gigot grillé au romain; friendly service; large courtyard open all year. £15. Closed Sun.

DON LUIGI, 33c King's Rd. T 730 3023. Must be admired for its friendly efficient professional manner. Italian food is good, too. £14.

HUNGRY HORSE 196 Fulham Rd. T 352 7757. British to the core, with kedgeree, roasts, pies and puddings. Good as ever after fifteen years. £14. Apart from Sun lunch, open evenings only.

BUSBY'S 79 Royal Hospital Rd. T 352 7179. Newer, but equally British; just the place to take foreign visitors. *Prix fixe* £3·50 menu, but with cover, drink, VAT, coffee, service, more like £5 a head. Evenings only, closed Sun.

Among the favourite restaurants of Chelsea dwellers are:

SAN QUINTINO, 44 Radnor Walk. T 352 2698, and SANTA CROCE, 112 Cheyne Walk. T 352 7534. Both owned by stylish San Frediano group. San Quintino is small and friendly with more of a neighbourhood feel about it than the others in this group – possibly because our friendly old Poet Laureate shuffles in from his house up the street for the occasional plate of Insalata di Mare. Santa Croce is more glossy, but still charming. Menus in both very similar and cooking is invariably good. £12. Both closed Sun.

ASTERIX, 329 King's Rd. T 352 3891, first place in London to do real Breton crêpes. £4 drinking cider with two courses.

KING'S ROAD JAM, 289a King's Rd. T 352 5390. Sells wine by the pint (£1·80), serves bistro type food, popular with the young. £6, but three-course special £2 excluding wine. Evenings only.

WILLIAM F, 140 Fulham Rd. T 373 5534. Also sells bistro food but to a slightly older clientele. The place to see theatrical people, pretty waitresses, and be soothed. £12. Closed Sun.

LA FAMIGLIA, 7 Langton St. T 351 0761. Most popular newcomer; Italian, everyone seems to love the food *and* the family. £10.

BAGATELLE, 5 Langton St. T 351 4185. Another smart, new place. Beautifully decorated, with fondant-coloured tablecloths; high marks for fish and the vegetables, French cooking. £19. Closed Sun.

Picnics

Chelsea Embankment Gardens offer a good view of Albert Bridge. Royal Hospital grounds and adjoining Ranelagh Gardens are delightful but closed to walkers and destroyed each May in the name of horticulture by the Chelsea Flower Show. Dogs are barred from Ranelagh, so you can sit on the grass.

WHERE TO DRINK

MAN IN THE MOON, 392 King's Rd. Watney's house serving traditional fined bitter and offering punk rock groups on Sat, jazz on Tue, comprehensive pub grub every day save Sun. Beautiful cut glass mirrors should occupy those not interested in food or punk.

THE ROEBUCK, 354 King's Rd. Courage pub serves real ale, an unusually wide selection of malt whiskies and excellent buffet food in 'restaurant area'. Haunt of Chelsea artists and resting theatricals.

THE RED HOUSE, 2 Elystan St. Watney's fined bitter, a selection of bottled and canned beers including Schlitz and Fosters, and the friendly atmosphere of a real local. Video games, jukebox, all-day food and serious darts and backgammon cults.

KING'S ARMS, Sloane Sq. Complex of bars, including saloon serving excellent hot food at all times, which somehow retain a genuine English pub atmosphere despite trendy location (next to Royal Court Theatre).

SLOANE'S WINE BAR, Sloane Sq. Beneath King's Arms. Interesting selection of wines, good range of hot and cold food.

MARKHAM ARMS, 138 King's Rd. Large, circular interior with small garden at rear and unusually mouthwatering hot food; usual sandwiches.

THE PHOENIX, 23 Smith St. Pleasant little Watney pub with fined bitter, bar snacks including hot food lunchtime except Sun, and outdoor tables where you can sit in summer and watch chauffeurs looking for somewhere to park the Bentleys and Ferraris.

CROSS KEYS, 2 Lawrence St. Small, often very crowded pub with little garden at the rear. Cheyne Walk locals trying to look inconspicuous mingle with lost American tourists. Good cold table and some hot food; real ale, too.

KING'S HEAD & EIGHT BELLS, 50 Cheyne Walk. The large saloon bar is bit tacky, noxious muzak. Claim restaurant is cheapest in London.

WORLD'S END DISTILLERY, 459 King's Rd. Impressive gilt and tiled exterior conceals tidy but somewhat spartan bars featuring jukebox, bar skittles and Watney's and Truman's keg beers. Lunchtime hot food.

WHERE TO SHOP

Once known as the heart of 'swinging London', shops are colourful, reflect inhabitants' and visitors' wealth; many cater to artists' needs, many run by their owners.

Sloane St Links Sloane Sq., with its bewitching fountain by Gilbert Ledward, with Knightsbridge.

GENERAL TRADING CO., No. 144. T 730 0411. Three Royal Warrants held for range of gifts – traditional, conventional designs; Far East exotics; cutlery, toys, souvenirs. Large, interesting range of home and garden items. Very geared to wedding presents.

PRESENTS, No. 129. T 730 1750. Zany presents for all ages and all types. Soft sculpture; household and decorative items; wide range of mirrors. Free gift wrapping.

Lower Sloane St: MEXICANA, No. 89. T 730 3871. Pricey but beautiful brightly coloured Mexican cotton garments with pin tucking and lace insertions, £40–£120.

LAURA ASHLEY, No. 71–73. T 730 1771. Immensely popular range of pretty small-print hand-printed fabrics. Women's and children's clothes in-spired by and adapted from Victorian designs. At this branch, dress fabrics and Bargain Shop.

MITSUKIKU, No. 73a. T 730 1505. Kimonos of all lengths, flowered or plain fabrics, Japanese sandals, toys, mobiles, rice bowls and chopsticks.

DAVID MELLOR, 4 Sloane Sq. T 730 4259. Functional and attractive ironmongery, kitchen equipment and tableware. Many designs by David Mellor, famous for his cutlery.

King's Rd Boutiques come and go at an alarming rate. *The* place for jeans – Soldier Blue, Jean Machine, Jean Junction and Jeans Centre; men's fashions – Quincy, Thackeray, Squire Shop and John Michael; and leading shoe chains – Ravel, Russell & Bromley and Dolcis. Sat afternoon enjoy watching way-out fashions parade up and down.

PETER JONES. T 730 3434. Part of the John Lewis chain of department stores, more up-market because of its position.

CHELSEA COBBLER, No. 54. T 584 2602. In the sixties created a collection of ready-to-wear boots in coloured leathers and fabrics that revolutionized men and women's footwear. Next came handmade shoes and sandals; now branches all over .

ACE, No. 185. T 351 1917. Really wild clothes. Diamanté T-shirts; jeans appliqué with tropical plants, palm trees and spotted leopards, £70; appliqué shorts, £35; Carmen Miranda dresses made from layers of old fabrics – anything made to order. Daily Blue velvet trousers in every colour.

GIVANS IRISH LINEN STORES, No. 207. T 352 6352. Old-fashioned draper strangely out of sync with today's bustle. Top quality Irish and Swiss linens, enormous towelling bathrobes.

TIGER, TIGER, No. 219. T 352 8080. Beautiful window display of grand dolls' houses, realistic and life-size soft toys, glove and string puppets makes shop look very expensive, but it has seventy-two baskets of pocket money toys.

RETRO, No. 229. T 352 2095. Nostalgic thirties and forties clothes, mostly American. Day and evening wear, accessories. Alterations done.

MEENY'S, No. 241. T 351 4171. Colourful, fun sporty clothes for children and adults imported from America. T-shirts, cowboy, basketball, sweatshirts with team names; dungarees, lots of work jeans; cords, goosedown jackets, leather jackets for adults. Also playwear – baseball outfits, cowboy hats and boots. Pretty clothes for girls up to six years old.

DESIGNERS GUILD, No. 227. T 351 1271. Co-ordinated fabrics, wallpapers and accessories with soft, subtle look. Sell off-cuts co-ordinated for patchwork, also remnants for napkin and cushion making.

CHELSEA ANTIQUE MARKET, No. 245a. T 352 9695. Large and rambling, miss many stalls if not careful. Large and small antiques of all types; some period clothes.

ANTIQUARIUS, 15 Flood St/King's Rd. T 351 1145. Over 200 stalls, everything from art deco tea sets, Victorian silver jewellery to thirties copies of *Vogue*.

PIPE SHOP. T 352 3315. Antique pipes and smokiana.

OSBORNE AND LITTLE, No. 304. T 352 1456. Beautiful and original wallpapers and fabrics. 450 designs in stock. Hand-printed papers, printed hessian, hanging gardens, metallics, friezes.

HABITAT, No. 206–222. T 351 1211. Largest and most spectacular branch of Terence Conran's great idea for furnishing the middle classes.

BOY, No. 153. T 351 1115. Latest in utility, military, strap and heavy duty wear. Vinyl dungarees, harness jacket and matching trousers to tempt you.

TERRY DE HAVILLAND, No. 323. T 352 9866. Snazzy spangley ladies' fashion shoes; stiletto heel mules, canvas boots, lots of gold.

HARRIET WYNTER, No. 352. T 352 6494. Scientific instruments, mainly pre-1830s. Also books on history of science, and applied arts.

KICKERS, No. 331. T 352 7541. Devoted entirely to popular French casual bootees and shoes for men, women and children. Twenty-four designs, but be warned – they're not cheap.

TAMESA FABRICS, No. 343. T 351 1126. Manufacture all their fabrics, display samples in showroom/shop. Tend to use natural fibres, hand screen-print, do a range of exotic fabrics using elaborate weaving techniques. Designs 'modern' rather than traditional.

World's End/King's Rd: BEAUFORT MARKET. T 352 2161. Predominantly clothes, often designed or made by stallholders. Military/punk gear, fifties and sixties clothes; art gallery, skateboard section, clairvoyant, leather clothes.

THE GLORY HOLE offers stained glass by Bronson Shaw; SUMATRA sells pipes, chillums, incense, kohl.

EMPEROR OF WYOMING, No. 404. T 351 0504. All the western gear you can think of, even saddles and blankets.

ESSENCES, No. 410. T 352 0192. Large stock and fast turnover of 1890s–1940s clothes all in good order. Victorian nightdresses, camisoles, petticoats. Small but exquisite range of handmade, one-off designs in antique fabrics and lace.

STRANGEWAYS, No. 502. T 352 9863. Somewhat bizarre furniture and ceramics – egg cups with feet, denim tea set, lifesize plaster sheep.

Langton St: TIBET HOUSE, 490a King's Rd/Langton St. T 352 1080. Wool jackets, embroidered felt boots, blouses, dresses, shirts, rugs, some jewellery, shoulder bags, incense, books, prints. Most made by Tibetan refugees.

OXUS, No. 11. T 351 1925. Tribal rugs,

textiles and embroideries made by nomads from Persia, Afghanistan, Turkey, Morocco, Russia, Asia and other rug-producing countries. Most antique; average £150 but up to £1000.
HOBBY HORSE, No. 15. T 351 1913. Lively craft shop supplying individual items and lots of kits for beading, leatherwork, macramé, etc.; craft books. Large discounts on bulk purchases.

Park Walk: GANESHA, No. 6. T 352 8972. Ann and Maarten Timmer import textiles, jewellery and basketware and artifacts from Burma, Cambodia, Indonesia, Laos, Malaysia and Thailand. Crammed with lovely but functional items of all kinds.
FRAILS, No. 20. T 352 5277. No trousers; clothes very feminine. Fid is main designer, uses Liberty cottons, silk, chiffons and rayon jersey to create interesting designs. From £30. Also cheap Indian dresses, Deco-style jewellery.

Old Church St: ZAPATA SHOE CO., No. 49–51. T 352 8622. Superb handmade contemporary shoes for men and women by Manolo Blahnik.
L'AIGLON, No. 44. T 352 8650. Functional and decorative ceramics and other handicrafts from Portugal.
MAXFIELD PARRISH, 4 Woodfall Court, Smith St. T 730 4867. Classic designs for range of garments in soft washable suede and top quality leather by Nigel Preston. Also collection in natural un-dyed silk.

Radnor Walk: CHELSEA POTTERY, No. 13. T 352 1366. Established twenty-six years. Hand-thrown, hand-painted pots, virtually everything one-off, and they undertake special commissions. Well known for 'Sgraffito' decoration technique.

Chelsea Green Very pretty and now pricey little complex.

Cale St: FABRIC SHOP, No. 6. T 584 8495. Pretty shop sells fabrics from all over the world at reasonable prices.

If they haven't got what you want, they will get it.
COLIN DENNY, No. 18. T 584 0240. Marine works of art early 1700s–1920. As Mr Denny has preference for clipper ship era 1850–1875, most marine paintings from that period. Nothing modern; restoration.

Elystan St: SIGN OF THE TIMES, No. 17. T 589 4774. Stock at Cathy McGowan's secondhand men's, women's and children's clothes often includes cast-offs of the likes of Gary Glitter, Elton John and Adam Faith. Also more ordinary wear.
CHELSEA GREEN SPORTS, No. 31. T 584 0776. Tennis and squash racquets, darts, training shoes, cricket bats, footballs for children and adults.

Fulham Rd: LAURA ASHLEY, No. 157. T 584 6939. (See Lower Sloane St.)
PAPERCHASE, No. 167. T 589 7839. Imaginative varied wrapping papers, boards, cartridge and other papers. Also mobiles, stationery, books, posters, pretty paper gifts.
BROTHER SUN, No. 171. T 589 6180. Hand-printed Provençal fabrics, by the metre and made up into a wide range of items for women. Also espadrilles for men and women.
HEAD OVER HEALS, No. 183–189. T 352 7931. Casual fashion wear for men and women. Unusual and exclusive clothes, leading fashion names like Fiorucci, Italian boots and shoes.
CONDOTTI, No. 50. T 589 3108. Interior decoration of the finest quality: Italian cane furniture; decorative antiques from India and the Far East; light luggage, ties, belts.
MONSOON, No. 54. T 589 9192. Delightful dresses, skirts, blouses, matching scarves and nightwear made up in hand-block printed fabric from Jaipur. Vegetable dyes. Also silk hand-printed dresses, blouses and skirts from Calcutta; dresses from Afghanistan; hand-embroidered, hand-crocheted cotton clothes from Romania.

PARROTS, No. 56. T 584 5699. Presents for all age groups: china, glass, toys, amusement items, leather, pictures and prints priced from 5p up to hundreds of pounds.

BUTLER AND WILSON, No. 189. T 352 3045. Deco jewellery, objects, twenties' scarves, bags, bracelets, boxes, bangles, cigarettes cases, brooches, pendants, ivory, enamel and silver jewellery.

CROCODILE, No. 60. T 589 4235. Classic knitwear by Rosilind Joffe; Hardware Clothing – jackets, suits and trousers, accessories. Some cheap items, most very expensive. PIERO DE MONZI, No. 68–70, and CERRUTI, No. 72. T 589 8765. Elegant expensive selections of French and Italian men's and ladies' classic style clothes. Mainly day wear but everything tailored. Also accessories: belts, bags, shoes and umbrellas.

ARGENTA GALLERY, No. 84. T 584 1841. Modern jewellery. Very beautiful and detailed pieces like miniature sculptures, imported silver jewellery from Scandinavia. Diamond jewellery chosen from manufacturers selected by De Beers. Will take commissions.

BOMBACHA, No. 104. T 584 5381. Two canopied shops. One sporty wear: drainpipe velvet and cotton jeans, wide choice of colours; crushed linen skirts; string jerseys; fun current fashions. The shop next door stocks pretty feminine clothes.

TULLEYS, No. 289–297. T 352 1078. Old-established upholsterer and re-production cabinet maker. Feather cushion sofas covered in any fabric; writing desks in mahogany and yew.

TATTERS, No. 152a. T 373 2084. Victorian and Edwardian lace embroidered tea dresses and petticoats; white lawn blouses.

PAN BOOKSHOP, No. 158. T 373 4997. Over thirty paperback publishers, all Pan books in print, good selection large format coffee table books and children's books.

FOOD SHOPS

PARTRIDGES 132 Sloane St. T 730 0651. Better quality groceries; fresh bread daily; English and French cheeses cut from whole; cold meats including a whole turkey, Alderton ham; pâtés, quiches, salads. Ice-cream, fresh cream pastries. Own table wine; wines, liqueurs.

LE COCHON ROSE 83 Lower Sloane St. T 730 2898. Delightful charcuterie with daily specials. Also pâté, cold meats, salads, breads, groceries.

King's Rd: BEATONS, No. 134. T 589 6263. Baking on the premises for seventy years. Breads, cakes, pastries, treacle tarts.

PORTCH BROTHERS, No. 405. T 352 4464. Most fresh fish, poultry and game in season. Also selection of shellfish and smoked fish.

Cale St: COOKSHOP CATERERS, No. 16. T 589 8388. Excellent delicatessen, French cheeses cut from whole, French salami, own pâté and tara-masalata, savoury and fruit pies, sausage rolls, scotch eggs. Fresh bread, some health foods, homemade jams, etc.

CHELSEA FISH & POULTRY SHOP, No. 10. T 589 9432. Fish in season on the slab. Also smoked fish, chicken, other poultry.

Fulham Rd: APPLE CORE, No. 298. T 351 3191. Above-average general supermarket. Mon–Sat 10pm, Sun 9pm.

MOORE BROS LTD, No. 248. T 352 8466. Brass scales and old coffee grinders, beautifully decorated tea containers. Wide choice freshly ground beans, equipment for all methods of coffee making.

WAINWRIGHT & DAUGHTER, No. 359. T 352 0852. Only the very best quality meat and fish. Beef from Scotland (hung for fourteen days), lamb from Canterbury and game in season. Finest Scotch smoked salmon, fresh and smoked fish daily.

LUIGI'S DELICATESSEN, No. 349. T 352 7739. Italian delicatessen with wines, wide range of pasta, salami, cheeses.

CURNICK, No. 170. T 370 1192. One of the best butchers in London. Free-range chicken always available; also great for pork sausages.

MAISON VERLON PATISSERIE, No. 178. T 370 1338. Croissants, brioches and fancy breads baked on premises in one of the oldest surviving Chelsea bread ovens (1742). Savarins, gateaux St Honoré, Austrian cheesecake, Black Forest cherry tart, Verlon Torte among their mouth-watering specialities.

SUMMERS, No. 323. T 352 8286. Mr Freeman bakes wide range of Danish pastries, fresh cream gateaux, cakes, Florentines and rum babas; granary French bread, granary and ordinary croissants, plaited chollar.

CHELSEA CATERING CO., No. 305. T 352 2261. Groceries, delicatessen and self catering for buffets. Fifty different English, French and Italian cheeses cut from the whole.

WHITTARDS, No. 111. T 589 4261. Seventeen blends of coffee roasted on the premises. Wide range of teas.

KEEPING AMUSED

BIRDS NEST CLUB 195–197 King's Rd. T 352 9255. Club ground level, pub below, function room upstairs. Live jazz every Mon, disco other nights. Mon–Wed midnight, Thur–Sat 1am, Sun 10.30pm. Lovely unexpected garden leading from pub, wrought-iron street lamps, circular fish pond. Club capacity 300. Lunch noon to 3pm.

SWIMMING BATHS AND SPORTS COMPLEX Chelsea Manor St. T 352 6985. 78–80°F heated pool open all year round. Balcony for observers. 19p adults, 8p children, Mon–Fri 9am–7.15pm (last ticket); 28p adults, 9p children. Sat 9am–5.15pm, Sun 9am–11.15am. Also facilities for squash, indoor tennis, badminton, five-a-side football, basketball and table tennis.

CHELSEA DRUGSTORE 49 King's Rd. T 730 8838/1682. Large entertainment complex including boutiques and pub. Disco up spiralling stairs to top floor. DJ and topless go-go dancers every night. 7.30–11pm Mon–Sat, 7–10.30 pm Sun; also 12.30–3pm Sat. 20p weekdays 50p weekends.

ZELLA 9 2 Park Walk. T 351 0588. Limited edition prints of 120 artists in two-floor gallery/shop. 200 prints can be displayed; unframed average £20–£40. 30-minute framing service. Open until 9pm seven days.

KING'S ROAD ART EXHIBITION King's Rd/Royal Ave. Every summer Sat local artists exhibit work. 11am–6pm.

ROYAL COURT THEATRE Sloane Sq. T 730 1745. Home of English Stage Company, dedicated to new plays. £1–£3. Small studio theatre (capacity up to 100), very good and experimental shows. £1·50.

CAFE DES ARTISTES 266 Fulham Rd. T 352 6200. Disco/restaurant. Live acts Fri, Sat; records other nights. From 50p, non-members welcome.

GOOD FOR KIDS

NATIONAL ARMY MUSEUM, Royal Hospital Rd. History of British Army from Yeomen of the Guard in 1485 to 1914 (when the Imperial War Museum in Lambeth takes over) plus Indian Army to 1947 and some Commonwealth regiments. Uniforms, weapons, colours and trophies, the skeleton of Napoleon's favourite charger. Mon–Sat 10am–5.30pm, Sun 2–5.30pm. Free.

BATTERSEA PARK Just across the river, with an attractive boating lake, a children's zoo and frequent special events and exhibitions.

HOW TO GET THERE

UNDERGROUND Sloane Square, Fulham Broadway.

BUSES 11, 14, 19, 22, 31, 39, 39A, 45, 49, 137, 249.

The City

This was the nicest place in London to live in because everything could be reached on foot, down alleys and passages. Like all county towns it had a bit of every trade. I was lucky enough to live in Cloth Fair where there was still a shop which sold cloth. On some weekly nights there was bell-ringing from the Tower of St Bartholomew the Great, just such bells as the walled city must have heard when there were 106 churches in its square mile. Behind me was Smithfield meat market with its cheerful, Chaucerian characters and medieval-looking hand barrows. The hellish noise of articulated lorries coming in from Europe in the small hours drove me out. Just over the boundary were the rag trade and the print, and down in Clerkenwell the clocks. Southward, the City became a river port with wharves and cobbled quays and a smell of fish from Billingsgate where alleys plunged steeply to the river.

There was still a sense of sewers where Fleet Ditch flows under Farringdon Street and Fleet Street climbs westward through the journalists to the Temple and the Law. East of the City at Aldgate Pump I could sense the Orient, and at Beaver Hall on a Sunday business was brisk in the fur trade while the rest of the City was silent. What makes the City so different from all London is its secrecy. It is really a village of about 400 people who know each other and whose word is their bond. If they break their word they are out. All this secret life is sealed by those medieval guilds, the City companies with their livery halls, bumbledom and beadles.

The character of the City has been nearly killed by old-fashioned tower blocks and inhuman scale.

John Betjeman

WHAT TO SEE

MUSEUM OF LONDON London Wall. T 600 3699. Combined collections of Guildhall and old London Museums, newly housed in SW corner of Barbican. Fascinating displays of relics from pre-history to present day, costumes, domestic and shop interiors. Roman, medieval and Tudor sections superb. Great Fire Experience, models of Tudor London and Lord Mayor's coach. Tue–Sat 10am–6pm. Sun 2–6pm; free.

GUILDHALL King St. T 606 3030. Centre of civic government for more than 1000 years, much of the building dates from the early fifteenth century. Mon–Sat 10am–5pm, (Sun May–Sept only, 2–5pm); free. Library, housed in new west wing, has unrivalled collection of records, manuscripts, books, maps and prints illustrating the history and development of London.

MONUMENT Monument St. May–Sept Mon–Sat 9am–5.40pm, Sun 2–5.40pm; Oct–April Mon–Sat 9am–3.40pm. Adults 20p, children 10p. Commemorating the Great Fire of 1666, this hollow column provides a breath-taking view from 202ft, providing one has any breath left after climbing up the 311 steps.

ST PAUL'S CATHEDRAL Church, crypt, galleries, observation balcony with marvellous view. Mon–Sat 10.45am–3.15pm, also April–Sept 4.45–6pm. Crypt 30p, 15p children; galleries ditto. CITY CHURCHES Some pre-Fire churches survive. Oldest St Bartholomew the Great in Smithfield, smallest St Ethelburga, Bishopsgate. The Great Fire destroyed eighty-seven churches of which fifty-one were rebuilt under Wren's supervision. Many brilliantly restored after Blitz. (See Keeping Amused).

SMITHFIELD MARKET Wholesale meat market – there was a cattle market on the site back in the fourteenth century. ST BRIDE PRINTING LIBRARY Bride Lane. T 353 4660. All aspects of print and related subjects, exhibition room of early presses and types. Mon–Fri 9.30am–5.30pm; free.

DR JOHNSON'S HOUSE 17 Gough Sq. T 353 3745. Interesting Queen Anne house in which the great dictionary was compiled. Mon–Sat 11am–5.30pm (Oct–April 5pm). 30p, children 15p.

PUBLIC RECORD OFFICE Chancery Lane. T 405 0745. Small public museum of historic documents, from actual Domesday Book on. Mon–Fri 1–4pm. Free.

TEMPLE. T 236 8462. Once the property of the Knights Templar, military crusading order accused of witchcraft and dissolved 1312. Lawyers moved in shortly after. Finest of five surviving round churches in England, with effigies of medieval knights and grotesque heads, Mon–Sat 10am–5pm (4.30pm winter), Sun 2–4pm (Aug–Sept 10am–5pm). Middle Temple Hall is Tudor, with magnificent double hammerbeam roof. Mon–Fri 10am–noon, 3–4.30pm, Sat 10am–4pm; free. Inner Temple Hall Mon–Fri 10.30am–noon, 2.30–3.30pm; free.

WHERE TO EAT

If you want a good meal in the City, it had better be a weekday lunch: as few people live there, restaurants mainly do a roaring trade 1–2 pm, then close shortly afterwards. A few stay open outside these hours; for example, the Gallipoli, Bishopsgate Churchyard (T 588 1922) with belly-dancers (12 noon–3pm, 6pm–3.30am); and the Spartan, 175–177 Queen Victoria St (T 248 5567) with live Greek music. Sample prices are for average three-course meal for two with drink. *Open for weekday lunches only* unless otherwise indicated.

SWEETINGS 39 Queen Victoria St. T 248 3062. Oysters, salmon, halibut and herring most popular dishes, plainly done. Noise, bustle and speed terrific, but an experience no City connoisseur should miss. £9.

GOWS 81 Old Broad St. T 588 2050. Began life in Victoria's reign, serving oysters to men in a hurry. Their 1¼lb plaice on the bone (£2·10) is famous. Eat at the bar, in old-fashioned stalls, or more modern restaurant. Excellent steaks, cutlets and cold roast meats. £7·50.

GREAT EASTERN HOTEL Liverpool St. T 283 4363. Edwardian rooms create happy illusion of being back in days of steam. Three restaurants lunchtime, two in evening. Diehards can still find mashed swedes and rice pudding. Beaufort Room for real bigwigs. Twigger's (coffee house) does good Sun lunch £2·90 per head (handy for Petticoat Lane). Coffee house £5 to Beaufort £15. Snack bar in Abercorn Bar.

LE MARMITON 4 Blomfield St. T 588 4643. More in the style of today, and French with it. The patron Michel has good reputation. Huge French cheeseboard, wine list reasonably priced. £10–£12.

LE POULBOT 45 Cheapside. T 236 4379. Owned by Roux brothers. Upstairs brasserie food, £3 a head. Downstairs altogether and literally more plushy (dark red). French food and cooking of the highest standard; wines £8–£46 a bottle, thus £28 not unusual for a meal *à deux*.

LE GAMIN 32 Old Bailey. T 236 7931. Also Roux brothers. This excellent restaurant caters for ordinary people as well as millionaires. A perfectly cooked large ham omelette, salad and glass of wine costs £1·80.

CITY FRIENDS 34 Old Bailey. T 236 4111. Chinese, open seven days a week, lunches and dinner. Crowded, but Cantonese food very good. £6 with lager if you stick to chef's suggestion for two – soup and four dishes which are different each day. Otherwise £3·50–£15 a head.

SLENDERS 41 Cathedral Pl. T 236 5974. Unlicensed, good choice of delicious vegetarian food. Fruit juice, muesli, carrot soup and lasagne Verdi [*sic*] would cost about £1·50 a head. 8.30 am–6.15pm weekdays.

THE COURT 116 Newgate St. T 600 1134. Across the road from the Old Bailey, designed to give lunches with a touch of privacy to members of the legal profession. Well known for steak and veal dishes with three fresh vegetables all for 60p, and a reasonable wine list; the menu is English and Continental; also one curry dish daily. Owner and efficient overseer is Mrs Allibhai. £8–£9.

CHARTERHOUSE GRILL 33–37 Charterhouse Sq. T 606 7392. Choose your own steak and watch the chef cook it on original grill. Very crowded at lunch, less so evenings when you can eat only in the Charter Room (606 9482), and pay more. £10 for lunch, £16 for dinner. Closed weekends.

MERMAID THEATRE RESTAURANTS Puddle Dock. T 248 2835. Downstairs, called Gutz at lunchtime, main dish about £1·20; Tavern at night, £10 for dinner – or you can have set dinner with theatre ticket £5·95 a head. Riverside upstairs has a fine view of river, does more elaborate meals £14. Last orders 7.30pm, closed Sat lunch and all day Sun.

BUBB'S 329 Central Markets, Smithfield (corner of Snow Hill and Farringdon Street). T 236 2435. Dinner as well as lunch, packed night or day. French cooking excellent, beautifully presented. Also quick-service no-booking brasserie. £14 restaurant; £2 a head brasserie. Last orders 9.30, closed weekends, Aug.

LE GAULOIS 119 Chancery Lane, T 405 7769. LA GERMAINERIE downstairs at same address. T 405 0920. First class French food; more elaborate at Le Gaulois, which also does dinners, £10. More easy-going at La Germainerie, which is renowned for steaks, £9. Both do excellent cheeses. Closed weekends. THE NOSHERIE 12 Greville St. T 242 1591. Just off Hatton Garden and 'kosher enough not to offend anybody'. Meals continuously 8am–6pm, packed 1–2. Salt beef, fresh salmon, pot-roast brisket and latkes famous. £4–£5. Closed weekends.

Picnics

Maze of old cobbled alleys and tiny courts, many leading to a minute patch of green, often a churchyard that's lost its church. The modern buildings, whatever their failings, usually incorporate a spacious piazza with plenty of seating.

WHERE TO DRINK

YE OLDE LONDON Ludgate Hill. William Younger's pub serving usual selection of strong northern brews. Dim but congenial interior. Lunchtime cold food and hot grills prepared before your eyes.

OLD KING LUD 78 Ludgate Hill. Comfortable Victorian-style pub offers hand-pumped Whitbread's ales and good hot and cold food. Service always fast, even at crowded lunchtimes.

THE BLACK FRIAR 174 Queen Victoria St. Free house serving real ale and excellent range of bottled beer. Food limited to rather dreary sandwiches but worth visiting for its copper murals, marble columns.

CORTS WINEBAR Old Bailey. John Mortimer, QC, takes his Old Bailey lunch breaks here. Large, freshly made salads complement the usual selection of wines, plus excellent ports and sherries.

YE OLDE CHESHIRE CHEESE Wine Office Court, Fleet St. Charismatic seventeenth-century pub with restaurant on three floors where legal types wolf down large quantities of roast beef and steak and kidney pie. Marston's bitter on tap, choice of wines.

JAMAICA WINE HOUSE St Michael's Alley, Cornhill. Hard to find but worth visiting, this was one of London's original coffee houses, rebuilt in 1668 after Fire. Will still serve coffee as well as wines and keg beers; free house. Hot and cold snacks lunchtime.

THE PUMP 185 Bishopsgate. Near Petticoat Lane/Liverpool St station, Edwardian-style Whitbread's pub serving excellent Marlowe ale as well as keg beers; hot and cold snacks.

EL VINO'S Fleet St. Traditional watering hole of London's journalists and is also popular with lawyers from nearby Temple. Some excellent (and often rare) wines. Good restaurant in basement.

THE SHIP TAVERN 27 Lime St. Reputedly oldest City pub, dates back to mid 1400s. Good selection of malt whiskies as well as keg and real Truman's ales. Hot snacks lunchtime only, good cold food otherwise.

MOTHER BUNCH'S Old Seacoal Lane. Cellar winebar with sawdust on the floor and an interesting cold table – game pie highly recommended. Worth booking lunch, though quiet in evening.

THE OLD WATLING 29 Watling St. Seventeenth-century ale-house was allegedly Wren's 'office' whilst construction of St Paul's was in progress. Two bars and a restaurant serving steak and oyster and pigeon pie.

THE GEORGE 86 Fenchurch St. Charrington's real ales. Variety of hot and cold bar food, also carvery restaurant at back.

WHERE TO SHOP

Shops are usually closed on Sat.

Holborn: BLACKS CAMPING AND LEISURE, No. 146. T 405 4426. Known world-wide; also equipment for climbing, lightweight pot holing and walking, accessories, outdoor clothing. Expert advice. Open Sat.

JODIES DRAPERY STORE, No. 143–144. T 242 2649. Full range cheap designers' fabrics. Fine selection of old buttons plus sixty varieties of pearl buttons.

JOHN BRUMFIT 337 High Holborn. T 405 2929. Established 1864, pipe specialists. Also wide range English and imported cigarettes, cigars, snuffs, pipe tobacco, lighters and gifts.

Holborn Bars: SANFORD BROS, No. 3. T 405 2352. Precious stones, watches, etc. at fifty-year-old jewellers and silversmiths.

Hatton Gdn Street full of dealers in silver and precious stones – often loose and uncut. Much close trading, so many shops do not welcome browsers.

THE JEWEL HOUSE, No. 113. T 242 4317. One of the first dealers to go retail. About 2000 items on display, including men's jewellery. £15–£4000. All jewellery new; make to order; repairs.

R. HOLT AND CO., No. 111. T 405 5286. Every gem, diamonds to agate, displayed; mineral display and lapidary workshop.

A. R. ULLMANN LTD, No. 10. T 405 1877. Secondhand and antique jewellery. Fine display Georgian and Victorian silver pieces, silver chain bags, *objets d'art*, scent bottles, brooches.

Greville St: FELT & HESSIAN SHOP, No. 34. T 405 6215. Felts in all colours, by the metre or in squares; hessian in next door warehouse where cut to order. Also soft toys 50p–£40.

Leather Lane Flourishing noisy street market; clothes, shoes, chamois leather fabrics, bags, records, toys, haberdashery, plants, hardware and umbrellas. 10am–2pm Mon–Fri. (See Buying Food.)

Farringdon Rd: FULLERSCOPES, No. 63 Telescope House. T 405 2156. For over 150 years all-brass telescopes handmade here; virtually everything to do with astronomy.

BOOK MARKET At Clerkenwell Rd end, from early morning until mid afternoon, weather permitting. Old books and newspapers.

DARIUS ARTS 105 Clerkenwell Rd. T 242 3741. Range of onyx items.

Cloth Fair Tiny street opposite St Bartholomew the Great owned by Landmark Trust who ensure nothing modernized.

MITCHELL, INMAN AND CO., No. 39. T 606 8708. Wholesale woollen merchants but happy to retail. Mahogany counters and cupboards from 1800, stock of felts and cloths stacked in huge rolls looks unchanging, too.

PRIORY ANTIQUES, No. 45. T 606 9060. Small antiques, antique and modern jewellery; repairs. Next door to only building in the street that survived Great Fire.

Newgate St: NEWGATE GALLERY, No. 114. T 606 3955. Large gallery, wide selection prints of all styles £15–£200. Frame on premises while you wait.

J. A. L. FRANKS 140 New Fetter Lane. T 405 2170. General stamp dealer; collection of postcards.

Chancery Lane: LANGFORDS, No. 46/47. T 405 6402. Delightfully chaotic shop. Antique and old silver, Sheffield plate, old model ships and scientific instruments.

SWEET AND MAXWELL, No. 23. T 583 9855. Publishers and booksellers. Legal, technical, some business books.

SOTHEBY'S, No. 115. T 405 7238. Auctions of books from 1830 onwards. Special emphasis on illustrated, travel and children's books. Sales every two weeks, Thur and Fri from 1pm, viewing until midday. Ring for a catalogue.

SILVER VAULTS. Entrance on side of Southampton Buildings. Over 150 years old, vaults look like a series of prison cells. Over fifty silver dealers, so marvellous choice. Not the place for bargains, but fair prices for quality pieces.

Moorfields: EDWARD MARCUS, No. 7.

T 638 0390. Optical instruments, some secondhand. Binoculars, telescopes, microscopes, barometers.

PHOTOMARKETS LTD, No. 16. T 628 0837. Enormous cut-price, full-range photography store.

London Wall: LYNTONS, No. 41. T 628 9036. General chemists. Also range of Biba cosmetics.

W. THURGOOD, No. 161. Salisbury House. T 628 5437. This sixty-year-old shop sells cigars from all over world, cigarettes, pipes, tobacco.

Gresham St: THRESHER AND GLENNY, No. 50. T 606 7451. Tailors and shirtmakers, holds earliest Royal Warrant issued to private trader. Make to order and sell off the peg; all designs traditional English.

HARRY B. HART. Now incorporated into Thresher and Glenny, handmade, traditional style ready-to-wear men's shoes.

Cheapside: APSLEY PELLATT CO., No. 47. T 248 4917. Leading English names in fine china and crystal.

WOODERSON, No. 123/124. T 606 5829. The Shop Under the Tree, established 1894. Make shirts to order and sells ready-made. Also accessories.

GORDON GROSE SPORTS 7 Ludgate House, St Bride St. T 353 0082. Weight training and lifting equipment; clothing and equipment for bowls, cricket, golf, tennis, badminton, squash swimming, rugby, soccer and hockey. Mainly adults.

Fleet St: MONTY CRISTO, No. 180. T 242 9417. (See Cheapside.)

COBHAM NUMISMATICS, No. 147. T 353 9447. Modern and Oriental coins, bank notes, bonds and numismatics books; albums, accessories.

GEOGRAPHIA, No. 63. T 353 2701. Wide range of globes, maps and atlases.

OYEZ, No. 191. T 405 2847. Law books, stationery, small selection general books.

BUYING FOOD

Leather Lane Fruit and vegetables, eggs and tinned produce at lively market 10am–2pm Mon–Fri.

COLESONS, No. 91. T 405 2526. Breads and pastries fresh-baked on premises.

GRODZINSKI, No. 22. T 405 9492. French and English breads, range of fresh-baked pastry and patisserie.

CONTINENTAL STORES, No. 90. Wonderful corner shop selling every kind English and Continental groceries; coffee.

HEALTH AND BEAUTY BAR, No. 56–58. T 242 9685. Good range of health foods, Loseley yoghourts, cereals, ginseng, vitamins. Also cosmetics.

Farringdon St: MACKENZIE BROS, No. 508. T 253 2703. Fresh fish displayed daily, selection of smoked fish.

BACON AND HAM SHOP, No. 506. Bacon sold by the pound or in large pre-packed quantities.

J. T. HART & SONS. Corner of Charterhouse St. T 236 0055. Linked small shops selling good-value meats, poultry, game, vegetables, cold meats and some delicatessen, bacon, cheese and groceries.

DAKIN, No. 333. T 236 2275. Off-licence and selection of high-class groceries and confectionery plus coffee beans.

GOLDRINGS OF HOLBORN Caxton House. T 253 5488. Bread, pastries, cream cakes; can eat on premises.

WALKERS 43 London Wall. T 638 1578. Restaurant with a delicatessen and grocery. Ardenne and mushroom and turkey pâté, whole hams, quiches with homemade pastry, pastries.

Fleet Street: NEWMANS CHOCOLATES, No. 31. T 836 5151. All handmade. English and Continental. They will send by post.

SHARATON PATISSERIE, No. 97. T 624 9287. Breads, tarts, cream cakes, gateaux fresh daily.

KEEPING AMUSED

GUILDHALL SCHOOL OF MUSIC AND DRAMA. T 628 2571. Well-known training ground for future 'greats'. Several student productions of excellent quality open to the public. Send sae to The Box Office, Guildhall School of Music and Drama, Barbican, EC2Y 8DT, for free tickets.

CITY UNIVERSITY St John St. T 253 4399. Concerts, plays, dances, cabaret nights, discos open to general public during school terms if signed in at door.

LONDON WALKS Experienced guides show 'hidden' areas. No booking required, for list send sae to: London Walks, 20 Alexandra Road, Hornsey, London N8. Approx 1½-2 hours, 70p.

OFF-BEAT TOURS OF LONDON 66 St Michael's St. T 262 9572. Range of forty walks lasting 1½ hours. Mid-May to mid-Sept Mon–Fri evenings; winter Sun afternoons. Adults 70p, students 60p.

LIVERY HALLS All around the City. Details and tickets from City Information Centre, St Paul's Churchyard, EC4M 8BX (T 606 3030).

STOCK EXCHANGE Old Broad St. T 588 2355. Mon–Fri 10am–3.15pm. Exhibition area, cinema and visitors' gallery to watch 2500 jobbers and brokers on trading floor.

ROYAL EXCHANGE Cornhill. T 606 2433. Present building dates from 1844, courtyard and ambulatory Mon–Fri 10am–3.45pm, Sat 10am–noon; free. Various art societies hold regular exhibitions here to which public are admitted free.

MERMAID THEATRE Puddle Dock. T 248 2835. On banks of Thames, includes a 498-seater auditorium, and two restaurants (see Where to Eat). Occasional late-night performances, otherwise first-runs.

OLD BAILEY (Central Criminal Court). Visitors' Gallery to the twenty-three courts 10am–4pm (closed 1–2pm) Mon–Fri. Free.

LAW COURTS (Royal Courts of Justice) Strand. Admission to fifty-five courts. 9am–4pm. Free.

CITY CHURCHES Lecture and music recital details in monthly 'Events in the City of London', from Information Centre, St Paul's Churchyard. T 606 3030. (See What to See.)

GOOD FOR KIDS

ST PAUL'S CATHEDRAL Whispering Gallery is an established favourite, Stone Gallery has marvellous view. (What to See.)

NATIONAL POSTAL MUSEUM King Edward St. Stamp-collector's paradise with comprehensive collection of, 350000 British and foreign stamps, including Phillips collection of nineteenth-century British stamps. Mon–Fri 10am–4.30pm (Thur 7pm). Free.

MUSEUM OF LONDON (See What to See.) WATCH AND CLOCK MUSEUM Guildhall Library. T 606 3030. Over 700 exhibits including watches, clocks and marine chronometers, tell the story of 500 years of timekeeping. Mon–Fri 9.30am–5pm; free.

HOW TO GET THERE

BR Blackfriars, Cannon St, Broad St, Liverpool St, Holborn Viaduct, Farringdon, Barbican.

UNDERGROUND Chancery Lane, Farringdon, Barbican, Moorgate, Liverpool St, St Paul's, Mansion House, Bank, Monument, Blackfriars.

BUSES 6, 8, 9, 9A, 10, 10A, 11, 15, 17, 18, 21, 22, 25, 40, 40A, 43, 44, 45, 46, 63, 76, 86, 95, 104, 109, 133, 141, 149, 155, 168, 168A, 171, 176A, 184, 214, 221, 243, 259, 271, 277, 279, 279A, 501, 502, 513.

Covent Garden

I first came to work here about a third of my life ago. I walked from the tube station down Floral Street, passing a lorry with enough sprouts on it to feed a *corps de ballet*, and I heard a tenor doing his scales in a dressing room. Before the night was out an extremely drunken journalist had asked me to be goal keeper for his team in the park the next day. I refused, but felt that I had experienced Covent Garden – veg, art and 'the print'.

The 'art' remains but most of the veg and print have gone and in their place new businesses are springing up. You can choose kites or hire barrows, buy make-up, rent theatrical costumes or find a French horn when sated with Japanese food and sake. There are old bookshops and new ones, shops that sell inks and nibs, scent, maps, paper toys. There are dozens of eccentric little businesses, new art galleries, photographers' studios and graphic designers – even punk rock.

It is a village of individualists, but I saw the men with theodolites measuring up the Japanese Garden for a nice new tower block. We have our eccentrics like the man who is convinced that the state of

England is due to the alcoholism of the Archbishop of Canterbury ('All those big cellars under Lambeth Palace'). We have our friendly policeman, our churches, the Floral Hall, the Piazza, our good pubs, good restaurants and, above all, our fervent hope that we won't be concreted over.

Charles Campbell

WHAT TO SEE

THE PIAZZA London's first square, 1670–1974 centre of Covent Garden market. Magnificent Victorian central market building being converted into arcade of shops, studios and workshops, part of Jubilee Hall will soon be a sports centre; plans to house London Transport Collection and British Theatre Museum in old Flower Market. Enthusiastic Staff of GLC Information Centre, 1–4 King St, will give details. ST PAUL'S CHURCH Bedford St. Designed by Inigo Jones as focal point of Piazza. Startlingly simple but very attractive interior, with monuments to many great actors.

ST GILES-IN-THE-FIELDS, St Giles High St. Founded 1101 as leper hospital chapel. Present building 1734, by Flitcroft, well restored after bomb damage.

GOODWIN'S COURT 55/56 St Martin's Lane. Enchanting alley of perfectly preserved eighteenth-century bow-windowed houses.

WHERE TO EAT

Area is filled during day with people from local offices, art galleries, rehearsal rooms, design studios; equally full at night with patrons and performers from theatres and Opera House. Many grand and spacious old warehouses being successfully converted to restaurants. Sample prices are for average three-course meal for two, with wine. Open for lunch and dinner seven days unless otherwise indicated. RULES 35 Maiden Lane. T 836 5314. Opened 1798 – past customers included Dickens, Thackeray and Prince of Wales with Lily Langtry. Rooms delightfully Edwardian in appearance (ditto waiters); menu reassuringly British. £20. Closed weekends and last three weeks Aug.

SHEEKEY'S 28–32 St Martin's Court. T 836 4118. Serving fish since 1896. Since takeover by Scott's, grill as well as boil. Other welcome innovations hollandaise sauce and longer hours – last orders Mon–Fri 11pm, Sat 11.30pm, Sun 10.30pm. £16.

CHEZ SOLANGE 35 Cranbourn St. T 836 0542/5886. Favourite with theatre-goers, very French and lively, food good too. £18. Closed Sun.

MON PLAISIR 21 Monmouth St. T 836 7243. Nearest thing to a real French bistro, run with terrific bonhomie by young owner, Alain Lhermitte. Excellent food, £12 unless bonhomie leads to more drink. Closed weekends.

FOOD FOR THOUGHT 31 Neal St. T 836 0239. Simple vegetarian wholefood dishes of the bean, lentil, yoghourt-based type. Cheap and healthy; not licensed, £3. Mon–Fri 12 noon–8pm.

AJIMURA 51–53 Shelton St. T 240 0178. Nicest, most authentic, most reasonably priced Japanese restaurant in London. Set menus £2·20–£4·50 a head. Worth it for charm, unusual food, and skill of cooks who can be watched. Closed Sat lunch, all day Sun.

POONS 41 King St. T 240 1743. Cantonese restaurant in which you can see the whole kitchen at work. Impossibly long menu; sea-food and dried meats recommended. £12.

BLITZ 4 Great Queen St. T 405 6598. Very cheap, homely food. Blitz has 'become a cult place for fashion people and college types'. Towards the end of the week Biddie, Eve and Richard sing forties' songs at the piano amid decor reminiscent of a wartime railway station. £8–£9 dinner, £2 for lunch without drink. Closed Sat lunch, all day Sun. Last orders 1.30am.

THE GRANGE 39 King St. T 240 2939. Hicks decor does clever things with mirrors and the tops of old confessional boxes. Pigeon pie, saddle of lamb and athol brose – good food for the squirearchy. Set menus £6·50–£9·30 a head include half a bottle wine. Closed Sat lunch, all day Sun.

NEAL STREET RESTAURANT 26 Neal St. T 836 8368. Cool, clean, beautiful. Contemporary pictures make it a favourite place with painters, dealers and art lovers who also have an enthusiasm for good food and wine. Renowned for prawns in bacon, game, grills and crème brûlée. £17. Closed weekends, last three weeks of August.

TUTTONS 11–12 Russell St. T 836 1167. Design and atmosphere cross between French brasserie and American bar/restaurant. Chairs and tables on pavement facing Piazza outside. Clean, friendly and informal with very switched-on young staff. Menu of varied items instead of formal courses, excellent large desserts, good range of drinks. Two-course lunch for two with wine, £5. No reservations. Open all day, closed Sun.

FRIENDS 30 Wellington St/21 Catherine St. T 836 5520. Smart but informal, attractively designed on conservatory theme with lots of plants; 'summerhouse' is bar. Emphasis on use of interesting fresh vegetables and fruit. Dinner £20. Closed Sun.

Picnics

Covent Garden is not one of London's prime picnic spots. A family were seen recently digging into their Tupperware in a back pew of nearby St Martin-in-the-Fields, but this is not recommended. The Italian Garden on the east side of the Piazza has some seats, and St Paul's and St Giles both have attractive churchyards. Embankment Gardens and Trafalgar Square are within easy walking distance, but full of rather pushy pigeons.

WHERE TO DRINK

OPERA TAVERN Catherine St. Unspoilt theatrical pub with posters and other ephemera all over the walls. Ind Coope house with draught Burton bitter; hot and cold food at lunchtime.

MARQUESS OF ANGLESEY Bow St. Pleasant, unfussy Young's house with plenty of seats to rest weary tourists' feet. Hot and cold bar food with pizza counter as lunchtime novelty.

THE GLOBE Bow St. Next door, smaller but gastronomically formidable. Sumptuous array of hot and cold food at all times including the best pub sausages for miles. Selection of champagne, too! Ind Coope beers.

BRAHMS & LISZT Russell St. Rhyming slang for you-know-what, and it's easy enough to overindulge in the wide range of well-kept wines both in the cool Market Bar downstairs, and wine bar proper at street level. Food is varied and generally good, especially fish. Closed Sun.

WHITE LION James/Floral St. Notable for selection of cold cuts served at all times, also serve hot bar snacks. Charrington beers and Aussie lager. Upstairs doubles bar with pool table and darts.

THE FRIGATE Upper St Martin's Lane/Little Newport St. Impossible to miss the massive ship's figurehead adorning the corner. Inside the theme remains nautical with ropes and gantries everywhere. Cold snacks in main bar, salads too in downstairs bar which sells wine as well. Restaurant upstairs.

SALISBURY St Martin's Lane. Beautiful windows and mirrors featured in many films. Serves a wide range of cold meats cooked on premises, cheese salads, hot snacks and main courses on its marble-topped bar and is something of a haunt for gay theatricals.

WHITE SWAN New Row. After you've been for a fitting to Moss Bros, call at this cosy if slightly dim hostelry for good hot food and real Charrington's ale.

MARQUIS OF GRANBY 51 Chandos Place. Near Charing Cross station, this Ind Coope house serves meat and cheese salads in the upstairs snug, and hot food as well.

PENNY'S PLACE King St. Attractive wine bar behind St Paul's Churchyard.

Fair selection of wines, hot food, grills and unusual specialities such as ham and chicken mousse, with salads available in wine bar and restaurant downstairs.

LAMB & FLAG Rose St. Small, low-ceilinged, old pub bustling with young ad-men and their secretaries who come at lunchtime for the excellent hot and cold food. Courage house. Theatrical clientele dominates in the evenings.

WHERE TO SHOP

Rabbit warren of tiny streets and alleys. Many specialist shops, some unchanged over 100 years. Traditional crafts still practised, since the Market moved to Nine Elms many new craft shops and workshops have come to area (see What to See).

Neal St Large proportion of newer shops can be found here.

NEW NEAL STREET SHOP, No. 23. Plants, bulbs, a range of unusual plant pots, macramé plant holders, Culpeper herbs, gardening and cookery books, dried flowers and leaves; preserves, prettily presented sweets and chocolates, small gifts, basketware from China. Also antique Chinese jewellery and embroidery, silk kimonos, paintings on silk – some antique, some modern, lacquer work. No. 29. T 240 0136. Wide range of items imported from China. Modern jewellery, painted paper kites, baskets, wicker bowls, children's books. Lots of decorative household items and little gifts. Open 11am, close 7pm Thur.

WAREHOUSE, No. 39. T 240 0931. Stock largely imported from India, China and Sri Lanka. Big range of small toys, 1p–£1, beads, Indian fabrics, small kitchen items; coconut matting in wide choice of colours, basketware, enamel plates, terracotta flower pots, pottery mugs, milk coolers; cheap clothes, some rattan furniture.

COPPER SHOP, No. 48. T 836 2984. English manufactured copper goods from plant troughs to jelly moulds, good quality cooking pots and preserving pans. Also handmade coal scuttles.

CLIVE SHILTON, No. 58. T 836 0809. Bags, hand luggage, leather jewellery, wallets, strappy evening sandals, boots handmade to order from a range of leathers and suedes.

R. I. HARDING & CO., No. 61. T 240 2860. Some of earliest cameras can be seen but not bought. Repairs to modern cameras only.

KITES, No. 69. T 836 1666. Everything necessary to build kites. Also a wide range of kites and kite books.

COVENT GARDEN BICYCLES, 41 Short's Gdns. T 836 1752. Linked to warehouse. Sell bikes from simple to exotic, also Chinese bicycles. Pretty basic but splendidly dignified, similar to old-fashioned English bikes. Secondhand bikes, repairs.

Endell St: CORNER HOUSE BOOKSHOP, No. 14. T 836 9960. Radical education, women's movement, socialism, nonsexist children's books, third world education pamphlets, enormous range of magazines and pamphlets on related subjects. Only London outlet for ACE's *Where*.

Earlham St: BLACKMAN HARVEY, No. 29. T 836 1904. Long established framer with Print Centre, sells modern graphics and reproduction prints of all periods. Offer forty-eight-hour framing service, and hire out pictures.

ARTHUR BEALE 194 Shaftesbury Ave. T 836 9034. Ropemakers on the banks of the Fleet 400 years ago, now leading yacht chandlers; more geared to sailing than motor boats.

Monmouth St: PAPER RAINBOW, No. 17. T 240 3664. Stationery and gift items of lively, unusual style. French enamel door number plates, enormous glass French storage jars, books, Gordon Fraser and Nigel Quiney wrapping papers.

RUSSELL AND CHAPPLE, 23. No. T 836

7521. Don't be put off by trade look – inside is a treasure house of ropes and twines, artists and theatrical canvas, coconut matting, green baize, hessian deck chair covering, cotton and jute twills. Make boat covers to order.

CATHAY ANTIQUES, No. 47. T 240 0458. Eighteenth- and nineteenth-century Oriental antiques: ceramics, paintings, bronze and lacquer work, some small furniture.

COLLECTORS CORNER, No. 63. T 836 5614. Classical and operatic records, including imports and exclusive items. Small secondhand section.

GEORGE PARKER & SONS 12 Upper St Martin's Lane. T 836 1164. Established in 1851. Finely made saddles, all aspects of saddlery.

Henrietta St: LONGMANS PLANT HOUSE, No. 4. T 623 8414 (ask for this branch). Tropical house plants, especially ones with shiny dark green leaves.

GRIFFITHS HANSEN PIANOS, No. 11. T 240 2204. Agents for most UK upright and grand pianos. Also tin whistles, accordions, violins, cheap folk guitars, musical accessories.

Maiden Lane: HARRIS PUBLICATIONS LTD, No. 42. T 240 2286. Stamp collectors paraphernalia: books and magazines (part of Stamp Collecting Group).

BOOKSMITHS, No. 33. T 836 3341. Bargains of publishers' remainders at half price or less.

Floral St: DANCE CENTRE, No. 12. T 836 6544. Tights with or without feet in twenty colours, leg warmers ten colours, leotards, Greek sandals and ballet, tap and jazz shoes.

FALKINER FINE ARTS, Mart St. T 240 2339. Small trade-style shop where Gabrielle Falkiner supplies specialist papers for artists and craftsmen: bookbinders, calligraphers, picture framers and fine printers. Doesn't mind browsers, or selling small quantities.

PROJECT HAND SHOP 38 King St. T 836 6941. Only handicrafts from unexploited small co-operatives in developing countries. Everything cheap and beautifully made. Mohair rugs from Lesotho, basketware from Bangladesh, Ethiopia and Africa, beads, musical instruments and batiks. (See Keeping Amused.)

COVENT GARDEN GALLERY 20 Russell St. T 836 1139. English and Continental drawings, watercolours and paintings from eighteenth and nineteenth century can be seen and bought.

C. &. W. MAY 9–11 Garrick St. T 836 5993. Fancy dress hire section of Moss Bros.

Bedford St: MOSS BROS. T 240 4567. Morning and evening men's dress hire, also sell 'everything for the man's wardrobe'; enormous Special Offer Room sells cancelled orders at bargain prices.

ROYALE STAMP CO., No. 41/2. T 836 6122. Stamps from all over the world bought and sold; specialize in stamps from Great Britain.

New Row: SCOTTISH MERCHANT, No. 16. T 836 2207. Rainbow and plain Shetlands, hand-knitted Fair Isles, machine-knitted patterns, Guernseys and other seamen's jumpers, shawls, gloves and hats. Some pottery and glass.

THOMAS BLAND & SONS, No. 21. T 836 9122. Established 1840 as gunmaker. Today 90 per cent of guns and rifles factory made; rest hand-crafted by Bland.

JAMES ASMAN, No. 23a. T 240 1380. One of leading jazz record shops. Mr Asman started collecting at the end of twenties and boasts fine collection, new and secondhand.

THEATRE ZOO, No. 28. T 836 3150. Hire out animal costumes. Sell hats, stage jewellery, grotesque and unusual face masks, false feet and hands and moustaches, stage make-up.

Bedfordbury: SUNFLOWER, No. 28. T 836 6564. Tibetan wool jackets, shirts and waistcoats; books on medicine and alternative technology, sympathetic novels, science fiction comics, Furry Freak comics and cards. NOSTALGIA, No. 29. T 240 5238. Men's and women's twenties to fifties day and evening wear; lots of Edwardian and Victorian whites. Also new mohair jerseys and dresses, Fair Isles knitted from old patterns.

GOODWINS GENERAL STORES, No. 25. T 836 5072. Canopied corner shop selling a little bit of everything.

Southampton St: SAMUEL FRENCH, No. 26. T 836 7513. Attempts to stock all plays and books on the theatre and related subjects that are in the English language. Also sound effects records, opera libretti and opera books. 100-page catalogue of technical books on request.

MAPSELLER, No. 37. T 836 8444. Antique maps from fifteenth century onwards for the collector. Also related books, early atlases; framing service.

Tavistock St: HARVEST, No. 40. T 240 0694. Changing exhibitions of full range of British crafts, prices £1–£100. All craftsmen commissionable.

LITTLEWOOD BROS, No. 13. T 836 6224. Been going 210 years. General tools and gardening equipment, domestic and hardware. Also clay flower pots up to fifteen inches high.

Wellington St: GOLF GEAR, No. 40. T 836 6514. Everything for enthusiasts: clubs, shoes, socks, balls, etc.

GALICIA, No. 24. T 836 2961. Best in classic designed French and English women's fashions. Swiss silk shirts, Stephen Marks blazers, Roland Klein evening wear, silk day wear by Scali, Jean Rychter knitwear, Berluc summer dresses, reasonably priced Joose separates.

PENHALIGON'S, No. 41. T 836 2150. Established 1870, handmake on premises all perfumes, toilet water, aftershave, shampoo, deodorant, bath oil and hair dressings to original formulas. Preparation can be watched.

Essentially a man's house, but many items popular with women. Beautiful catalogue on request. Also sell antique bottles containing Penhaligon products, antique dressing table articles and dressing cases.

TOYE KENNING & SPENCER LTD, 19–21 Gt Queen St. T 242 0471. Jewellers and silversmiths, medallion insignia, regalia manufacturers and tie, trophy and badge specialists with a Royal Warrant. Sharing premises is HOUSE OF DENT who undertake clock and watch repairs.

Drury Lane: ANELLO AND DAVIDE, No. 30. T 836 1983. Theatrical shoemakers. Shoes and boots of any style or period to order, also stock of one-bar shoes in most colours, ballet and tap shoes. Next door sale shop; men and women's sandals and shoes from Italy plus some Anello and Davide lines.

PHILIP POOLE & CO., No. 182. T 405 7097. Old-fashioned shop with collection of fountain pens, pen wipers, inkwells on display. Sells modern fountain pens, all eighteen varieties of nibs made today, steel pens, blotters, inkwells. Also commercial stationers.

Long Acre: BRODIE AND MIDDLETON, No. 79. T 836 3289. Run as a family business for 137 years. Supply theatrical and arts trade with powder-colours, pigments, glitters, curtains and drapes, everything necessary to make scenery.

BELL BOOK & RADMALL, No. 80. T 240 2161. English and American modern fiction, modern poetry and literature first editions.

J. W. BOLLOM, No. 107–115. T 836 3728. All types of paints, wall coverings and fabrics. Within Bollom's is THE LONDON GRAPHICS CENTRE, largest Letraset dealer in the country, stocks of all fine art and graphics materials.

VIDEO CASSETTE RECORDERS, No. 112. T 240 0126. Really a trade concern supplying studios, but will sell to public. Machines from £650. Cassette players/recorders, TV games, cassettes. GLASSHOUSE, No. 65. T 836 9785. Sells work of group of young glass-blowers, who can be watched making pieces.

MADE IN HEAVEN, No. 18–19. T 836 4056. Manufacture enormous range of jeans in wide range of fabrics. Ranges of separates in soft-coloured voiles and in plain and striped linen; knitted cream skirts; exclusive floral print cotton range. Also sell track-suits in bright colours and choices of fabrics, baggy sweatshirt tops, swim-wear, handbags, shoes; surfboards, golf clubs, tennis racquets, etc.

STANFORDS, No. 12. T 836 1321. *The* London map shop. Complete range of Ordnance Survey maps for UK and several other countries; wall, militaria, RAC, professional and nautical maps; *Observer* maps of Zoo, Roman and Art Britain in full colour; atlases and globes.

HOWIE, No. 138. T 240 0896. Lynne Franks, leading fashion PR, behind zany clothes, accessories and fun items. Low prices.

Denmark St: RHODES, No. 22. T 836 4656. Mostly electric guitars, key-boards, drums and accessories; range of amplifiers, extremely large range of effects.

ZENO, No. 6. T 836 2522. Books on every aspect of Greece and the Islands: guide books, dictionaries, fiction, etc.

TOP GEAR, No. 5. T 240 2118. Electric and acoustic guitars, amplifiers, accessories.

The Unexpected

SALVI, 55 Endell St. T 836 0788. Italian Salvi harps £1900–£5600. Also harp books, music, records and accessories.

PAXMAN, 116 Long Acre. T 240 3647. Only horn-maker in this country, and sole outlet for their horns. Mr Paxman makes some on the premises but most of thirty-eight models made in their factory. £540 for a Series II to about £1200 for Full Triple Horn. All horns made from brass (yellow or gold) or nickel silver. Also, accessories, records and music.

CLIVE SHILTON, 58 Neal St. T 836 0809. Accessories – shoes, bags, jewellery – using lush satin and finest kid. Shell motif everywhere. Every-thing is exquisitely handcrafted – and incredibly expensive – but just looking in the window is an experience.

BUYING FOOD

COLESONS 1 Monmouth St. T 836 2066. Fresh bread daily, rolls, cakes, pastries.

Neal Yard: WHOLEFOOD WAREHOUSE, No. 2. T 240 1154. Grains, pulses, nuts, dried fruits, seeds, flours, cereals, pasta, salt, tea and jam; all cheaper in quantity. Also honeys and freshly made peanut butter.

WHOLEFOOD BAKERY, No. 6. T 240 1154. Own storeground flour; bread, quiches, flans.

New Row: DRURY LANE TEA & COFFEE CO., No. 3. T 836 1960. Twenty-two blends of own-roast coffee, ground to order. Also eight of own teas plus a range bought in. Teapots, caddies, coffee-making equipment.

COLISEUM DAIRY, No. 7. T 836 1031. Whole English, Welsh and Dutch cheeses, plus packaged French and Italian. Freshly cut ham, tongue, pork, beef and chicken. Also garlic sausage, salamis, cream cakes and buns; wide range groceries.

JUBILEE MARKET, Southampton St. Arrival of enormous half open air market coincided with Nine Elms move. Good for fruit and vegetables, farm fresh eggs, poultry, bacon, irregular fish stall. Daily meat auc-tions.

DRURY LANE TEA & COFFEE CO. 37 Drury Lane. T 836 2667. (See New Row.)

FRUITY FLORIST Long Acre (by Covent

Gdn tube). Retail produce at wholesale prices. Daily special offer of one or two fruits or vegetables incredibly cheap. Unusual fruit and veg.

KEEPING AMUSED

BRITISH CRAFTS CENTRE 43 Earlham St. Gallery displaying work of leading British artist-craftsmen. Mon–Fri 10am–5.30pm, Sat 10.30am–3.30 pm.

WAREHOUSE GALLERY 52 Earlham St. Shows little-known artists; also some highly successful special exhibitions. Mon–Sat 10am–6pm. Free. No. 48 for Artists Market.

PHOTOGRAPHERS' GALLERY, 8 Gt Newport St. Excellent regular exhibitions, wide range of prints and books on sale. Tue–Sat 11am–7pm, Sun noon –6pm. Usually free.

ANTHROPOS GALLEY 65–67 Monmouth St. T 836 8162. Ethnic tribal art from all over the world, 700 items on five floors. Always show Eskimo, New Guinea and African art, Indian temple paintings and miniatures. Mon-Wed 10am–8pm, Thur–Sat 10am–noon, Sun 1–7pm.

ANTHONY STOKES 3 Langley Court. T 240 1804. Shows paintings and sculptures of young artists. Mon–Fri 11am–6pm, Sat 11am–2pm.

HARVEYS AUCTIONS, No. 22–25. T 240 1464. Antique and general furniture, pictures, silver, bric-à-brac and Oriental furniture auctions every two weeks. Viewing Tue 10am–4pm; auctions Wed beginning 10.30am. Catalogues available.

ROCK GARDEN 6–7 The Piazza. T 240 3961. 'It ain't the Ritz but it's good' as the blurb goes. Restaurant, rock venue, lunchtime and evening theatre, photographic and art exhibitions, real ale bar. Noon–midnight every day; Sun jazz.

ROXY 41–43 Neal St. T 836 8811. Former sweaty haven for all New Wave punk bands, now under new management as general rock venue.

Hard to find it. Prices according to attraction.

BUNJIE'S 27 Litchfield St. T 240 1796. Long-established folk club. Casual atmosphere, food available.

COVENT GARDEN CINEMA CLUB 29 King St. T 836 1426. Unusual or little-shown films. Double feature Thur to Thur. Membership 20p per annum, seat £1. Worth searching for.

SOUNDS CIRCUS Portugal St, Kingsway. T 405 8004/5. Former Royalty Theatre revamped into rock venue. 1000-seater auditorium, disco, restaurant (open lunchtimes as well) and snack bar. 6.30pm–2am. Entrance ticket provides access to all facilities. Circus motif, pub prices. Resident summer musical from USA.

LYCEUM BALLROOM Wellington St. T 836 3715. Beautiful old plush theatre now houses everything from olde time music hall to occasional rock/reggae concerts.

AFRICA CENTRE 38 King St. T 836 1973/76. Information and discussion centre; frequent films, dances, lectures workshops and exhibitions open to anyone. Traditional food in restaurant.

ARTS THEATRE CLUB Great Newport St. T 836 3334/2132. Slightly wider scope than conventional West End venues. Home of Unicorn Theatre (see Good for Kids). Snack bar open during the day, Membership 15p.

ROYAL OPERA HOUSE Covent Garden. T 240 1066. (24-hour recorded information, T 240 1911.) Ballet, opera, Proms. Telephone credit card bookings accepted.

OASIS SWIMMING POOL Endell St. T 836 9555. Indoor and outdoor pools. Adults 30p; children 8p weekdays, 10p weekends. Ticket gives access to either pool. Mon–Fri 9am–6.45pm, 7.45 outdoor pool. Sat 9am–4.45pm, Sun 9am–5.45pm. Two-hour sauna £1·80.

THEATRES See Press for what's on at the many theatres in this area.

GOOD FOR KIDS

UNICORN THEATRE The Arts Theatre, Gt Newport St. Box Office T 836 3334 (Tue–Sat 10am–5.30pm, Sun 12.30–5.30pm). Professional theatre for children presenting an extensive variety of plays for those between four and twelve every weekend and during school holidays: term-time performances for school parties every weekday afternoon. Plays, puppet shows, conjurors, mime shows, dance companies, concerts and films. Also theatre workshops and club activities. Tickets 70p upwards plus 5p for temporary membership. Various types of long-term membership available, T 240 2076.

TRIDIAS Toy shop Extraordinary, 44 Monmouth St. T 240 2369. Small but packed with grand dolls' houses and furniture, tricks, models, Pollock's Toy Theatres.

HAMBLINGS 29 Cecil Court. Wagons, trackside signs, other accessories to overwhelm any model railway buff.

PLAYGROUND. Small area of fixed play equipment behind St Giles-in-the-Fields.

OASIS SWIMMING POOL (See Keeping Amused.)

HOW TO GET THERE

BR Charing Cross.

UNDERGROUND Covent Garden, Leicester Square, Tottenham Court Road, Trafalgar Square, Embankment.

BUSES 1, 1A, 6, 7, 9, 9A, 11, 13, 14, 15, 19, 22, 24, 25, 29, 38, 55, 68, 77, 77A, 77C, 170, 172, 176, 188, 239, 501.

Fulham

This area is largely a Victorian working class development of terrace houses in a generous curve of the river, broken now and then by small factories. The village centre is Waltham Green, an odd island with a church and some early Victorian shops and cottages in the final stages of decay. It had a theatre that was pulled down a year or two ago, but a friend of mine remembers seeing Nancy dance there in an Arab belly dancer's get-up with a gold sequin in her navel, and has ever since longed to be Nancy (now fat and sixty-odd, drinking gin and tonic in our local).

There are only two really beautiful buildings. One is Hurlingham House which is a private club, and the other is the Bishop's Palace in Bishop's Park – secret and wonderful and open to the public.

I feel Fulham has enormously profited from the middle-class invasion. Those areas of red-brick terraces with William Morris inspired scrolls around the doorways are now brightly painted in pink or yellow. Little urns full of flowers have appeared on doorsteps. Yet, in spite of this, the core of Fulham is still working class and the market place in the North End Road is the meeting place – where politics, gossip and idioms such as 'It's so hard to be good when everything is so expensive,' are freely exchanged. There are families who have lived here for generations and have never felt the need to go very far.

I live near the gasworks and watch the containers rise and fall with the light catching their silvery sides. Because of the low skyline (hardly any of the houses are more than three storeys) the sunsets are marvellous. Just nearby is a tiny, secret square of two-storey cottages called Imperial Square, with only one entrance. It was built at the turn of the century by Polish immigrants who had been brought over to labour in the gasworks.

From the window where I sit I can see a chestnut tree, lilacs in bloom, one white, one mauve, lots of clematis, some rows of lettuces, lavender bushes, yellow jasmin, a wisteria, a pink climbing rose, lupins, delphiniums (not yet in flower) and several washing lines.

I love it here. There is nothing much stopping me from living anywhere in the world, yet I live in Fulham.

Nell Dunn

WHAT TO SEE

FULHAM PALACE For centuries the country house of the Bishop of London. Not at all palatial, early sixteenth-century with dark red brick diamond patterned walls, ornate eighteenth-century bell-turret, peaceful central courtyard with goldfish pond and fountain. Bishop's Park very pleasant with lots going on (see Good for Kids). Avenue of tall plane trees beside river, with a view over to Putney boathouse.

SIR WILLIAM POWELL'S ALMSHOUSES near All Saints'. Row of golden stone, single-storey 1869 with lots of Gothic detailing, set in little flowery garden.

FULHAM GAS WORKS Have the oldest gas-holder in the world with Grade II preservation order – 'everything a gas-holder should be' says GLC historic buildings' department. Pick it out from the other rusty giants that hog the skyline over King's Rd by pointed turrets. Surrounded by more immediately attractive terraces of small brightly painted early nineteenth-century houses.

IMPERIAL SQ. Tiny, secret square of two-storey cottages – see Nell Dunn's intro. Still lived in by North Thames Gas employees. Urban planners should take a look: each house has a small fenced front garden, everything on a modest scale but very satisfying.

PARSON'S GREEN Late eighteenth-century terrace facing green, Nos 237–47 New King's Rd, Lady Margaret School handsome early Georgian house. Look out for lions in the streets round here. They are perched incongruously on turn-of-the-century gables, balconies and porches – mis-shapen but appealing.

WHERE TO EAT

Fulham people feel sufficiently detached from the rest of London to refer to anywhere east of their village as 'up in Town'. Confusion abounds as to where Fulham ends and Chelsea begins, for the two main restaurant-bearing arteries – Fulham and King's Rd (plus New King's Rd) – flow parallel right through both villages. However, the frontier is the railway line at Stamford Bridge – in Fulham the restaurants become far more friendly, informal, smaller, cheaper and homelier. Because the area is largely residential, it is quite difficult to find somewhere open for lunch, and most places close on Sun or Mon. Sample prices are for average three-course meal for two with house wine. Open for lunch and dinner seven days unless otherwise indicated.

CARLO'S PLACE 855 Fulham Rd. T 736 4507. Going for twelve years with same trio – owner Carlo, pudding maker Malcolm and Breton chef Jean. Fish soup, avocado cocktail, duck à l'anglaise and exquisite desserts are all firm favourites. Evenings only, closed Mon. £12.

RED ONION BISTRO 636 Fulham Rd. T 736 0920. Equally popular with the neighbourhood, though recent inclusions in guides have brought droves of outsiders. Dark and informal ambience. Menu includes blinis, charcoal-grilled lamb steaks and baked bananas with butterscotch sauce. £8. Evenings only, closed Sun.

FINGAL'S 690 Fulham Rd. T 736 1195. Newest arrival on this patch; usefully open for lunch when best buy must be fresh salads made by Tina, an expert wholefood cook, with Eastern European influence, excellent boeuf stroganoff. Bistro menu lists meat dishes. Tiny garden at the back for eating out in fine weather. Pale piney scrubbed kitchen furniture and panelling. Lunch £4–£6, dinner £10–£12. Closed Sun and Mon.

THE TRENCHERMAN 271 New King's Road. T 736 4988. Busy, relaxed and friendly atmosphere in dark sixties surroundings. Specialities such as gratin Thermidor, bouillabaisse, suprême de Volaille à la Périgord. Another welcome haven for lunch, set menu at £1·95 a head (ex VAT, service, coffee). A la carte lunch £7, dinner £12. Set Sun lunch £2·55 a head. Closed Sat lunch, Sun dinner.

BAS AND ANNIE'S 58 New King's Rd. T 731 2520. Snug and cosy, with a large walled garden for eating in fine weather, very comfortable dark cocktail bar downstairs. Bas, who was a barman at the Playboy for five years, mixes expert classical cocktails; sister Annie controls restaurant. Menu French-Italian; calves' liver particularly good. Cocktails average 95p each, sixty to choose from. £13. Evenings only, closed Sun.

BISTRO CARLOTTA 144 Wandsworth Bridge Rd. T 736 2418. Run by Ada and Mario, with the help of chef/manager Carlo. Real family place, where customers can order specials in advance and feel truly cosseted. Menu includes delicious Italian specialities as well as Irish stew. Excellent desserts, especially lemon meringue pie and chestnut pot. £8·50. Closed Sun.

BLUE'S TRATTORIA 1 Walham Green Court, Fulham Rd. T 381 0735. Takes its name loyally from Chelsea football club's colours, the grounds being almost opposite. Owner chef is Luigi, who makes his own tortellini and tagliatelle verde. Steaks charcoal grilled, the rest of the menu typical trattoria style. Highly recommended, small, intimate and pretty; necessary to book. £8–£9. No lunches, closed Mon and for summer holidays.

RIVE GAUCHE 541b King's Rd. T 736 7644. Cuisine and wine list truly South of France (the chef comes from St Paul de Vence). House wine delicious. Herbs, wine and garlic emphatically used in excellent cooking. *Prix fixe* menus £5·95 (£2·95 lunch only). Decor red, white and blue with masses of geraniums and daisies in windowboxes. Fully booked every night, less busy for lunch, closed Mon.

WHERE TO DRINK

PRINCESS ROYAL Waterford Rd. Very much a local for the modern flats opposite and terraced houses behind, this is a smoky, friendly place with Watney's fined bitter, skittle billiards, darts and unobtrusive jukebox. Hot and cold main courses and snacks lunchtime, just snacks in evenings.

DOG & PHEASANT Billing Rd. Small but extremely attractive pub tucked behind Chelsea football stadium. Untarted panelled interior, real ale and a chatty landlord who's willing to tell you all you need to know about alimony.

IMPERIAL ARMS 577 King's Rd. In an area blessed with few notable pubs, the Imperial makes a valiant stab at enticing ambience with cosy saloon bar and a darts-oriented public bar with pool table. Watney's beers, draught lager. Hot and cold main courses and snacks.

HAND & FLOWER 617 King's Rd. Ind Coope pub with jukebox, smoky but convivial atmosphere and a clientele which mixes builders converting bijou residences with their well-heeled owners. Hot and cold snacks available at lunchtime.

DUKE OF CUMBERLAND 235 New King's Rd. Large Victorian pub with tiled exterior and attractive windows overlooking Parson's Green. Interior equally impressive, Young's real ales. Hot and cold snacks lunchtime.

WHERE TO SHOP

Home decoration and interesting food shops rub shoulders with long established corner shops. Smart antique shops popular in Parson's Green, while bargains are plentiful in junk/bric-à-brac shops in Fulham's backstreets.

PETER TOPP WALLCOVERINGS 343

Fulham Palace Rd. T 736 4821. Wallcoverings from over eighty English and foreign firms can be viewed, amongst them – Sanderson, John Oliver, Osbourne and Little & Coles. Special effects showroom with silks, grass cloths, simulated suede, foil, hessians and murals.

Fulham High St: ALLSPORTS, No. 32. T 736 6075. Equipment and clothing for all sports except fishing and underwater swimming. Re-stringing service. TRADE UNLIMITED, No. 51. T 736 7887. Pine furniture restored and finished by them to high standard. Showroom at No. 41 for Welsh dressers, from £100.

D. AND H. OAKLEY, No. 53–55. T 736 4573. Double window displays lots of copper and brass, new and old.

New King's Rd: COBRA, No. 220. T 736 4710. Art deco and nouveau objects and furniture. Also European and particularly French glass.

GARDEN CRAFTS, No. 158. T 736 1615. Life-size cast stone and marble figures and garden ornaments outside. Cast aluminium Victorian pattern garden furniture.

LUNN ANTIQUES, No. 86. T 736 4638. Clothes and textiles 1890–1940, 50p–£50. Also Victorian and Georgian rummers, English and Continental prints, small Regency furniture.

ERIC KING ANTIQUES, No. 203. T 736 3162. Very good quality Oriental and Eastern furniture; early pine, wicker and bentwood furniture. Lots of lacquer and ivory boxes and small objects, also art deco.

GERALD FAIRHOLME, No. 285. T 736 4979. Reproduction nautical furniture: chests of drawers, desks, carvings.

MERCHANT CHANDLER, No. 72. T 736 6141. Orange painted shop has baskets of goods spread outside when it's fine. Kitchen furniture, equipment, lots of nice house things from England and France.

FIONA CAMPBELL, No. 259. T 731 3681. Everything made to order. Enormous collection of wallpaper and fabric pattern books for bedcovers, cushions, curtains, bedheads, valences. FULHAM POTTERY, No. 210. T 736 1188. Established 1670s to make bottles and drinking vessels. 1841 brick bottle kiln still standing. Now sell all equipment for potting, including kilns. A resident potter gives advice, or buy by mail order.

J. CROTTY & SON, No. 74. T 385 1789. Eighteenth- and nineteenth-century fireplace accessories – dog grates, fenders, fire implements; brass chandeliers and early hall lights; marble and wooden fireplaces and mantelpieces. Small amount of reproduction. AND SO TO BED, No. 7. T 731 3593. Reproduction and Victorian brass and steel bedsteads. New and old patchwork quilts and white crochet bedspreads.

King's Rd: FRED WARR, No. 611. T 736 2934. Britain's original Harley-Davison dealer. Magnificent line-up of the legendary machines.

CHRISTOPHER WRAY, all T 736 8008/5989. LIGHTING EMPORIUM, No. 600–602. Packed with old and reproduction lighting, most brass, some converted to electricity. LAMP WORKSHOP, No. 613–615. Spare parts: shades, brackets, wicks, burners, chimneys, etc. TIFFANY SHOP, No. 593. Reproduction Tiffany lamps made by Christopher Wray. POT SHOP, No. 606. Handthrown terracotta pots of all shapes and sizes. TERRACOTTA POTS, No. 591. Huge selection of antique terracotta pots of all shapes and sizes.

THROUGH THE LOOKING GLASS, No. 563. T 736 7799. English and Continental nineteenth-century framed mirrors, most in carved, decorative gilt. PARSONS TABLE LTD, No. 569. T 736 0007. Octagonal and rectangular mirrors of several pieces of mirror bordered in bamboo. Antique reproduction chairs, tables and four-poster beds.

VAN DER FANSEN 96 Waterford Rd. T 736 3814. Two sisters adapt twenties to fifties clothes and fabrics to own designs using mixture of materials. Some knitwear and accessories.

Fulham Rd: TOOKES, No. 614. T 736 1484. Selling all fishing tackle and accessories for over 50 years.

PLATFORM ONE, No. 594a (Kelvedon Rd). T 731 3119. Mainly vintage toys: Hornby trains, Dinky toys and tin plate toys. Also lead soldiers and animals, old games and old advertising tins. Only Fri–Sat.

CHELSEA FOOTBALL SOUVENIR SHOP, No. 468a. T 385 4913. General football clothing shop. Also rosettes and scarves from most of popular teams.

FROCK EXCHANGE, No. 450. T 381 2937. Wide selection of good quality fashionable secondhand women's clothes.

BIKE CENTRE, No. 849. T 736 7965. All Puch cycles for adults and children; Puch and Suzuki mopeds and motorcycles; accessories and spares. Lots of skateboards.

ABODE, No. 781. T 736 3161. New pine and cane furniture, Spanish chairs, bentwood furniture, household accessories.

TAURUS GALLERY, No. 637. T 736 1031. Antique engravings, ephemera, curios, assorted bygones, prints, pictures, miscellaneous and decorative items from the seventeenth century.

POLLYANNA, No. 811. T 731 0673. Children's mix and match practical tough clothes 2–12; boiler suits, dungarees, clogs.

Jerdan Pl.: LEISURE CRAFT CENTRE, No. 2–10. T 381 2019. Kits of all kinds: candle-making, self-hardening clays, enamelling, soft toys, macramé. Related bits; craft books. Most craft accessories.

WOOD AND WIRECRAFT SUPPLIES, No. 19a. T 385 2910. Old-established shop, now only wirecraft side. Mrs Kreeger sells lampshade frames, natural parchment, raffia, occasionally chair cane. Excellent source of basketware.

Dawes Rd: THE DOLLS' HOSPITAL, No. 16. T 385 2081. Actually a normal toy shop but 100-year-old business specializes in repairing Victorian and Edwardian dolls, will give advice – send sae. (Few spares available for modern dolls.)

VERE AND FLEMING, No. 125–129. T 385 8866. Over 60 English and American antique patchwork quilts, plus French pine, wicker and bamboo furniture, thirties china.

Munster Rd: CHRISTOPHER'S ANTIQUES, No. 213. T 381 3524. Victorian and Edwardian bamboo furniture, all authentic and all restored.

SUNNY'S, No. 191a. T 385 5025. Search crowded shelves for quirky knick-knacks and bric-à-brac. Also secondhand records from skiffle to punk.

EUROFRAMES, No. 127. T 736 2167. All types of frames made to order plus all the equipment for DIY.

NAYLORS, No. 131. T 731 3679. Novelty bric-à-brac and antiques. Old tin boxes, walking sticks, Victorian nightwear, cheese dishes, jelly moulds.

CORNUCOPIA, 93 Lillie Rd. T 385 4591. Kitchenware gift shop selling English and Portuguese glass, china and pottery. Also basketware, candles, cards.

RICHARD MORRIS, 142 Wandsworth Bridge Rd. T 736 1448. One of many pine furniture shops in street. Large corner shop with furniture spreading onto the pavement.

The Unexpected

GNOMES 329a Fulham Rd. T 351 4232. Ceramic hand-painted six to seven-inch-high gnomes can be laughed at or ordered to your own design. Brainchild of Robin Guild.

BUYING FOOD

New King's Rd: DIBZEE, No. 275.

T 731 0716. Delicatessen, off-licence and grocery. Also fresh vegetables and meat, coffee beans, fresh bread. Open till midnight.

THE GOURMET, No. 53. T 736 0521. Oriental and Continental delicatessen and grocery. Smoked ham on the bone, salami, bacon, pâtés, olives, fresh vegetables and tinned and frozen groceries.

LUIGI'S, No. 60. T 731 4994. Easily the best delicatessen in the street with a range of salamis, hams, pâtés, Continental cheese, cold meats, Italian wines, salads and a wide range of pasta.

HEALTH FOODS, AETHERIUS SOCIETY 767 Fulham Rd. T 736 8848. Wide range of health foods with a homeopathic section and homeopathic chemist on the premises.

DANISH PATISSERIE 156 Munster Rd. T 731 3877. Delicious range of croissants, French stick bread, white and brown loaves, Danish pastries and pastisserie.

North End Rd Stalls line for a quarter of a mile, one of London's best food markets. Daily except Thur pm and Sun. Also haberdashery, secondhand and new clothes, hardware.

KEEPING AMUSED

RIVERSIDE STUDIOS Crisp Rd. T 741 2251. Formerly the biggest TV studios in Europe, used by the BBC, now an arts centre. Theatre, concerts, dance, exhibitions, late night films, etc. Food and drinks available. Along the road, painted fingers point the way. (See Good for Kids.)

FULHAM BATHS North End Rd. T 385 7129. Mixed pool plus ladies' private pool. 9am–7pm Mon–Fri, 9am–5pm Sat, 9–11.30am Sun. Adults 10p, weekends 12p; children 5p, weekends 6p.

COMMUNITY RESOURCES CENTRE 31 Fulham Palace Rd. T 748 3020. Poetry readings and other cultural functions. Also silk screen workshop, organized by Bradford Art College, for public use.

CRAVEN COTTAGE T 736 5621. Home of Fulham Football Club, grounds date from 1879, stadium holds 40000, Aug–May £1–£2·50.

STAMFORD BRIDGE T. 385 5545. Stomping ground for Chelsea Football Club, this turn of the century club boasts 50 000 capacity stadium. Aug–May £1·30–£3·20.

HAMMERSMITH TOWN HALL King St. T 748 3020.

FULHAM TOWN HALL Fulham Broadway. T 385 1212. Comprehensive range of entertainments and activities in both town halls, including old-time dancing, films, art exhibitions, afternoon variety shows, and performances by Group One Theatre, Fulham Light Operatic Society, Hammersmith Symphony Orchestra, and others. Further details Arts, Sports and Entertainments Department, Hammersmith Town Hall.

BISHOP'S PARK OPEN-AIR THEATRE Bishop's Ave. T 736 7181. On banks of Thames by Putney Bridge, provides a wide range of cultural activities for the whole family. Several guest appearances by well-known personalities. Jazz, folk, 'Big Band', Spanish music and disco common, along with magic shows, military bands and occasional ballet.

GOOD FOR KIDS

BISHOP'S PARK Lovely play area for young children near Bishop's Ave entrance; big sandpit, paddling-pool like miniature lake – island in the middle, grassy playground with swings, roundabouts and slides. Now allows skateboarding in bandstand area when no bands. Field for cricket and kicking balls about.

HANDICAPPED CHILDREN'S ADVENTURE PLAYGROUND Fulham Palace Gdns (in Bishop's Park). T 731 2753.

Imaginative new building for indoor activities and carefully designed adventure playground with tempting-looking tree-houses and walks.

RIVERSIDE STUDIOS Crisp Rd. T 741 2251. Sun afternoon children's films, developing older children's activities. (See Keeping Amused).

HOW TO GET THERE

UNDERGROUND Putney Bridge, Parson's Green, Fulham Broadway.
BUSES 11, 14, 22, 28, 30, 31, 74, 74B, 91, 220, 295.

Greenwich

My flirtation with this area went on for about a quarter of a century. When I lived in the country, first in Kent then in Sussex, I regularly found excuses (education of the young or edification of overseas visitors) to stand on that majestic little hill beside Wren's Observatory and look down upon Britain's most elegant palace, the Queen's House, and up-river to the unique angle-shot of St Paul's framed by Tower Bridge.

I swear I didn't start living in the place just for the view. In fact we were not house-hunting when we side-slipped into Greenwich. We just saw an ad in *The Observer* and with quiet precipitation came to live in part of the property once owned by the parents of James Wolfe, who left it a major-general at the age of thirty-two and returned embalmed from the triumph of Quebec in 1759 to lie in state for some days on the ground floor. One of his letters described it as being 'the prettiest situated house in England'. I was a bit carried away myself, discovering that I could see St Paul's from the back loo and Westminster's Victoria Tower (flag and all sometimes) from a window we reinstated in my study. Views are bad for writers and when the chestnut candles came out that spring I became convinced I should never set pen to paper again.

That was soon overcome by the realization that Greenwich is a working place. Rich in vistas and history maybe, but enjoying a uniquely varied and brisk contemporary life. It is a commuters' suburb where, nevertheless, foreign seamen frequent some of the bars. There is active industry – things are still made in the borough – yet it is a venue for international tourists. It has a live theatre, an open market, an increasing number of restaurants and an ever-increasing battery of juggernaut traffic. A lot goes on. It's a good all the year round place to live with no danger of becoming a bourgeois ghetto – and I have not had to re-brick up my study window with the view.

John Pudney

WHAT TO SEE

ST ALPHEGE'S Handsome bold exterior designed 1712 by Nicholas Hawksmoor. St Alphege is Greenwich's own martyr – an eleventh-century archbishop murdered here by Danes.

ROYAL NAVAL COLLEGE, King William Walk. English architecture at its most formal and magnificent – Wren, Vanbrugh and Hawksmoor all contributed to design of the naval hospital. Domes and colonnades make splendid vistas from both the river and the hills of Greenwich Park. The Painted Hall is sheer theatre – Thornhill's teaming wall paintings work brilliantly. The Chapel has far less impact – an impersonal, secular atmosphere, but fine intricate late eighteenth-century detailing. Painted Hall and Chapel open every day except Thur 2.30–5pm; free. (See Keeping Amused).

NATIONAL MARITIME MUSEUM, Romney Rd. Full of treasures – great marine paintings, battle scenes, maps and charts, beautifully made, mysterious navigational instruments, new galleries devoted to Nelson and Cook, hundreds of model ships, the largest and finest collection of globes in the world, and recently reopened Barge House with splendid royal barges. Museum open Mon–Sat 10am–6pm, 5pm in winter, Sun 2.30–6pm. Free.

THE QUEEN'S HOUSE The first Renaissance house in England and centrepiece of the museum. Inigo Jones designed it, Henrietta Maria loved it and called it her 'house of delight'. Pure and strict inside and out, the great hall – a perfect cube – and the 'tulip staircase' are both very beautiful.

CUTTY SARK and GIPSY MOTH. Both in dry dock near Greenwich pier. Splendid *Cutty Sark* was last of the great tea clippers – she could sail 360 miles in a single day. Collection of figureheads below decks; explore captain's cabin and saloon with its coal fire and panelled walls and the

crew's quarters. Mon–Sat 11am–6pm; adults 40p, children 20p. *Gipsy Moth*, in which Sir Francis Chichester sailed single-handed round the world, looks comparatively insignificant but compact living quarters and specially designed equipment fascinating. Open as *Cutty Sark*, but closed Fri. Adults 15p, children 10p.

ROYAL OBSERVATORY Top of hill in Greenwich Park. Odd and charming building designed by Sir Christopher Wren for Charles II. Prime meridian of the world runs across the courtyard. Greenwich Mean Time clock mounted on the gatepost and inside Flamstead House are old telescopes and astronomical instruments. Same hours as Maritime Museum. Free.

VANBRUGH'S CASTLE East side of Greenwich Park. A make-believe fortress with turrets and towers designed and lived in by Sir John Vanbrugh – the first mock-medieval folly in England.

CROOM'S HILL Road of many fine and varied Georgian houses on west side of park. Gloucester Circus – urbane eighteenth-century – leads off it.

RANGER'S HOUSE West edge of the Park at Blackheath end. Built about 1688, elegant red brick mansion where the pedantic wit the Earl of Chesterfield lived and wrote the famous improving letters to his son. It houses the Suffolk Collection of sixteenth–eighteenth century English portraits. Open daily 10am–5pm (4pm Nov–Jan) Free. T 348 1286. (See Keeping Amused.)

WHERE TO EAT

Places with a rich historical background are often poor in eating places, but Greenwich is a fully alive place and caters for all tastes. Sample prices are for average three-course meal for two with house wine. Open for lunch and dinner seven days unless otherwise indicated.

MEANTIME 47 Greenwich Church St. T 858 8705. Menu adventurous, verging on French. Dinner £14; set lunch £3·50 a head without wine. Sat dinner only, Sun lunch only, Mon closed all day.

LE PAPILLON 57 Greenwich Church St. T 858 2668. Pretty, warm interior, dark brown and bright red. Good roasts, very large portions. Anglo-French menu. Dinner £15; set lunch £3·50 a head, but some extras. Closed lunch Sat, all day Sun.

BARNARDS AT GREENWICH THEATRE Nevada St. T 858 1318. Independent part of theatre, open to all comers, quick lunches and snacks (salads and quiches plus one hot dish like boiled beef and carrots). Dinners more elaborate with waitress service. English menu. Actors eat here, too. Set dinner with theatre seats at £5·50 or £6 a head; lunches about £1·20 for main dish and glass of wine. Closed Sun.

DIKS 8 Nelson Rd. T 858 8588. An owner-chef concern where the food is decidedly homely, but not ordinary. Excellent hors d'oeuvres, casseroles, brandy cake, good cheeses. Menu changes daily. Simple decor made remarkable by the addition of some forty homemade lampshades, with lights in, hanging from a black ceiling. Lunch £4, dinner £10. Closed Tue.

MARKET DELICATESSEN. 16 The Market. T 853 1296. Mainly for take-away food, ideal for picnics; also prepare hampers for parties of any size if phone in advance. London-born Turkish chef makes first-class kebabs and hamburgers on a charcoal grill. Good ices, Greek and Turkish cakes. Excellent cheeses, salamis and locally baked French bread. Packed with tourists in summer, but very popular with the locals, too. 9am–midnight. Kebabs and hamburgers 50p–£1, pizzas 30p–£1, filled rolls 30–45p.

LA CUCINA 275 Creek Rd. T 858 9412. Italian trattoria, off the tourist track and full of locals, especially business men. Very simple and informal, with pasta cooked to order, as are most dishes. £12. Closed Sat lunch and all day Sun.

GODDARD'S PIE SHOP 45 Greenwich Church St. Real eel and pie shop, founded 1890 by the present Goddard's grandfather, patronized by plenty of East Enders who cross river by foot tunnel. All pies baked on the premises and filled with good beef. Stewed and jellied eels Thur–Sat only. Good bargains, pie with mash 34p. Open 11am–3pm, closed Sun.

MACDONALD'S 17–18 King William Walk. T 858 0871. Not one of the hamburger chain but large clean cafeteria with home cooking and menus in five languages. Clean, friendly, no nonsense. Butter, cream and jam in plastic packs, but cream tea 65p, full set meal £1·95, freshly cooked fish and chips £1·10, bacon and egg 80p. Licensed. Summer 10am–6pm; winter 10am–4pm, closed Mon.

Picnics

Footpath with seats along edge of river in front of Royal Hospital – nice contrast between rusty cranes, barges, decaying docks and grand buildings behind. Sometimes old Thames sailing barges can still be seen on this stretch of the river. Or sit on grass among cannons in front of Maritime Museum, or under Spanish chestnuts in Greenwich Park.

WHERE TO DRINK

CUTTY SARK TAVERN Ballast Quay. Protected building dating to the turn of the eighteenth century houses a Charrington's house. Main bar in the style of a ship (naturally the *Cutty Sark* stands near). Upstairs restaurant and bar snacks.

TRAFALGAR TAVERN Park Row. Stands on the site of the Old George Inn but was renamed in honour of Nelson. There are two restaurants and two bars, one decorated in nautical style à la *Cutty Sark*. Watney's real ale and high class cuisine.

THE YACHT Crane St. Greenwich has few notable pubs and all the good ones are old ones. The Yacht is one of the oldest, reputedly from early seventeenth century but rebuilt in modern style with panoramic Thames views. Big choice of American and Continental beers and Watney's keg. Bar snacks available.

WHERE TO SHOP

Nelson Rd: GREENWICH GALLERY AND SPREAD EAGLE ANTIQUES, No. 22. T 858 9713. Two shops, one sells varied and interesting antiques, unusual small effects, the other old watercolours and oil paintings, with regular supplies of model ships.

POCKETTS, No. 25. T 858 1231. Gift shop full of touristy items; silkscreened pub mirrors, jewellery, adult games, Snoopy toys, greetings cards.

MERIDIAN BOOKS, No. 2. Antique, secondhand and new books related to the sea.

RELCY ANTIQUES, No. 9. T 858 2812. Marine and scientific instruments, quality furniture, good bric-à-brac, model ships, oil paintings and prints.

MERIDIAN ART GALLERY, No. 10. T 858 9884. Contemporary oil paintings, reproductions, original wood and steel engraving prints, copper etchings, pewters, mirrors, framing, artists' materials and heraldic plaques.

GREENWICH CHIMES, No. 11. T 858 3706. Eighteenth- and nineteenth-century wall and grandfather clocks; eighteenth- and nineteenth-century furniture.

BRASS RUBBING CENTRE, No. 15. T 858 2141. Make your own brass rubbings; replicas, books, guides and all necessary materials. Also ceramics and glass.

PICKWICK PAPERS AND FABRICS, No. 6. T 858 1205. Large range of fabrics: Heal's, Warner, Sanderson, etc. Also range of tools for home decoration.

Turnpin Lane Narrow alleyway easily missed. Has several antique and interesting shops.

GREEN PARROT, No. 2. T 858 6690. Unusual small antiques: down perilous stairs furniture, china, jewellery and small decorative items from Far East. Cheap Afghan furniture.

GREENWICH DISPLAY CENTRE, No. 15. T 853 1727. Fine arts and crafts, stoneware pottery, batiks, jewellery and other crafts. Pictures, limited edition prints, other contemporary studio work.

SPREAD EAGLE ANTIQUES 8 Nevada St. T 692 1618. Cheaper, junkier section of Spread Eagle Antiques. Old costumes, books and oddities – you never know what to expect at this Aladdin's cave.

GREENWICH BOOKSHOP 37 King William Walk. T 858 5789. Paper and hardbacks for all tastes and ages; good children's section. Also maps and greetings cards. Sell 'Royal Greenwich' (*the* guide to Greenwich), written by Nigel Hamilton who owns shop.

CHARLTON MARINE LTD 22 College Approach. T 858 1446. Yacht chandler. Very attractive brass and copper paraffin and electric ships' lamps. Also brass name plates: Cabin Boy, Store, etc.

Greenwich High St Every Sat waste ground adjacent to High Street car park becomes open-air antiques market. Victoriana, bric-à-brac, some craft.

GLASSBLOWING CENTRE 324 Creek Rd. T 853 2248. Handblown glass mostly decorative, some functional. Delightful paper weights. (See Good for Kids.)

BUYING FOOD

MARKET DELICATESSEN 16 The Market. T 853 1296. The area's only delicatessen: range of English and

Continental cheese, cold meats, groceries, coffee beans, range of cakes, French stick loaves and various snacks including burger in pitta with salad. Italian ice-cream in summer.

BOULTON 34 Greenwich Church St. Excellent fishmonger selling everything in season, displayed on the slab. Live and cooked crab, lobster, their own fillet and smoked haddock, also kippers, bloaters.

DAVY'S WINE VAULTS 165 Greenwich High Rd. T 858 7204. Hundreds of wines including house claret, burgundy and Neirsteiner; specialize in fine clarets and vintage ports.

KEEPING AMUSED

ROYAL NAVAL COLLEGE King William Walk. Entertainments Office, 25 Woolwich New Rd, Woolwich, T 854 5250. Major orchestral concerts including RPO, held in lavish setting of chapel throughout year. £1–£3.

RANGER'S HOUSE Chesterfield Walk. Entertainments Office as above. Sun night classical concerts sometimes held in intimate eighteenth-century salon. T 348 1286.

THE TRAMSHED 51 Woolwich New Rd. T 854 3933. Converted tramshed with different happenings each night of the week–plays, cabaret, music hall, jazz, folk music and rock. Ticket price varies with attraction. (See Good for Kids.)

GREENWICH PIER Boats to: Westminster – every 20 min in summer, 11am–5.45pm. Adults 90p, children 45p. Journey 45 min, return fare £1·20. Charing Cross – every 30 min 11.15am–5.30pm. Adults 90p, children 45p. Tower Hill – every 30 min 11am–5.30pm. Adults 70p, children 35p; return fare adults £1, children 50p.

GREENWICH BATHS Trafalgar Rd. T 858 0159. Mon–Sat 8am–8.30pm, Sun 8–11.40am. Weekdays 26p adults, 12p children; weekends 30p adults, 15p children; gymnasium 20p per hour.

Two pools, one covered during winter for roller skating, soccer, badminton, table tennis.

GREENWICH THEATRE Croom's Hill. T 858 7755. Former Victorian music hall, presents plays of high quality, frequently on a 'first-run' basis using established actors. £1·25–£2·75, previews and Sat matinees £1·25. Bars and eating area open lunchtime for hot and cold buffets. Combination dinner/theatre ticket for £5·50 and £6. Also Bowsprit Company (Greenwich Young People's Theatre, see Good for Kids); art gallery of contemporary work; occasional Sun jazz; Greenwich Film Society presentations.

TRAFALGAR ROWING CENTRE Crane St. T 858 9568. Temporary membership 20p a visit plus 10p for clubhouse and use of its bar on riverfront.

WARWICK LEADLAY GALLERY 5 Nelson Rd. T 858 0317. Mon–Sat 9am–5.30pm and most Sun. Antiquarian map and print gallery, specializing in Greenwich and other 'watery' locales. Maps are lovely, good for gifts; from £1·70 for a small print. Research commissions undertaken.

GOOD FOR KIDS

THEATRE Greenwich Young People's Theatre, The Stage Centre, Burrage Rd. Organizes all sorts of workshops for 7–25 year olds. Lots of special events and shows for kids, T 854 1316. More children's entertainments Sat mornings at The Tramshed, 51–53 Woolwich New Rd, T 855 3371.

NEW NEPTUNE HALL Best place to start discovering treasures of the Maritime Museum. There is *Reliant*, a paddle tug with its big wheel still turning – you can walk about on deck, peer at the engine and the crew's quarters. Also small boats from all over the world, figureheads, the first class cabin of a grand liner; *Port Liberty* is like navigating a ship into port with lighthouses and radar. Museum also puts on film shows and projects for kids in the holidays. Check details and subjects, T 858 4422. Free.

BOATING POOL Park Row entrance of Greenwich Park. A chance to captain your own craft. There is playground nearby and steep paths in park are great for skateboarding.

THE PLANETARIUM, near the Observatory, has shows in the holidays explaining all sorts of aspects of the night sky. Children 5p, adults 15p. Contact Educational Services Dept, National Maritime Museum. T 858 4422.

GLASSBLOWING 324 Creek Rd. Can watch glassblowers at work – furnaces roaring, cheeks bulging. Edward and Irene Hill also sell charming dolls' house decanters, rolling pins, tumblers, etc. (See Where to Shop.)

THE FOOT TUNNEL Near *Cutty Sark*. Strange, exciting feeling to be running about under the Thames. Inside redbrick domed building, down spiral staircase is a white echoing tunnel that leads to the Isle of Dogs. From there Greenwich looks marvellous. Exactly the view Canaletto painted in 1750 – picture is in Maritime Museum.

HOW TO GET THERE

BR Maze Hill, Greenwich, from London Bridge.

BUSES 1A, 70, 108B, 177, 180, 180A, 180B, 185, 188.

Hampstead

Hampstead's no village but that richer agglomeration, a small cosmopolitan town of considerable, if nordic panache – say, a Weimar – and we who live there are townspeople not villagers, wanting and getting town-life's gains: privacy, urbanity and style, to start with; friendship and wide acquaintance, not imposed but to hand.

We've a proper small-town civilization, theatre, cinemas (art and pop), churches for concert-halls, public libraries for galleries, town gardens opened for charity and appropriately bourgeois houses to enter, like exquisite Fenton House and tragic Keats's. We've even got a market now, and say nothing against our boutiques, our exotic little bazaars, though a Marks and Spencer would help.

And we've our festivals, like the open-air art show and the galumphing Bank Holiday Fairs; no Punch at the moment, but still the donkey rides, and you can still drink at the chalybeate springs, our earliest tourist attraction. Despite the pejorative 'Hampstead intellectuals', no one could claim we're high on intellectual rigour, but there's a full gamut of creativity from arts to crafts, though no longer craftsmanship – alas, our leatherwork and pots!

All good towns, even walled ones, have one side open, and for us there is the splendid Heath, lovingly tended by the GLC, filthed by too high a proportion of tourists. If Camden Council cared, they'd save us from murder by motor, by the parking commuters and the through traffic, but Camden Council, though high on social service, is sadly low on aesthetics. You should see some of the things they've let get built, including probably the most expensive council houses in the world on promised open space. But they seem to have the usual Left-middle-class hatred for middle-class highish culture, and they notably fail to make quiet enclaves by blocking of roads higher in Hampstead (though lots lower down (the hill). If they did, we'd have the best urban walks in London and a view, at the top, not of parked cars but of the Heath.

But the spring flowers are still later and the air fresher as you climb the hill, and many a May there's still a nightingale.

Marghanita Laski

WHAT TO SEE

FENTON HOUSE Hampstead Grove. Fine late seventeenth-century house contains Benton-Fletcher collection of early keyboard instruments, Binning collection of porcelain, exquisite furniture, needlework, engravings, paintings. Delights of the collections may be enhanced by students' use of the harpsichords and virginals. Formal concerts sometimes held in evenings. Wed–Sat 11am–5pm, Sun 2–5pm (or dusk). Closed Dec. 60p, accompanied children 30p.

KEATS HOUSE (Wentworth Place) Keats Grove. Poet's home 1818–1820, last and most creative years of his short life. Originally two houses, one of which was occupied by his beloved Fanny Brawne. Mon–Sat 10am–6pm, Sun 1–5pm. Free, but donations gratefully received. Keats Memorial Library, which contains many relics and some portraits (and Kate Greenaway Collection in public library next door), can be seen by appointment with custodian. Delightful Regency church of St John on corner of Keats Grove and Downshire Hill.

THE HILL off North End Way. (Small signpost north of Jack Straw's Castle.) Bewitching and beautiful garden: wisteria, roses and clematis trail over a pergola.

ADMIRAL'S HOUSE Admiral's Walk. Eighteenth-century nautical folly on the roof of which Admiral Matthew Barton, becalmed at last, walked the deck with telescope in hand and greeted news of national triumphs by firing a cannon.

CHURCH ROW. One of the most elegant streets in London, mostly *c*. 1700. Former residents include George du Maurier, H. G. Wells. At parish church of St John-at-Hampstead, Constable lies in old churchyard, Hugh Gaitskell and Kay Kendall are buried in the newer part.

WHERE TO EAT

No one can complain of lack of restaurants here. Hungry patrons, whether fresh from a bout of physical exercise on the Heath or intellectual exercise in their studies, may choose from the cuisines of several nations at prices to suit every pocket. Prices given are for average three-course meal for two with house wine. Open for lunch and dinner seven days unless otherwise indicated.

KEATS 3–4 Downshire Hill. T 435 3544/1499. The only restaurant to offer real *haute cuisine* and it *is* expensive – £30. Superb wine list, special gastronomic evenings. Evenings only, closed Sun.

VILLA BIANCA 1 Perrins Court. T 435 3131 & 794 4017. Best bet for first-class Italian food. Packed with regulars, lively and cheerful. £13.

TURPINS 118 Heath St. T 435 3791. Pretty eighteenth-century house with garden. Menu includes pies with all sorts of fillings from duck and cherry to sole and prawns. £10–£12. Closed Mon and Sun evening, lunches Sun only.

VERONA ANTICA 108 Heath St. T 435 6397. Very popular, attractive display of Italian food in window. £12. Closed Sun.

LA GAFFE 109 Heath St. T 435 4941/ 8965. Ebullient poetry-writing Italian patron. Favourite stoking-up place for people on their way back north £14–£16, closed Mon.

GILLY'S 80 Heath St. T 794 6431. Newest place, wine bar and restaurant food with slant towards French provincial style. Good value for money. Glass of wine, cheese and fruit at bar for £1 a head; full lunch £4; dinner £8. Closed Mon.

FAGIN'S KITCHEN 82 Hampstead High St. T 435 3608. Popular with discerning diners, candlelit and Dickensian in keeping with its name, but French menu. £13–£14. No lunches.

GULESTAN 73 Heath St. T 435 3413. Good Tandoori restaurant, paying special attention to their sauces so that one dish does taste different from another. Crisp samosas, moist nan. £12. Food served all Sat and Sun.

MAXWELL'S 76 Heath St. T 794 5450. Serves fast American food in what was once an old dairy and cow shed. Very popular with baseball teams after a game on the Heath, pool room bar for beer or cocktails, patio outside. £5. All day at weekends.

PIZZA EXPRESS 64 Heath St. T 435 6722. Good value, nice place to be, especially when the string quartet plays on Mon evenings. Large courtyard at back. £3 pizza and glass of wine for two. Noon–midnight every day, Fri, Sat, Sun–12·30 am.

LOUIS 32 Heath St. T 435 9908. Favourite tearooms and patisserie hard to pass by with children in tow. Open seven days a week, 9·30 am–6.30pm all prices.

HILL HOUSE 216 Haverstock Hill. T 794 4125. Suburban thirties villa with a costermonger's cart in the front garden is unlikely setting for a restaurant with a most sophisticated menu. Solicitous service and reasonable prices at the lower end of the scale while the more expensive things are outstandingly good, giving the place a mention in most good restaurant guides. £5–£6.

Picnics

The Heath – where else?

WHERE TO DRINK

HORSE & GROOM 68 Heath St. Recently redecorated Victorian pub. Offers Young's excellent draught ales to attract its mainly young clientele. Sandwiches at all times.

NAG'S HEAD 79 Heath St. The young but not necessarily indigenous Hampstead real ale lovers vacillate between the Horse & Groom on one side of Heath St and Nag's Head on the other. This latter hostelry is owned by CAMRA and therefore features a splendid array of unusual brews including Godson's, Sam Smith's, Brakspear's and Greene King. A concrete surfaced 'beer garden' contains the overspill from the two large bars and the place is full of large bellies and loud voices.

HOLLY BUSH 22 Holly Mount. Tastefully converted from an early nineteenth-century stable which accounts for its oddly shaped but cosy bars. Ind Coope draught beers sold and a reassuring contingent of locals add to the attraction.

JACK STRAW'S CASTLE North End Way. Dating back to the 1380s and named after the rebellious Wat Tyler's second-in-command who lived on the site, the Castle was rebuilt in 1964 with weatherboard exterior and Victorian-style bars. Charrington's beers. Hot and cold pub food, also good restaurant upstairs. Crowded at weekends, mainly by outsiders who appreciate the view over the Heath.

SPANIARDS INN Spaniards Rd. Most of building dates from 1580, tables in large, pleasant rose garden with aviary. Charrington's beers. Luncheon rooms serve hot business lunches in the winter, salads in summer. Also hot and cold bar snacks.

FREEMASON'S ARMS 32 Downshire Hill. Cheerful place with pool table and comfortable armchairs inside and plenty of metal ones outside. Food available and only a short stroll from the Heath.

THE FLASK 14 Flask Walk. Usually crowded with an engaging mixture of arty locals and theatricals. Young's draught and some rare malt whiskies behind the bar; bar snacks, too.

MAGDALA TAVERN 2a South Hill Park. Charrington's and Bass on draught, pub games and a bustling atmosphere conveniently near the Heath.

WHERE TO SHOP

Something for everyone here. Fashion shopping centred in Heath St, many bookshops and minority interest shops in narrow backstreets, food shopping centred in High St.

JARVIO 244 Haverstock Hill. T 794 4997. Cheap, colourful cotton, rayon, corduroy separates, dresses and jeans, mostly made in factory above shop.

ROSSLYN HILL BOOKSHOP, No. 62. T 794 3180. Old prints of birds and animals decorate the window of this antiquarian bookshop. Children's, travel, art, German, French, early detective books.

Hampstead High St: H. KNOWLES-BROWN LTD, No. 27. T 435 4775. Established 1891, old-fashioned jeweller, silversmith, clock repairer and seller.

CUTE KIDS, No. 77. T 794 1343. Branch of King's Rd shop selling casual clothes, six months to fourteen years.

HIGH HILL BOOKSHOP, No. 6. T 435 2218. Excellent bookshop covering virtually every subject in paperback and hardback.

COLTS, No. 5. T 435 7387. Four to sixteen-year-old boys' clothes. Mostly casual: T-shirts, sweatshirts, jeans.

MONSOON, No. 1. T 435 1726. Delightful range of dresses, skirts, blouses, scarves and nightwear made up in hand-blocked printed fabric from Jaipur. All dyes are vegetable. Also silk hand-printed dresses, blouses and skirts from Calcutta; dresses from Afghanistan; hand-embroidered, hand-crocheted cotton clothes from Romania.

Heath St: HAMPSTEAD BAZAAR, No. 30. T 794 6862. Ethnic clothes for women selected with style: antique Chinese shawls, hand-stitched blouses from Hungary and Romania, full-skirted and colourful dresses from Afghanistan and matching outfits and dresses from India.

HAMPSTEAD ANTIQUE EMPORIUM Covered market of 30 stalls sells books, furniture, glass, jewellery, lamps, mirrors, silver, clocks, Victoriana, bric-à-brac and African craft.

THAT NEW SHOP, 1a–5a Perrins Ct (off Heath St). T 435 4549. Enormous gift shop offering a selection of china, glass, pottery, wood, candles and lampshades, stationery, toys and adult games, linen, kitchenware, straw, rugs and women's clothes, bags, belts, jewellery, scarves, key rings and kites.

PARKER'S, No. 13a. T 435 8629. Shirley Parker designs exclusively for her shop. She mixes antique lace with new fabrics to give an unusual finish to her clothes.

SMALL WONDER, No. 75. T 794 3635. French and Italian good quality clothes for up to twelve-year-olds. Jeans, shorts, sweatshirts, dungarees, check shirts, ski suits and pretty print dresses for smaller girls.

JIGSAW, No. 83. T 794 3014. Jeans by Inega, T-shirts, skirts, dresses and accessories all with a casual, colourful sporty look.

CHIC OF HAMPSTEAD. T 435 5454/5. Cream of British collections, matching lingerie and fine fashion shoes. No. 74: shoes, boots and sandals; No. 78: lingerie, dressing gowns and under things, and No. 82: day and evening wear, smart separates and coats, elegant knitwear and leather accessories.

A BUTTON SHOP, No. 91a. T 794 9604. Hand-painted buttons; Victorian and mother-of-pearl buttons; ducks, cats, flowers, ships, faces and fruit; wooden toggles and glass buttons from 2½p to £1 each.

Kingswell Heath St. Two-storey modern shopping complex built round pedestrian precinct.

VIVA, No. 10. T 455 7870 (ask for Hampstead branch). Classic design women's clothes from France and Italy: separates, dresses, coats and macs, silk scarves, belts, bags and a few hats.

CARPET BAGGERS, No. 14. T 435 9910. Old and new handmade Oriental carpets from Persia, Pakistan, Afghanistan, Turkey and China. Various sizes from £50.

VILLAGE GAMES, No. 15. T 435 3101. Children's and adults' games: over 500 word games and 300 war and fantasy games, also traditional games like backgammon and chess, mah-jong, Go and jigsaws. Enormous range of Tarot cards and knick-knacks.

RONALD KEITH, No. 16. T 435 8800. Mainly women's casual shoes, wide range of wedge heel espadrilles. Also desert boots and clogs for men and women.

VIVA FOR MEN, No. 18. T 794 2717. French and Italian men's separates. Co-ordinated casual look.

South End Rd: F. HEGNER, No. 13. T 435 0786. Excellent artists' material shop displaying as much as the limited space allows: Rotring pens, brushes, inks, paints, Pentels, watercolour papers, sketch pads and pencils. Also framing service.

DOVES, No. 15. T 794 8015. Own design pure cotton prints, made up into smocks, blouses, dresses and skirts that suit all ages. Comfortable and easy to wear. Also own design pure wool sweaters, range of cord items, variety of natural materials.

ANTHEA PROUD, No. 61. T 435 0236. Imaginative clothes for one to fourteen age group. Jeans and T-shirts for girls; pretty Liberty print dresses.

WELL WALK POTTERY 49 Willow Rd. T 435 1046. Established over twenty years. Many pots made behind shop. Mostly functional domestic ware but also elaborate and splendid working fountains.

Flask Walk: OWL AND THE PUSSY CAT, No. 11. T 435 5342. Soft toys, puppets, books, pocket-money toys, novelty toys, greeting cards and wrapping papers for the nought to ten age group.

A CARD FOR ALL REASONS, No. 12. Greeting and post cards for all occasions including Jewish and Catholic feast day cards. Wrapping papers, some gift items and stationery.

CULPEPER, No. 9. T 794 7263. Herbal delights and remedies, spices, pure essential oils and perfumes, scented pillows, dried herbs. Selection of honeys and of potted herbs in season.

FLASK BOOKSHOP, No. 6. T 435 2693. General antiquarian book dealers with leaning towards art and literature; range of modern first editions.

Finchley Rd: FAIRFAX KITCHEN SHOP 1 Regency Parade. T 722 7646. Wide selection of English, French, German and Italian kitchen equipment. Unusual specialities include a pasta machine, asparagus cooker and fish kettle. Supply the catering trade.

TIMOTHY SHAW, No. 277. T 435 3092. General stocks of good condition antiquarian and secondhand books mostly 1750–1850. Open afternoons and Sat am only.

JOHN BARNES. T 624 6000. Part of John Lewis department chain. Fashions perfumery and fashion accessories, china, glass, silverware, gifts, lighting and hardware. Closed Mon.

The Unexpected

TONY BINGHAM AT THE SIGN OF THE SERPENT 11 Pond St. T 794 1596. Antique and old musical instruments. musical prints, new and secondhand books on musical instruments, old sheet music and some records of music played on old instruments. Everything labelled with name, date and price.

BUYING FOOD

DELICATESSEN 56 Rosslyn Hill. T 794 9210. Good delicatessen; homemade breads, quiches, ricotta, Saxby's pies free-range eggs, cooked lasagne dishes, etc., fresh coffee, off-licence, some general groceries.

QUESTA, 7 Pond St. T 435 1541.

Excellent delicatessen. Cooked cold dishes, delicious and imaginative salads; fresh coffee, French bread, patisserie, wine. Tue–Sat 10.30am–7.30pm winter, also Sun in summer.

South End Rd: HAMPSTEAD PATISSERIE & TEA ROOMS, No. 9. T 435 9563. Austrian and Italian pastries, cakes, croissants, brioches, scones, Danish pastries and cheesecake baked on the premises. Tue–Sat 9am–9pm, Sun open 9.30am.

DELICATESSEN, No. 23. T 435 7315. Large selection of salads, taramasalata, humous, very best whole English farmhouse cheeses, olives, homemade quiches, meat and fish pâtés, twelve blends coffee beans, loose herbs and nuts, French and Greek and wholemeal breads, a range of groceries including selection of teas.

COFFEE AND TEA WAREHOUSE 2 Flask Walk. T 435 0959. Homemade breads, pastries and savouries, coffee and coffee-making equipment plus wide range of health foods.

High St: FOOD FAIR, No. 30. T 435 0622. Grocery and provision store catering for all nationalities. Coffee beans, ground, wide range of delicatessen, off-licence.

HAMPSTEAD COMMUNITY MARKET. Wet fish stall with good selection, fresh farm eggs, bacon and English cheese and a fruit and vegetable stall can be found in tiny alleyway.

PIPPIN WHOLEFOODS, No. 83. T 435 6434. Wholefood shop, make bread from whole flour produced on own farm, also daily changing pastries, own apple juice, organically grown vegetables. Self-service wholefood restaurant; upstairs another restaurant, self-service lunchtime, waitress service in evenings.

LOUIS PATISSERIE 32 Heath St. T 435 9908. Hungarian patisserie, brioches, croissants, breads and delicious range of cream cakes, pastries and tarts are baked on premises. Very busy, 9.30 am–6.30pm including Sun and most holidays.

Finchley Rd: JOHN BARNES. T 624 6000. Basement food hall especially good for its wet fish counter, delicatessen and wines. Closed Mon.

BEVERLY'S, No. 189. T 624 2840. Wide range of coffee beans, also caffeine-free coffee, blends of tea and range of coffee-making equipment.

LOUIS PATISSERIE, 12 New College Parade. T 722 8100. Branch of Louis Patisserie where prices marginally cheaper.

KEEPING AMUSED

CAMDEN ARTS CENTRE Arkwright Rd. T 435 2643/5224. Large exhibition area for paintings, sculpture, craft. Also picture-lending library. Mon–Sat 11am–6pm (8pm Fri), 2–6pm Sun.

EMBASSY THEATRE & STUDIO TWO THEATRE Both Eton Ave, Swiss Cottage. Central School of Speech and Drama, T 722 8186. Embassy thirteen productions a year, wide variety full-length plays; 60p pensioners and students 30p. Studio Two short and experimental plays, cabaret; free. Advertisements in press.

SWISS COTTAGE UNISEX SAUNA 2 New College Parade, Finchley Rd. T 586 4422. Well equipped. Open twenty-four hours, seven days a week. Sauna £2·25, sauna and half-hour massage £6, one-hour massage only £7·70, sauna and one-hour massage £9·25, facials £5 with free sauna.

SWISS COTTAGE BATHS Winchester Rd. T 278 4444 x 3035. Two large heated pools in sophisticated modern complex. Pool open Mon–Fri 8am–7.30pm, Sat 8am–6.30pm, Sun 8–11.30 am and 2–5.30pm. Adults 25p, juniors 8p; weekends 35p and 10p. Weekend family tickets available. Squash and badminton; judo and karate.

EVERYMAN CINEMA Nr. Hampstead tube. T 435 1525. One of most intimate and cheapest (80p) cinemas in London;

programme changes every three to four days, little-shown or 'specialist' films. Art exhibitions in lobby; occasional concerts. (Used to be old variety theatre – Noel Coward acted there.)

SUMMIT GALLERY 116 Heath St. T 435 4005. Sculpture, lithographs, paintings and period and contemporary drawings. Mon–Fri 10am–6pm, Sun 11am–6pm, closed Thur, Sat.

OPEN-AIR ART EXHIBITION Whitestone Pond, Heath St. Every weekend and Bank Holiday, May–end Aug; contemporary pottery, prints, paintings and jewellery. 11am–7pm.

FLEET PEEP SHOW Fleet Community Education Centre, Agincourt Rd. T Janet Mokades 485 9988. Plays at Cockpit and Fleet theatres; also shows for children, hospitals and festivals. Weekly workshop open to everyone.

LIDO OUTDOOR SWIMMING POOL Southeast corner of Hampstead Heath/ Parliament Hill. T 485 3873. Popular pool 36yd by 33yd, 9ft deep. Summer 7–9.30am, 10am–7pm; adults 20p, children 10p. Winter 7.30–10am; free.

HAMPSTEAD POND East Heath Rd. T 485 4491. Large pond 20–25ft deep. Summer seven days, men and boys 6–10am, mixed 10am–11pm (or sunset). Winter Sat and Sun, men and boys 7.30am–1pm.

PARLIAMENT HILL ATHLETIC TRACK. T 435 8998, park manager T 485 4491. Also open for public use outside meetings.

HAMPSTEAD GOLF CLUB Winnington Rd. T 455 0203. Founded in 1893, nine-hole course has a history of famous members from political, legal and entertainment professions. Must be member of another club, then facilities (including club rental, use of clubhouse and dining room) £3·50 until 5pm, then £2·50, Sat and Sun fee £5 until 5 pm, then £3. Open seven days from 9am. Par for hilly course 68.

GOOD FOR KIDS

HAMPSTEAD HEATH Wild, rugged GLC park with more than 800 acres of hills, ponds and pathways, glorious for kite-flying, riding, swimming, bird-watching and almost every healthy outdoor pursuit known, including donkey rides. Whitestone Pond at summit (440ft above sea-level) popular for model boats, paddling. Nearby Golders Hill Park, just beyond West Heath, has deer enclosure, modest zoo.

HAMPSTEAD OBSERVATORY, Lower Terrace. Small astronomical observatory run by Hampstead Scientific Society near Whitestone Pond Sat 8–10pm Oct–April (weather permitting).

HOW TO GET THERE

BR Hampstead Heath, Finchley Road & Frognal.

UNDERGROUND Hampstead, Belsize Park, Swiss Cottage.

BUSES 2, 2B, 13, 24, 26, 28, 46, 113, 187, 210, 268.

Highgate

Officially Highgate does not exist – except in the eye of the Post Office to whom we owe our postal district 'N6'. Otherwise the bureaucrats have carved us up, which is what helps to give Highgate its special character: parliamentarily and in local government we divide into four slices with the High Street as the main boundary: for education, for our electricity, our gas, our police – it's a straight split.

Outsiders link us inextricably with Hampstead, but invariably as the junior partner. Thus only the more adventurous tourists reach Highgate, hindered by guidebooks that falter after mentioning Coleridge and Whittington. But their reward is to discover roads such as The Grove, an avenue of old trees obscuring a grand semi-terrace of Georgian houses, and glimpses of the parish church which dominates the rambling Victorian cemetery stretching downhill towards Kentish Town. We are proud, too, of local people, and places, and connections, of Andrew Marvell, of Highgate School, of Gerald Manley Hopkins, of Charles Dickens, of John Betjeman, of Kenwood House.

Despite the temptations of heath, park and woodland, the post-war developers bypassed it, no doubt misled by the buses which ply to what London Transport calls Highgate, but everyone else knows as Archway. Thus the hill-top remains very much as a century ago, with private houses among the shops in the High Street (no multiple stores, but lacking only a fishmonger among life's staples).

Pubs abound – eleven by my count – with the Flask a publican's dream on hot summer weekends as customers throng the courtyard. Some bemoan the paucity of restaurants despite the presence in the neighbourhood of Christopher Driver, the *Good Food Guide*'s moving spirit.

Highgate's self-reliance is evident in its thriving community life. At one end is the egalitarian Jackson's Lane Community Centre, in the middle the Highgate Society (president Yehudi Menuhin) which with 1500 members claims to be the largest amenity society in Britain, and next door the far older Highgate Literary and Scientific Institution (founded 1839) with a library that flourishes because none of Highgate's constituent boroughs thought fit to provide a free public library that might have been used by ratepayers other than its own.

The list need not end there: a choral society, a theatre club and a horticultural society that still offers that increasingly rare spectacle, a grand summer show in a gigantic marquee: of flowers, vegetables, handicrafts, food, homemade wines and all.

No wonder we call it Highgate Village.

Ion Trewin

WHAT TO SEE

KENWOOD HOUSE Hampstead Lane. Remodelled by Robert Adam 1767–9, library one of finest surviving interiors. Outstanding collection of paintings includes works by Rembrandt, Vermeer, Reynolds, Romney, Gainsborough, Boucher. Daily 10am–7pm (5pm Oct, Feb, March; 4pm Nov–Jan). Surrounded by attractive parkland with *trompe l'oeil* bridge, Dr Johnson's summer-house from Streatham, superb beech trees and rhododendrons. Open daily 8am to dusk.

HIGHGATE CEMETERY Swain's Lane. Total population *c.* 45 000. Russian visitors go east, where Karl Marx lies. Old cemetery on west side of lane is overgrown and romantic, includes Catacombs – half hidden by vegetation, the Egyptian style entrance leads into a crumbling and creepy rotunda lined with vaults. Unfortunately vandalism has forced authorities to keep cemetery gates closed except on open days organized by Friends of Highgate Cemetery.

WATERLOW PARK Given to Londoners by Sir Sydney Waterlow in 1889, 'to be a garden for those who are gardenless'. Attractive, much restored Lauderdale House may become museum. Terrace has herbal sundial and lovely view over the park.

ST MICHAEL'S CHURCH South Grove. Fine stained-glass window by Evie Hone (1954). Line on wall just inside main door marks level of top of cross on St Paul's dome.

THE GROVE. Delightful street of late seventeenth-century houses includes No. 3 where Coleridge lived 1823–34. Not far from 31 West Hill, where Sir John Betjeman lived as a child, 'Safe in a world of trains and buttered toast'.

WHITTINGTON STONE Highgate Hill. Stone cat with chipped ear marks the spot where young Dick may or may not have heard the bells of St Mary-le-Bow summoning him back to the City and his glorious future.

WHERE TO EAT

Dearth of eating places as inhabitants rarely seem to eat out here. Sample prices are for average three-course meal for two with house wine. Open for lunch and dinner seven days unless otherwise indicated.

SAN CARLO 2 High St. T 340 5823. Smart Italian, large, clean, noisy and alive. Food and service highly professional. Beautiful hors-d'oeuvres display raises hopes of good meal to follow – usually does. £10–£12. Closed Mon.

DRAGON SEED 66 High St. T 348 6160. Cantonese cuisine almost up to Gerrard St standards. Exceptionally helpful waitresses. Clean, spacious with Chinese classical music just audible. Good place to take children. £12. No break between lunch and dinner Fri, Sat, Sun.

LONDON STEAK HOUSE 7 South Grove. T 348 0302. Same as all others. £10.

KENWOOD HOUSE. T 348 4286. Eating places have marvellous premises (Coach House cafeteria and Old Kitchen restaurant), but food a let-down. Crisps and salads, packeted cakes and pies. £2 cafeteria; £5 Old Kitchen which does lunches and set teas only at weekends (Sun only in winter). Closed evenings.

SAN SIRO 2 Highgate West Hill. T 340 5856. Transport caff famous because boxer John Conteh uses it for breakfast after training. Steak, liver, bacon, egg and chips. Excellent value, under £1 a head. Open 8am–6.30pm, closed Sun.

Picnics

Lots of benches near Kenwood House, but otherwise difficult to improve on Hampstead Heath.

WHERE TO DRINK

THE FLASK 77 West Hill. Unspoilt Ind Coope pub with large forecourt and excellent lunchtime food. Dating from 1663, the Flask allegedly harboured Dick Turpin; atmosphere still very friendly to non-locals.

YE OLDE GATE HOUSE North Rd. Large brassy corner pub with thick glass windows and comfortable interior. Hot and cold food in snack bar lunchtime and evening. Younger's ale and a precarious route across two main roads for those who indulge too much.

PRINCE OF WALES 53 High St. Watney's pub selling fined bitter. Small and comfortable with chintz and wood-panelling. *The* village local. Back entrance is quiet and almost traffic-free with outside tables in tranquil and spacious Pond Sq. No music to interfere with high-powered Highgate conversations.

DUKE'S HEAD 16 High St. Hot and cold food available at this pleasant Charrington's house.

THE BULL 13 North Hill. Ind Coope Burton draught served to a predominantly young crowd who are also pandered to by a well-programmed jukebox.

WHERE TO SHOP

Perched on a hill, Highgate has a strong village feel to its shops, many of which have fronts which are wooden porches extending on to the pavement. There's something for everyone in among the varied and pleasant cluster.

High St: CENTAUR GALLERY, No. 82. T 340 0087. Speciality eighteenth- and nineteenth-century paintings, but behind the heavy old pine door there is a series of small rooms crowded with unusual, large decorative antiques such as old English domestic and farming implements. Also ethnic jewellery, Polish wood carvings, dried flowers. Contemporary paintings exhibited in large gallery in pretty garden.

COLERIDGE, No. 80. T 340 0999. Antique section has eighteenth- and nineteenth-century porcelain, silver, glass, jewellery, objets d'art, furniture. Modern section stocks all leading names in fine bone china and crystal ware.

CROMWELL HOUSEWARE, No. 62. T 340 3057. Excellent hardware, china and gift shop. Also sells pine furniture.

EARLY YEARS, No. 48. T 348 4401. French and Italian good quality clothes for nought to twelve-year-olds. Jeans, shorts, sweatshirts, dungarees, check shirts, ski suits and pretty print dresses for smaller girls.

FISHER AND SPERR, No. 46. T 340 7244. Four floors with large general stock; rare antiquarian and old books, prints and maps: mythology, poetry, first editions of literary criticism, art, medical, biography, pocket editions, music, guides, Orientalia and mystics.

HELGATO, No. 50. T 348 3864. Prints and maps from 1670–1870. General antiques, especially porcelain, ceramics, glass and small objets d'art before 1840. Closed Sun and Mon.

HIGHGATE BOOKSHOP, No. 9. T 340 5625. General bookshop, paperbacks and hardbacks.

PUSS IN BOOTS, No. 11. T 340 9748. English, Italian, Spanish and Greek day and evening shoes, boots and sandals for men and women.

SATIN, No. 3. T 348 8362. Smart and pricey separates and dresses.

ACORN, No. 13. T 340 6781. Bow-windowed women's boutique, feminine dresses and co-ordinates to suit all ages. A few French and Italian items; handbags and costume jewellery.

ANIMUS, No. 84. T 348 7381. All stock on animal theme. Wonderful collection of imaginative soft toys, selection of pocket-money toys, ornaments, gifts, a few taxidermist's items, cards.

BAILEY & SAUNDERS, No. 64. T 340

3663. Delightful chemist selling many unusual lotions and potions, established in reign of George III.

Archway Rd Other shopping centre, near the tube, and less up-market than the Village.

ANTIQUE SHOP, No. 373. T 348 0897. One of many antique shops in Archway Rd, this one sells furniture, clocks, china and pictures.

BONAVENTURE, No. 259. Hundreds of old books covering many subjects. Also maps and prints.

BUYING FOOD

High St: A. WYLIE, No. 57. T 340 3851. All breads, rolls, cakes and pastries baked at Muswell Hill branch. Birthday cakes of all types.

WALTON HASSEL & PORT, No. 88. T 340 1118. Old-established grocery, offering good range plus unusual international foods. Range of Continental cheeses, also off-licence.

M. A. RANCE & CO. 4 South Grove. T 272 3227. Breads and pastries baked at Finchley branch. Cakes for special occasions; delicious gingerbread men.

Archway Rd: HOME EAST & WEST STORES, No. 367. T 348 2614. Delicatessen with Greek and Italian specialities like fetta cheese, olives, olive oil from Cyprus, Italy, Greece and Spain, salamis and cold meats. Also range of Continental cheeses.

DAIRY & HEALTH STORE, No. 308. T 340 5963. Range of health foods, English and Continental cheeses, cold meats, coffee beans, wholemeal breads and free-range eggs. Wide range of natural fruit juices.

KEEPING AMUSED

KENWOOD SWIMMING POND Fitzroy Park. T 340 5303. Ladies only, ten-foot deep pond open 7am–9pm seven days, 7.30–10am during winter for any who can stand it. Qualified swimmers only, admission free.

HIGHGATE POND Millfield Park. T 485 4491. Men only, more rugged swimming site (thirty-five-foot deep, two diving boards) open 7am–8.30pm seven days until 3.30pm during winter. Admission free.

KENWOOD HOUSE north-east corner Hampstead Heath. Grounds roll down to picturesque lake, site of open-air series of performances by Britain's finest symphony orchestras on Sat June–Aug. Contact Greater London Council Parks Department, T 633 1707 for prices and programme details. Iveagh Bequest spring and autumn recitals and poetry readings are held in the Orangery. (See What to See.)

WATERLOW PARK OPEN-AIR CONCERTS Highgate Hill. Free concerts in hilly park Sun 7pm in summer. Local symphony orchestras and light operas. Band concerts 3pm. Tennis courts. Further details available from the London Borough of Camden Libraries and Arts Department. T 278 4444x 2452.

HIGHGATE SAUNA CENTRE 283 Archway Rd (opp Highgate tube). T 340 7005/9992. Mon–Sat 11am–11pm, Sun noon–9pm. £2 sauna, £7 sauna and massage.

JACKSON LANE COMMUNITY CENTRE 271 Archway Rd. T 340 5226. Highgate Folk Club, concerts, two theatres, headquarters for the Gatehouse Theatre Club. Nominal membership fee for film club, bar and theatre performances.

HIGHGATE GOLF CLUB Denewood Rd. T 340 1906. 18-hole parkland course, 8.30am until dusk. Reasonably proficient visitor golfers welcome, green fee £3 per round or £5 per day. Clubs available for hire, consult the pro. Course par 69.

GOOD FOR KIDS

SPOT THE SPIRE. Views over the city from the Hampstead–Highgate ridge –

the highest part of London – are quite breathtaking on a clear day. About 200 yards east of Kenwood there's a small shelter with a guide to the skyline.

GYPSY CARAVAN. An old favourite which has been absent from its usual spot near Kenwood House undergoing extensive renovation. Should be back in position in 1978.

HOW TO GET THERE

UNDERGROUND Archway, Highgate. BUSES 143, 210, 271.

Islington

I came here because I found a house. I liked the house straight away. Islington took longer.

I hope it will forgive me, but there are prettier places. Not many, you understand (boroughs can be touchy), but some. At first glance it seemed flat and down-at-heel. The prevailing colour was a rather dirty yellow. One wide, low square looked much like another and weren't there *any* trees?

Furthermore, there seemed to be a permanent demo outside the estate agent who had brought me here, and there were ominous rumblings about gentrification. This meant outside persons moving in and painting their new front doors with Dulux Gloss. Who could they mean? The paint brush froze in my hand. . . .

But the place has grown on me. Not the prettiest borough? What do you mean? I've sorted out the squares now and they are all completely different and the yellow brick is beautiful. They call it old London stock and if you need any you'll find it costs a lot.

The demo is long gone and you hear less of gentrification. What we worry about now is a real ogre – Urban Blight. As for trees, of course there are trees, there are *several* trees. Isn't that one over there?

What's more, there are nice corner shops and good pubs and friendly neighbours and the ducks fly over from the New River and you can be in the West End in fifteen minutes and if you do miss the last tube it's near enough to walk home. I've never done it myself. But I met a man who knew a man whose father did.

George and Weedon Grossmith lived here. So did Evelyn Waugh. So did the Western Brothers. That's the sort of place Islington is.

Angus McGill

WHAT TO SEE

ISLINGTON GREEN Timber warehouse north of gardens was once Collins Music Hall, where George Robey, Marie Lloyd, Vesta Tilley and all the greats appeared. Unappealing Victorian statue commemorates one of London's greatest benefactors, Sir Hugh Myddelton, Welsh goldsmith who brought fresh water to the city with his New River (completed 1613). CANONBURY TOWER Canonbury Pl. Sixteenth-century building has remarkable history (Sir Francis Bacon, Oliver Goldsmith, Washington Irving and the ghost of 'a lady in grey' have all been tenants). Squat red brick tower and fine panelled rooms with beautiful plaster ceilings remain, as does mulberry tree said to have been planted by Bacon. Tower can be viewed by special appointment with resident warden, T 226 5111. Give two or three days' notice. (See Keeping Amused.)

NEW RIVER WALK St Paul's Rd to Canonbury Rd. Winding path planted with roses, potentilla, pansies. Weeping willows trail over lazy, murky stream; stagnant pools are an insult to Myddelton's memory.

MECCA SOCIAL CLUB 161 Essex Rd. Former cinema, now listed building and bingo hall. Marvellous Egyptian façade with lotus-bud capitals. Interior's gaudy glory is for members only.

DUNCAN TERRACE Some splendid Georgian houses but has Islington's special blend of discreet elegance and disintegration.

WHERE TO EAT

General 'coming up' of the area, with thriving antique business around Camden Passage, has led some good restaurateurs to set up there. Ethnic food is provided by the local Turks, and there are a few original eating places such as MANZE'S – still selling eels and pies up Chapel Market, in the same place with the same family after seventy years – and HOWELL'S – also selling eels and pies in White Conduit St. Sample prices are for average three-course meal for two with house wine. Open for lunch and dinner seven days unless otherwise indicated.

Camden Passage: CARRIER'S, No. 2. T 226 5353. Cookery book writer Robert Carrier's own restaurant; among top ten in London, if not the British Isles. Alas, expertise costs money and the set-price, four-course menu is now £10 *a head* for dinner, £8·50 for lunch (same menu) *without* drink, service or VAT. Worth it though. Closed Sun.

FREDERICK'S. T 359 2888. Elegant surroundings, delightful garden at the back. Good wine, French food hard to fault, but the place does lack a certain intimacy and friendliness. Popular for business lunches. Sat shoppers' lunch at £2·75 a head; £14 for dinner for two. Closed Sun.

PORTOFINO, No. 39. T 226 0884. First restaurant in the Passage, opened 1961; we should therefore be grateful to Aquilino Consigli for showing others the way. Now extremely popular with people from outside London, for reliable Italian food. £14. Closed Sun.

AQUILINO BAR, No. 31. T 226 5454. Cheap and quick in-and-out place owned by Portofino's proprietor, good bargain. £4. Closed Sun.

CAFÉ DU VIN, No. 45. T 359 5801. If you can master which days do lunches and which days do not; which end for self service and which for the waitress, you could find yourself eating good French provincial food, largely based on recipes from Elizabeth David. Reasonable wines, specializing in burgundies. Very good for Sun lunch, reduced prices for children. Breakfast on market days (Wed and Sat) at

9am. Dinner £8. Closed all day Mon, Tue lunch, Sun evenings. (Extension of take-away and delicatessen at 28 Upper St.)

M'SIEUR FROG 31a Essex Rd. T 226 3495. A welcome find in one of Islington's dreariest thoroughfares. Smell of garlic bread pervasive but encouraging. Middle courses tend to be less successful than firsts and lasts. French menu including frogs and snails; friendly service, but local enthusiasm slightly waning after one or two rather uncertain dishes. £12. Closed Sat lunch, all day Sun and Mon.

DUE FRANCO 207 Liverpool Rd. T 607 4112. Singing, sometimes with piano accompaniment (if the thing is not too heavily laden with sweets and hors d'oeuvres) lends jollity to the evenings. Very popular with the locals. Unswervingly Italian. £10–£11. Closed Sun and Sat lunch.

Upper St: JULIUS'S, No. 39. T 226 4380. Austrian owner-chef knows the catering trade inside out – each order is cooked in full view in his little glass-walled kitchen. Intimate, and of the neighbourhood. Impressive wine list, super cakes (order for special occasions in advance). Set two-course lunch £1·80 a head; dinner £10 for two. Closed Sun.

SULTAN'S DELIGHT, No. 301. T 226 8346/359 2503. Very handy for the King's Head Theatre, the marionette theatre and the Screen on the Green cinema. Turkish, very good food, homemade and available for take-away. Pretty decor, open late. £9. Closed Sun lunch.

ROXY DINER, No. 297. T 359 3914. Also handy for theatre, marionettes and Screen, basic American food, mainly hamburgers and chilli. Lots of local families at weekends, friendly, noisy. £6. Weekends noon–midnight.

YA MUSTAFA 11 Islington High St. T 278 8853. Misleadingly scruffy exterior; inside fit for a sultana. Food

very good, authentically Turkish and prepared on the premises. £7. Takeaway. Noon–1am Fri and Sat, closed Sun lunch. Booking advisable.

ANNA'S PLACE 69 Barnsbury St. T 607 7172. Miniscule stripped pine, 22-seater cabin run with tremendous attention to detail by Swedish brother and sister. Eric is a professional patissier, the cakes and pastries are sensational; Anna makes treats like pickled herring and grav lax, and all the bread. By closing three weeks at Easter, Aug and Christmas they keep sane, so check to see if they're open. Book anyway. £14. Closed Sun–Mon, all Aug.

Picnics

Gardens separating Duncan Ter. and Colebrooke Row are pleasant, rose-filled, oddly landscaped with rocks like most of Islington's open spaces. Other streets and squares with gardens include Compton Ter. and Canonbury Sq., but Highbury Fields suffer less from exhaust fumes.

WHERE TO DRINK

KING'S HEAD 115 Upper St. Theatre upstairs has modern and fringe productions; music in bar folky or at least acoustic weekdays, bands at weekends. American-Irish owner still rings up his till in old pence! Ind Coope, good draught beer and lunchtime menu.

NARROW BOAT 119 St Peter St. Charrington's. Very local local with nice terrace overlooking canal, bar shaped like narrow boat, friendly atmosphere, old and young. Hot lunches weekdays, roasted sandwiches at other times. Reasonably priced.

CAMDEN HEAD Camden Walk. Right by Camden Market with a lot of seating outside in summer. Can still see excellent woodwork and cut glass mirrors peeping out from behind brewery-installed red plastic.

ISLAND QUEEN 87 Noel Rd. Truly

weird with twice-life-size female models dressed in laceup underwear and black stockings above bar. Mixed selection of people playing pool, chess, etc. Charrington's uninspiring beer, but excellent cheap food such as quiche and salad.

ALBION 10 Thornhill Rd. Stuff of which Watney's ads are made. Ivy on walls outside and every inch of cosy inside jammed with horse brasses, oil lamps and other trad bar paraphernalia. Draught beer. Garden at back with stable bar for younger clientele, open 8pm.

RISING SUN 55 Brooksby St. Small Charrington's pub ruled by splendid local lady for twenty-five years – 'I've seen a few changes here.' Ceiling covered in stuffed birds and musical instruments. Excellent draught Bass and Guinness at exactly right temperature.

HOPE & ANCHOR 207 Upper St. Watney's house run by Laurel and Hardy pair who supply hot rock'n'roll six nights a week in sweaty basement. Large bar upstairs with best jukebox in town, very nice restaurant on first floor does main course plus starters and coffee for about £2.

WHERE TO SHOP

Islington's claim to fame is Camden Passage. Antique book and print shops spill into the surrounding streets where bargains are far more likely to be found. Many shops closed on Mon.

Essex Rd: AMBER ROSE ANTIQUES, No. 76. T 609 4238. Good quality pine furniture specialists, plus some china and bric-à-brac. Do all own restoration and finishing work.

R. & R. MILITARIA LTD, No. 70. T 359 8579. Ethnographical militaria with the emphasis on 1850 – modern day, Uniforms, badges, weapons.

ISLINGTON FRAMERS LTD, No. 14. T 359 8031. All kinds of framing and block mounting done within the day

if necessary. Also range of Christmas cards.

SPORTS DESIGN CENTRE 35 Islington Green. T 226 3824. Sporting art and antiques of all periods.

Upper St: NORTH LONDON JEAN CENTRE, No. 345/6 & 76. T 226 5696 & T 226 4502. Originally an army surplus shop, now sell jeans slightly below recommended retail prices. Own brand are cheapest of all.

WILLIAM BEDFORD ANTIQUES, No. 327. T 226 9648. Masses of Georgian furniture plus tea caddies, work boxes, candlesticks, clocks, pictures, mirrors and leather bound books.

BREW IT YOURSELF, No. 135/136. T 226 0252. Run by William Tayleur who's extremely knowledgeable on the subject. Kits, concentrates and everything needed for wine and beer making.

JASKO, No. 172. T 359 1906. Piles of Indian cotton bedspreads, cheesecloth Indian fashion clothes: shirts, blouses, skirts, dresses and leather sandals.

COMPTON BOOKSHOP, No. 271. T 226 4652. General secondhand bookshop with a bias towards English literature. Some first editions; better class paperbacks.

CANONBURY BOOKSHOP, No. 268. T 226 3475. General, with children's books. Also children's educational toys.

Islington High St: ISLINGTON ANTIQUES, No. 100. T 226 5673. British 1900–1940 prints, drawings, paintings and sculpture.

ANGEL BOOKSHOP, No. 102. T 226 2904. General, with children's books, books on antiques and art.

Camden Passage One of London's most attractive antiques centres. Shops line the paved-over street and the side streets. On Wed morning and all-day Sat an open-air antiques and bric-à-brac market takes place at either end of the street. Silver is concentrated in mid-way side streets. On Thur–Fri secondhand book market takes place and there are plans for a coin market on Tue. Three covered markets in Passage: ANGEL ARCADE for antiques, old clothing, glass and jewellery; FLEA MARKET ARCADE two floors of jewellery, brass, militaria, porcelain and furniture and GEORGIAN VILLAGE with thirty-four vaults for silver, fifty stalls for antiques, twenty-five antique shops and galleries.

FINBAR MacDONNELL, No. 17. T 226 0537. Comprehensive range of pre-1900 prints and engravings. Also views of London and the Home Counties, maps, cartoons and Japanese prints.

THE SNUFF SHOP, No. 8. T 359 9417. Fifty-six different varieties of snuff including Fribourg & Treyer and Wilson's; cigars, tobaccos, cigarettes and pipes. Speciality teas.

ANNIE'S, No. 10. T 359 2328. Women's original 1900–1945 clothes and accessories. Currently lots of whites: petticoats, camisoles, nightdresses, etc.

S. E. NICHOLLS, YE OLDE CLOCKE SHOPPE, No. 25. No phone. Established in 1869 and still run by the Nicholls family. Clock and watchmakers, also repairs and jewellery. Excellent source of fob watches.

CORNER CUPBOARD, No. 28. T 226 4539. Victorian decorative pin cushions, quilts, wool pictures, papier-mâché objects and stuffed birds in glass domes.

STRIKE ONE 1a Camden Walk. T 226 9709. Established eleven years ago and selling virtually every kind of eighteenth- and nineteenth-century English clock, all with a year's international guarantee.

BUYING FOOD

Essex Rd: STEVE HATT, No. 88. T 226 3963. Smoke fish on the premises, can be bought hot from the smoke-hole. Best quality wet fish in season.

DICKENS BAKERY, No. 68. T 226 3916. Brown and white breads and English cakes and pastries baked on the premises.

Greenman St Daily fruit, vegetable and flower market.

Popham St One very good old-fashioned vegetable stall daily.

BREAD & ROSES 316 Upper St. T 226 9483. Wholefoods, also café, books and some craft.

Chapel St 103-year-old market selling fruit, vegetables, meat, bacon, eggs and tinned groceries. Open Mon–Sat, closed Thur pm.

Penton St: OLGA STORES LTD, No. 30. T 837 5467. Italian delicatessen and wine merchant. Italian groceries, pasta, salamis and hams, parmesan, biscuits, breads and coffee.

RESTORICK, No. 18. T 837 6961. English baker who bakes breads only, including the French stick, on premises. Served from a small round wooden counter.

KEEPING AMUSED

TOWER THEATRE Canonbury Place. T 226 5111. Tavistock Pep have occupied this theatre for twenty-five years. Up to twenty productions annually, Sept–July. Tickets £1 and 80p. Theatre frequently hired out to other companies during summer. On Sat during Rep season parties of twelve or more can indulge in a meal, a seat at the show and a conducted tour of the lovely Canonbury Tower for £2·25 a head. (See What to See.)

UPPER STREET GALLERY 286 Upper St. T 226 9811. Tue–Sat 11am–5pm. Double-fronted gallery specializes in contemporary arts and crafts, with frequent one-man and mixed exhibitions.

SADLER'S WELLS THEATRE Rosebery Ave. T 837 1672. See Press for details.

HIGHBURY FIELDS Opp. Highbury & Islington tube. Band concerts in the park every Sun at 3 pm during summer.

SCREEN ON THE GREEN CINEMA Islington Green. T 226 3520. Usually a double bill of very good or rarely viewed reruns, late night shows well attended so get there early. Friendly atmosphere. Fri and Sat homemade food on sale in the foyer for late performances. Capacity 300. Ticket £1.

FISHING City Rd Basin, arm of Regent's Canal, is three acres of water, most four to six feet deep. General coarse fishing (lots of carp, perch) is allowed with a London Anglers' Association licence. Contact H. J. Wilson, 183 Hoe Street, Walthamstow, E17 3AP; T 520 7477. Rod licence also required from Thames Waterways Authority, T 837 3300.

GOOD FOR KIDS

ISLINGTON BOAT CLUB Wharf Rd. Lively waterborne youth club in City Rd Basin, 9–15 years old, casual visitors welcome. Must be able to swim fifty yards. During term time March–Oct Sat–Sun 11am–6pm (Nov–Feb to 4.30pm), Wed–Fri 4–7pm. In school holidays Tue–Sat 1–6pm, closed Sun. 15p to join plus 10p per day or 5p after school hours.

LITTLE ANGEL MARIONETTE THEATRE 14 Dagmar Passage, Cross St. T 226 1787. Performances 11am Sat for the very young (3–5), 3pm Sat and Sun for older children. Special weekday shows during school holidays.

HOW TO GET THERE

BR Highbury & Islington.

UNDERGROUND Angel, Essex Road, Highbury & Islington.

BUSES 4, 19, 30, 38, 43, 73, 104, 171, 172, 214, 277, 279, 279A.

Knightsravia

The Observer has discovered a new village: it has no name on the map, but we have called it Knightsravia. Its spine is Walton Street and the Fulham Road as far as Sydney Street, its northern frontier Brompton Road, its southern boundary the King's Road. Less formal and stuffy than Belgravia – though it has elegant crescents and places, Egerton, Pelham – less rackety than Chelsea, it yet has something of the village about it; a definable character, representing all sections of the community, a self-sufficiency and a variety of secret aspects within its identity. From almost everywhere you can see grass and trees. There are few human needs you cannot satisfy within a five-minute walk of its network of streets and squares.

Eyesores exist like the slum of Pelham Street along the railway line and the confused scufferies of South Kensington underground station, but in the thirty years I have lived there much of the good has remained virtually intact. One or two straw-hatted fishmongers and family butchers have been replaced by antique shops and boutiques, the number of restaurants has quadrupled, we have call-girls as well as Conran, and a brasserie. J. Gregory, QPR wing-half and off-licensee, is now Westminster Wine. But Simpson's the greengrocers are still there, as well as the Chelsea Glass Works, Whittards, purveyors of fine teas and coffee, the old post office that sells sweets and birthday cards, and on the corner of Sloane Avenue, the delectable Michelin building and P. Josiah, newsagent, with surely the smallest premises in London.

The dozen or so pubs, patronized equally by the council flats in Elystan Place and Marlborough Court, by the transient visitors from Chelsea Cloisters and the residents in the candy-coloured terrace houses of Hasket Street and First Street, are much the same, though one now announced topless dancers at lunchtime.

There are churches and mews, and in the early mornings the clip-clop of horses on their way to the Park. On summer evenings it is cool and scented, dogs are walked under overhanging trees, and what you cannot find to eat in the Indian, Chinese, French, Polish, Lebanese, Turkish and Italian restaurants, with their exiled patrons and employees, is scarcely worth bothering about.

Alan Ross

WHAT TO SEE

SOTHEBY'S, BELGRAVIA 19 Motcomb St. Comical Doric temple built 1830 in a charming road of stucco houses, antique shops and little art galleries. Auctions of Victorian paintings, furniture and all sorts of collectors oddities – clockwork toys, stuffed birds, ephemera. Not at all intimidating – a great place to wander round just looking. (See Keeping Amused.)

ST PAUL'S, Knightsbridge, Wilton Place. Rich Victorian interior – fine open timber roof and interesting details – strange chandeliers, font and organ case by Bodley.

ALBERT GATE/HYDE PARK HOTEL Two elegant bronze stags stand on the gateposts, the Italianate houses on either side of the gate are by Cubitt. One was the home of Hudson, the Victorian railway king. Nearby, a complete contrast, looms the Hyde Park Hotel, bright red brick with spiky gables and zig-zagging fire escapes.

HARRODS Knightsbridge. The food hall is one of *the* sights of London, a splendid Edwardian interior, white and gold tiles decorated with designs of peacocks and wild boar. Scores of hams and salamis festoon the ceiling and the counters are opulent still-lifes. Fish displays are masterpieces.

CADOGAN SQ/CADOGAN HOTEL Oscar Wilde sipped hock and seltzer in Room 53 of the Cadogan Hotel waiting for the police to come and arrest him. The whole area of Sloane St, Pont St, Cadogan Sq. has a very *fin de siècle* feeling. The tall terracotta buildings are of a peculiarly localized style defined by Osbert Lancaster as 'Pont St Dutch'. It hardly exists outside Knightsravia.

BELGRAVE SQ. Largest and grandest square in London, Full of embassies.

BROMPTON ORATORY Built 1884, triumphantly Catholic building with its baroque dome and trumpeting statues against the sky. It would be at home in Rome or Paris; in London it looks flamboyantly foreign. Interior – marble, candles, fine seventeenth-century statues, incense, pink silk hangings – equally impressive.

VICTORIA & ALBERT MUSEUM Cromwell Rd. Enormous, with endlessly fascinating collections of sculpture, furniture, textiles, ceramics, paintings, drawings, prints, jewellery, metal work, costumes, musical, instruments, etc. Frequent concerts and lectures – information from Educational Dept, T 589 6371 ex 261 or 247. Excellent shop selling books, reproductions, etc. and the work of today's craftsmen, not too expensive. 10am–5.50pm; Sun 2.30–5.50pm; closed Fri. Free except for special exhibitions.

THE MICHELIN GARAGE Fulham Rd/ Sloane Ave. Delicious late art noveau folly striped pale green and white, covered in tiles, with motor-tyres on the parapet, lots of lettering. The tile pictures all round the outside are amusing and gorgeous – intrepid men in goggles, scarves flying, puff along the Corniche in open sports cars or zoom on bikes past astonished peasants.

MEWS Expensive sports cars, Sloane Rangers, geraniums and Yorkshire terriers have replaced coaches and horses, but the mews of Knightsravia have retained an extraordinarily villagey, secret atmosphere. Their charm, even though often distinctly self-conscious, makes them worth searching out. Particularly pretty or intriguing are – Lennox Gardens Mews, especially the Milner St end, Old Barracks Yard, Wilton Row with the famous 'Grenadier' pub, Pont St Mews, Halkin Mews, Belgrave Mews North and Kinnerton St which has little yards off it like Ann's Close and very nice pubs.

WHERE TO EAT

The place to find true professionals,

but not all of it is that expensive; many restaurants give better value for money than anywhere else in London. The biggest choice is to be found in Beauchamp Place; while there is another cluster of eating places at the western end of Walton St and the northern end of Draycott Ave. Sample prices are for average three-course meal for two with house wine. Open for lunch and dinner seven days unless otheriwse indicated.

MA CUISINE 113 Walton St. T 584 7585. Half a dozen places can be described as having the best food in London and this place should be at the top of the list. Owner-chef Guy Mouilleron is a genius; his food cooked *à la nouvelle cuisine* is delicate, light and beautiful to look at. Perhaps tables *are* too close together, but this makes for some terrific eavesdropping. £18. Closed Sat–Sun.

LE SUQUET 104 Draycott Ave. T 581 1785. Most superior fish restaurant. Generous plat de fruits de mar at £4·50. Fans swear Le Suquet is the next best thing to being in France. £22. Closed all day Mon and Sat lunch.

AU FIN BEC 100 Draycott Ave. T 584 3600. An old favourite. Menu mainly French; on occasions customers' requests can be met even when not on the menu. £15. Closed Sun.

BEWICK'S 87–89 Walton St. T 584 6711/2. Very friendly, pretty, light and airy restaurant with a French menu; specialities include roast leg of lamb stuffed with herbs, mushrooms and garlic. Lovely puddings. Flute and lute type music kept to one end of the restaurant. £14. Closed Sun, last two weeks Aug.

LA BRASSERIE 272 Brompton Rd. T 584 1668. London's first brasserie, complete with newspapers on poles to read with your coffee. But for the licensing hours, indistinguishable from real thing. Andouilles and tripes au cognac very popular. Ideal for breakfast – French of English. Popular with families at weekends. 8am (Sat and Sun 10am) till 11.30pm. Dinner £12, but far less for snacks.

SAN LORENZO 22 Beauchamp Place. T 584 1074. All the customers look like tax exiles just ashore from their yachts (some are). The Bernis have been here fifteen ˙years; the food is lovely, and not at all like the usual London Italian food. Note the conchiglioni al gorgonzola and crudites con bagna cauda, and above all Mara's chocolate cake. Excellent Sardinian house wine. £15. Closed Sun.

ZIA TERESA 6 Hans Rd. T 589 7634. A real haven for those wanting reasonably priced meals which are served all day long. One of excellent Spaghetti House chain, offering fish and pizzas as well as the usual pastas and entrées. £8. Open 10am for coffee, meals noon–11pm; closed Sun.

LOOSE BOX 136 Brompton Rd. T 584 3344. Efficient self-service eating place with roof garden on top and wine bar below; highest standards, most reasonable prices. Everything freshly cooked and made on the premises. Buffet type food, especially generous with sandwich fillings. £4. Closed Sun.

SALE E PEPE 13/15 Pavilion Rd. T 235 0098. Chic and packed at lunchtime, but a Must for Serious Eaters. Best to book, Italian food, pasta cooked to order. £12–£14. Closed Sun.

TROJAN HORSE 3 Milner St. T 589 4665. Small neighbourhood Greek restaurant, here thirteen years and famous for the taramasalata. Huge helpings, with unusual items like sauté brains and chicken kebabs. £12. Dinner only, closed Sun and all Aug.

LUBA'S BISTRO 6 Yeomans Row. T 589 2950. Still going strong after twenty-four years with Luba in charge. Famous for piroshkis, borsch and cernic (a cold pancake stuffed with fruit and cream). Very Bohemian. No licence, so take your own drink (no corkage). £5. Closed Sun.

SLOANE'S 116 Knightsbridge. T 589 6873. Hamburger place serving American food, based on Hard Rock but much quieter. Famous pop stars eat here and perform if they feel like it. Hamburger with chilli con carne on top, fries and salad £1·65. Doorstep sandwiches gigantic £1·35–£1·45. Room for dancing, licensed till 3am. £5·50. Open 12.15pm–3am (Sun midnight).

MONTPELIANO 13 Montpelier St. T 589 0032/2753. Covered with greenery inside and out, fashionable diners eat in a garden-like courtyard with a sliding glass roof. 100 per cent Italian menu, wines and service. Specialities crab mornay with parmesan, veal Montpeliano and a cold crepe filled with exotic creams. £13. Closed Sun.

SHEZAN 16–22 Cheval Pl. T 589 7918/0314. Held by many to be the best Indian restaurant in London. In a basement, therefore noisy, but air conditioned. £18. Closed Sun.

EATON'S 49 Elizabeth St. T 730 0074. Good food in comfortable surroundings at reasonable prices, though it would be nicer if there was air conditioning. Chef and owner are ex-Inigo Jones, which accounts for excellent cooking and attentive service. £15. Closed Sat lunch, all Sun.

MOTCOMBS 26 Motcomb St. T 235 6382. Vinous restaurant and wine bar with no licence for spirits, a large dark friendly place with Spanish chef specializing in sea bass, cavré d'agnean. Live guitar music in the evenings, backgammon boards available in bar. Wine chosen by Harry Waugh. Lunches £8–£9, dinners £12–£14. Closed Sun.

DRONES 1 Pont St. T 235 9638. Unashamedly for the beautiful and trendy, with photos of the famous as children. Aimed at slimmers, with delicious salads, such as smoked chicken or spinach, bacon, prawn and chilli, and grills, with corned beef hash as well. £12.

UPPER CRUST IN BELGRAVIA 9 William St. T 235 8444. This deplorably named restaurant has been under same management since 1946. Popular with shoppers, food very good, reasonably priced and served fast. Menu traditional English, with thirteen types of pie, all at £1·75; veg and bread served as part of the cover charge. £7.

TERRACE COFFEE SHOP Chesham Place. Ladbroke Belgravia Hotel, T 235 6040 x 325. Specialize in quick lunches, hamburgers, steak sandwiches. £8. Open 7am (Sun 8am)–11pm.

Picnics

Difficult apart from Hyde Park. All the beautiful, leafy squares are firmly locked against outsiders, but there is an unexpected courtyard with trees, seats and Chinese statues at the Victoria and Albert Museum.

WHERE TO DRINK

BILL BENTLEY'S WINE BAR 31 Beauchamp Place. At quieter end of this rather twee shopping thoroughfare you'll find an exceptional selection of predominantly French wines allied to a range of edibles very much a cut above the average wine bar fare, such as pheasant pâté with brandy, lobster bisque and turtle soup. Champagnes and sherries are additional specialities.

THE GROVE 43 Beauchamp Place. Useful selection of draught lagers in cheerful Whitbread house, and there's a choice of cold meats cut off the bone as well as a proper restaurant upstairs serving trad English dishes. Play pintable or sit outside and watch impatient chauffeurs await their sartorially fastidious mistresses.

TEA CLIPPER Montpelier St/Montpelier Place. Well-run Watney's house with a small grill bar and alcove tables on a platform around the perimeter. Panelled walls are old enough to be almost convincing and a potted history of the tea clippers decorates the exterior.

THE NELSON Montpelier Place/Sterling St. Unspoilt and still very much a 'local', this tiny bar offers a cheerful welcome to all and sundry. Not much in the way of facilities, but bar snacks usually available.

LOOSE BOX Cheval Place. Backing on to Justin de Blank's up-market deli, this three-tiered wine bar sells the same succulent array of pies, quiches, pâtés, etc., plus a goodly choice of wines from all over the Continent. The cellar bar or roof garden are the best bet for those seeking cool respite from the hustle-bustle of Harrods.

TURK'S HEAD Kinnerton St. Charrington's house serving draught IPA, a small but well-chosen selection of wines and salad-garnished snacks at lunchtimes. Un-tarted, dimly-lit interior adds to the relaxed ambience.

NAG'S HEAD 53 Kinnerton St. Tiny but friendly pub that Ind Coope have decorated on the outside but not ruined on the inside. Well-heeled regulars harangue unwitting tourist on subjects as diverse as Scottish politics and blasphemy. Hot and cold snacks.

BUNCH OF GRAPES 207 Brompton Rd. Despite the slightly garish exterior, this well-run pub on the main shopping drag offers a comfortable, unpretentious atmosphere with lovely wood carvings, mirrors and a decent selection of beers. Hot food at lunch, sandwiches available.

WHERE TO SHOP

Brompton Rd: ALPINE SPORTS, No. 309 T 581 2127. Sea wear, skating boots, skateboards; clothes and equipment for badminton, tennis, skiing and squash. Adults only.

CAROLYN BRUNN, No. 211 & 287. T 584 1966. Classic cotton, towelling and wool fashion knitwear for women, fully co-ordinated. Washable silk shirts.

REJECT SHOP, No. 245. T 584 7611. End of line, samples, slight seconds. Deal with large manufacturers and can provide continuity of stock for later matching. Furniture, basketware, glass, china and kitchen equipment with gifty items.

KICKERS, No. 183a. T 589 2211. Twenty-four designs from France, shoes and bootees for children, men and women.

SCANDINAVIAN SHOP, No. 170. T 589 7804. Clothes, hand-knitted garments, glass, rainwear; Norwegian wool; gifts from Sweden, Finland, Denmark, Norway and Iceland.

NORWAY FOOD CENTRE, No. 166. T 584 6062. Sweaters (hand-loomed), gifts from Norway.

PERSIAN CARPET GALLERIES, No. 152. T 584 5516. Auctions of rare and antique Oriental rugs.

MARISA MARTIN DESIGNS, No. 148. T 486 7870. Unusual evening and wedding dresses with combinations of antique fabrics and trimmings, Chinese embroidered panels, rare lace and buttons.

FORCES HELP SOCIETY & LORD ROBERTS WORKSHOPS, No. 122. T 589 3243. Lacquer bedtrays, basketwork, tables, garden furniture and household brushes made by men disabled in wars.

KNIGHTSBRIDGE PAVILION, No. 112. T 581 0435. Pavilion of fifty Regency style shops selling comprehensive selection of antiques and fine art. LAPADA, the antique trade association, has its HQ here: enquiries from general public welcome.

JAEGER, No. 96. T 584 2814. Contemporary classics, everything colour co-ordinated. Knitwear and accessories.

INCREDIBLE DEPARTMENT STORE, No. 94a. T 589 0162. Denim, tartan and Scottish knitwear, thirties–forties and Victorian women's clothes, Indian fashion clothes, records, tapes, jewellery. Skateboards.

ST LAURENT, HOMMES, No. 84. T 584 4993. Complete range of clothes; shirts from £15, suits from £125. Also far more expensive Rive Gauche collection.

WAREHOUSE, No. 58. T 584 3855. Bulk-bought women's high fashion clothes. Jeans, shirts, T-shirts, skirts, dresses and separates from France, Italy and Hong Kong.

JOSEPH, No. 20. T 589 0698. Clothes, boots, shoes, sandals, bags, belts and other accessories; Man's Shop, clothes from the Margaret Howell collection and other leading designers.

SCOTCH HOUSE, No. 2. T 581 2151. Tartan everything and wide range of Shetland and other knitwear. Traditional day and evening Highland dress for men, long kilted skirts for women, children's department.

FIORUCCI, No. 15. T 584 4095. Clothes and accessories in garish but fun colour combinations; witty designs like dinner jacket T-shirts, see-through plastic jumpsuits.

ST LAURENT RIVE GAUCHE, No. 35. T 584 0561. Incredibly expensive handmade women's clothes: cotton two-piece £350!

CHARLES JOURDAN, No. 47–49. T 589 0114. Very best and most up-to-date shoes, sandals and boots. 'Classic' and 'young' collections. Also Christian Dior range.

BONHAMS Montpelier St. T 584 9161. Auctions virtually every day selling virtually everything. Regulars include: Wed prints, watercolours and bygones; Thur antique furniture, oil paintings; Fri porcelain.

LITTLE HORRORS Cheval Pl. T 589 5289. Large and practical collection of clothes for children aged 2–16. Many mix and match co-ordinates from French, Italian, Swiss leading designers. High prices. Out of season clothes available.

Knightsbridge: HARVEY NICHOLS. T 235 5000. Very old-established fash-ion and accessories store has emerged victoriously from a great re-vamp. Perfumery, Cartier boutique, Hardy Amies boutique, model hats, suedes and leathers, Jean Varon boutique, 21 shop – smart young fashion designs, linens, lingerie, cruise and resort wear all year round.

ALAN MCAFEE, No. 73. T 235 7218. Long-established bespoke and off-the-shelf men's shoes in seven fittings.

HARRODS. T 730 1234. Most famous store in the world living up to its motto 'everything for everyone every-where'. Started in 1849 by Charles Harrod as a double-fronted grocery, now employs over 5000 staff in building covering a square of almost five acres.

Beauchamp Place Bustling short street packed with women's fashion, jewel-lery, shoes and antiques.

MONSOON, No. 53. T 589 7737. Delightful dresses, skirts, blouses and nightwear made up in handblock-printed fabric from Jaipur. All dyes vegetable. Also silk hand-painted dresses, blouses and skirts from Calcutta, dresses from Afghanistan and hand-embroidered hand-crocheted cotton clothes from Romania.

CROCODILE, No. 58. T 589 4455. General sportswear, classic knitwear by Rosilind Joffe and Hardware Clothing – classic style jackets, suits and trousers and small amounts of accessories. Some very cheap items, most expensive.

JANET REGER, No. 2. T 584 9368. Sexy lingerie and nightwear in silk, satin de lys, crêpe and chiffon.

GAMBA, No. 55. T 584 4774. Famous theatrical shoemakers famed for ballet shoes: this branch sells fashionable ready-to-wear women's shoes.

MAP HOUSE, No. 34. T 589 4325. Maps galore – antique, moon, stars, Ord-nance Survey, Michelin, walking, aeronautical and navigational. Also guide books, atlases, gazetteers.

DELISS, No. 41. T 584 3321. Imaginative boots, shoes and handbags made in own workshops. Items can sometimes be made in twenty-four hours if necessary.

SYLVIA'S, No. 25. T 589 5284. Imaginative and 'special' jewellery. Range of cheaper costume jewellery, astrologically based jewellery, high fashion costume jewellery. Other small interesting items.

KATHERINE SUNG, No. 35. T 584 5953. Oriental fashions and Chinese couture. Own-design clothes, readymade and made-to-measure. Fabrics by the yard. Some Continental styles.

LUXURY NEEDLEPOINT, No. 36. T 584 0391. Everything for the tapestry maker from beginner to expert: also made-up work.

HUGGINS & HORSEY, No. 26. T 584 1684. French mid-nineteenth-century carriage clocks. Repairs and restoration.

Sloane St: LAURA ASHLEY, No. 40. T 235 9728. Distinctive small-print furnishing fabrics and matching wallpapers.

RODIER, No. 15. T 235 3417. French sportswear: sweaters, skirts, blouses, blazers, trousers, dresses and coats. Everything co-ordinates, is simply cut and well-sewn.

BROWNS, No. 6c. T 235 7973. Selection of international high fashion with names like Chloe, Maud Frizon and, Sonia Rykiel.

MAGLI SHOES, No. 207. T 235 7939. Classic and superbly crafted shoes and boots made in Bologna, matching bags, range of Magli scarves.

TRUSLOVE AND HANSON, No. 205. T 235 2128. General bookshop specializing in biography, fiction, children's books and current affairs. Also stationery, die-stamping and printing service.

Hans Crescent: MIDAS, No. 36. T 584 8913. Pretty, colourful and exciting cheap shoes, sandals and boots by leading designers like Manolo Blahnik at Zapata in Chelsea.

HARDY AMIES, No. 42. T 584 2180. Complete range of stylish, sporty wear for women, including accessories. No. 32. T 584 7998. Men's collection.

ARABESQUE 12 Motcomb St. T 235 7334. Superb Eastern clothes and accessories. Bias cut robes in raw silk and pure silk chiffon; drawstring harem and Turkish trousers, Lebanese shirts; antique robes and shawls of all kinds, including Chinese.

West Halkin St: MEDINA, No. 10. T 235 7179. Elegant versatile women's fashions. Complete collection of Gordon Luke Clarke. Caftan Room.

BEATRICE BELLINI, No. 11. T 235 3027. Knitwear combining traditional stitches with high fashion styling. Lots handmade, small collection machine knits. Couture handknits by Beatrice Bellini, Kaffe Fasset and Nicky Rea.

LA CUCARACHA 6 Halkin Arcade. T 235 6741. Mexican pottery, glass, furniture, chandeliers, wall lights and lanterns made in wrought iron, wood and handblown glass.

Walton Street: WALTON STREET STATIONERY CO., No. 97. T 589 0777. Beautiful writing papers, own inks, traditional At Home cards, own 100 per cent cotton paper in seven colours, Curwen Press wrapping papers.

BALLOON, No. 77. T 589 3121. Elegant maternity clothes; coats; long dresses; jeans, corduroy and gaberdine trousers; thick loose tops; bras and tights. Baby and children's clothes up to two; slings and baskets.

FRENCH PICTURE SHOP, No. 117a. T 584 6663. French twenties original prints, particularly early fashion plates, theatrical designs and landscapes. Most limited editions, many signed.

RUMAK, No. 109. T 584 2357. Romantic floor-length gowns. Lots of ribbons, lace and antique embroidery, flouncy delicate fabrics. Bridal wear.

GILLIAN SAW – MACOLIN – LONDON, No. 186. T 584 2233. Gifts for all ages. Good for wedding presents, personalized merchandise, greetings cards, soft toys.

Draycott Ave: MEENYS, No. 163. T 581 2163. American, colourful, fun sporty clothes for children and adults. Cowboy, basketball, sweat and T-shirts with team names; dungarees, lots of work jeans. Also playwear – basketball outfits, cowboy hats and boots. Pretty clothes for girls up to six.

Sloane Ave: THE JOY OF COLLECTING, No. 73. T 584 4381. Old and new quilts, books on quilting, exhibitions related to wall hangings and quilting. JANE HALKIN, No. 45. T 589 2919. Carefully chosen, individual selection of fabrics. English tweeds, prints of all kinds, mainly on cottons, Swiss voile. Also skirts, silk squares, ties, cravats.

BUYING FOOD

Brompton Rd: SCANDINAVIAN SHOP, No. 170. T 589 7804. Largest selection of Scandinavian foods in London. Range of herrings – called sild – in jars, tinned and homemade, wide range of cheeses, especially goat cheese, and range of flat breads.

NORWAY FOOD CENTRE, No. 166. T 584 6062. Norwegian delicatessen and groceries. Also restaurant and outside catering.

JUSTIN DE BLANK AT SEARCYS, No. 136. T 584 8144. Unusual vegetables displayed outside, their own breads, cheeses, including the very best farmhouse cheddar and double Gloucester, Stilton and French cheese, teas, coffee, oils, vinegar, mustards, brioches and croissants, own biscuits and groceries.

GLORIETTE, No. 128. T 589 4750. Austrian konditorei, patisserie, croissants, Danish pastries and cream cakes baked at Montpelier Mews.

HARRODS. T 730 1234. Worth a visit just to admire beautiful tiled roof and walls of food halls (see What to See). Coffee, widest range of cheeses in London, fresh fish – shellfish arranged round a small waterfall – breads and biscuits, salamis and cold meats and range of excellent groceries.

GERMAN FOOD CENTRE 44 Knightsbridge. T 235 5760. Range of foods from Germany.

Sloane St: BENDICKS, No. 195. T 235 4749. Handmade chocolates, thirty-two types but best known include Bittermints, Mint Crisps and Sporting and Military Chocolate.

ROBERT JACKSON, No. 6. T 235 9233. Excellent delicatessen and grocery, greengrocery, breads, licensed.

KEEPING AMUSED

SOTHEBY'S BELGRAVIA 19 Motcomb St. T 235 4311. At least twelve auctions monthly, open to the general public. This branch of Sotheby's covers 1830 to present day. Mon–Fri, 9.30am–4.30pm; occasional Sat viewing. Items can be viewed a minimum of three days before auction. Tue, paintings, drawings, prints; Wed, furniture, works of art, collectors' sales (postcards, music boxes, old telephones, cigarette cards); Thur, silver, ceramics, glass, Oriental works of art; Fri, photographic material and art nouveau/deco. (See What to See.)

HORSE RIDING Rotten Row, Hyde Park. Several riding schools use as exercise ground, but non-members must book.

BLUMS RIDING SCHOOL 32a Grosvenor Crescent Mews, T 235 6846, allows anyone to ride for £5 per hour. Seven days 5.30am–7.30pm, or dusk in winter. Approx thirty horses.

MINEMA 45 Knightsbridge. T 235 4225. Small, elegant and unusual, shows films not generally released. Weekend late-night programmes at reduced rates.

CRANE KALMAN GALLERY 178 Brompton Rd. T 584 7566. Two floors.

Mon–Fri, 10am–6pm, Sat 10am–4pm. One-man and mixed exhibitions with frequent examples of work by established artists.

SLOANE STREET GALLERY 158 Sloane St. T 730 5835. Large stock of modern paintings and sculpture. Mon–Fri 10 am–5.30pm, Sat 10am–1pm.

JOAN PRICE'S FACE PLACE 33 Cadogan St. T 589 9062. Salon run by former beauty editor of *Harpers and Queen* offers complete body overhaul, or merely spot treatment. Make-up sessions, sunlamp treatment, massages, facials, manicures, electrolysis, Mon–Fri 10am–6pm, also Sat am.

MARIA ANDIPA'S ICON GALLERY 162 Walton St. T 589 2371. More like wood-panelled cottage than smart art gallery. Icons scattered throughout, at prices from the reasonable to the ridiculous.

HARRODS Brompton Rd. T 730 1234. 'Top people's store' offers 'top to toe' beauty treatment at £16·95, saunas at £1·85, and massages for £3·50. Store also holds fashion shows, art exhibitions, demonstrations in the relevant department. Ladies' Room is a marvel of Edwardian luxury – glass, marble and mahogany. (See What to See.)

IBA BROADCASTING GALLERY 70 Brompton Rd. T 584 7011. Watch how a television programme is made. Guided tours starting at 10am, 11.30 am, 2.30pm, 3.30pm. Admission free. Best to book.

GOOD FOR KIDS

JULIP MODEL HORSES 18 Beauchamp Pl. Tiny basement shop, sells beautifully made, moveable model horses – all sorts from shires to Shetlands, plus riders, tack, jumps, stables, etc. Horsey little girls liable to get addicted.

HARRODS TOY DEPARTMENT Organizes competitions most holidays, e.g. painting, building with Lego, and it's a great place to browse in. The Pet Shop selling pedigree puppies, kittens, exotic fish, etc., also a treat.

STEAM AGE 59 Cadogan St. Specializes in magnificent scale models of steam trains, ships, traction engines, etc. – adult collectors' pieces but fun just to look at.

VICTORIA & ALBERT MUSEUM Costume court, the musical instruments gallery, the armour, the Great Bed of Ware, Tippoo's tiger, and a mirror that magnifies hugely in the Regency room on the upper first floor, are the most fun. (See What to See.)

HOW TO GET THERE

UNDERGROUND Knightsbridge, Hyde Park Corner, South Kensington, Sloane Sq.

BUSES 9, 9A, 14, 19, 22, 30, 39A, 45, 49, 52, 73, 74, 74B, 137.

Little Venice

Venice, Italy, a slowly sinking, claustrophobic tourist trap, with shops full of hideous coloured glass and music boxes, six orchestras playing selections from 'My Fair Lady' at different tempi in the square, would be impossible to live in; as would Venice, California, with its canals and oil derricks. But Little Venice, W2, is a different glass of water, a totally habitual stretch of urban preservation along the sides of the canal which links Uxbridge to the Zoo at Regent's Park, where reconstructed barges and sometimes gangsters float, and where the Church Commissioners have turned their old brothels into elegantly white painted Victorian houses which the police patrol constantly for the better protection of Lady Diana Cooper.

I am now in my fourth flat in Little Venice. The third moved thirstily a couple of feet nearer the canal in the 1976 drought and almost cracked in two. I was lying in bed in my first flat and a huge pumpkin was mistakenly delivered to me from Harrods, closely followed by Mr Barry Humphries, who turned out to live next door, wearing a bow tie that flashed on and off like a lighthouse and claiming his lost Australian delicacy. Little Venice is full of romance and surprise encounters.

It also has the best delicatessen in London, Pribik and Sterman in Clifton Road, which shuts at seven at night and opens at seven in the morning, at which time I am in it buying the lunch and discussing the decline of civilization with its owners. Opposite is a fishmonger named Mr Vandersluis, who wears a straw hat, with whom I discuss the decline of the wet fish business (who can you find who wants to spend a winter's morning castrating a skate nowadays?). There's a pub called the Warwick Castle where you can drink outside, Romano's, a very good Italian restaurant, or you can live, as we often seem to, on Chinese take-away from the Lotus House. From here you can get to Piccadilly Circus in eight and a half minutes, only I never want to go.

John Mortimer

WHAT TO SEE

BLOMFIELD RD Lovely for a summer stroll. On one side are fine nineteenth-century houses, mostly stucco, some with grand columns and curvy balustrades, all with flowery gardens; on the other, plane trees, brightly painted barges and the dark green canal. Near the bridge is a charming canal keeper's cottage that looks as if it could be in the middle of the country. Where the road curves, the water opens out into a wide basin, the centre of Little Venice with more boats and a tree-covered island.

ST MARY'S Paddington Green. Late eighteenth-century brick church with a Greek cross plan – formal and calm in spite of roaring motorway nearby. The interior, recently very well restored, has galleries and many fine eighteenth- and early nineteenth-century monuments. (In a previous church on this site John Donne preached his first sermon.) Mrs Siddons is buried in the churchyard and poor Benjamin Robert Haydon who, having failed ignominiously to become England's Michelangelo, cut his own throat, lies near in unconsecrated ground.

ST MARY MAGDALEN-IN-PADDINGTON Westbourne Green. Designed by Street and built in the 1860s, now centrepiece of a GLC housing scheme, its spiky steeple silhouetted against tower blocks. Go down into the crypt and discover beautiful jewel-like little chapel by Comper. Blue ceiling with gold stars, elaborately carved and painted woodwork – like the background of a Flemish altarpiece – rich stained glass.

CLIFTON COURT Edgware Rd. Stockbroker Tudor run riot, an immense block of flats all black and white half-timbering – quite bizarre.

CLIFTON NURSERIES Clifton Villas. Nice to wander round planning dream gardens, several big greenhouses to shelter in if it rains. Always have a huge stock, give helpful advice (see Where to Shop). Open 8.30am–6pm (Oct–Feb 5.30pm); Sun 9.30am–1.30 pm. T 286 9888.

LORD'S CRICKET GROUND St John's Wood. The most famous cricket ground in the world – gets its name not from aristocratic connections, but from its founder, farmer Thomas Lord. It was opened in 1814. Splendid sight on match days, especially the late Victorian pavilion – crowded white iron balconies, flags fluttering. The Memorial Gallery is full of interesting relics. (See Good for Kids and Keeping Amused.) Out-of-season conducted tours of the ground including members' rooms can be arranged. Ring curator, T 289 1611.

WHERE TO EAT

Although Little Venice proper covers not much more than a square half-mile, it has three very good restaurants and one or two handy caffs. Patrons come from all around, attracted by lack of traffic in the wide tree-lined streets and pretty walks along the canal. Sadly, nowhere, except the Maida Café and Feeding Time, a café boat moored on a canal which serves snacks such as egg and chips, is open on Sun. Sample prices are for average three-course meal for two with house wine. Open for lunch and dinner unless otherwise indicated.

DIDIER'S 5 Warwick Pl. T 286 7484. Pretty little restaurant. Cooking shared by two very able English ladies who bring good French home cooking to a highly professional level. Delicious terrines, grills and puddings. £12. Closed weekends, and two weeks from 27 Aug.

ROMANO'S 30 Clifton Rd. T 286 2266. Clean and cave-like, equally suitable for intimate meal *à deux* or jolly get-together. Reliable Italian food. £10.

CANALETTO 451 Edgware Rd. T 262 7027. Venetian blinds (of course) screen customers at ground level; below, the room is cool, elegant and beautiful. Nine years with same chef and a faithful clientele of discerning regulars indicate that traditional Italian food is likely to be excellent, and it is. £12. Closed Sat lunch.

Picnics

Sadly, the huge communal gardens behind many Little Venice streets which make living here such a pleasure are not open to outsiders. Small but charming public garden overlooks canal basin; seats beside the water in Blomfield Rd; pleasant recreation ground behind St Mary's Church.

WHERE TO DRINK

BRIDGE HOUSE Westbourne Terrace Rd. Comfortable Charrington's house adjacent to the canal, usually full of amiable locals at weekends. Hot and cold food available at the bar. Small patio at front.

WARWICK CASTLE 6 Warwick Pl. Hidden down a tiny side-street just two minutes' walk from the Bridge House, the smoke-stained wood panelling of the Warwick Castle houses a somewhat ritzier selection of local custom. Sandwiches, salads and limited hot dishes at the bar, good selection of beers and spirits and fascinating, often licentious, conversation to over-hear. Pavement seating on sunny days, too.

WARWICK HOTEL 106 Harrow Rd. Comfortable Truman's house, recently smartened up in a fairly attractive manner, including some hand-decorated wooden panels.

THE EAGLE 15 Clifton Rd. One large, well-upholstered saloon with jukebox, darts. A bit too bright and smart for some tastes perhaps, but at least it's *clean*. Truman's ales. Hot food lunchtimes and Fri and Sat evenings

WINDSOR CASTLE 3 Lanark Pl. Watney's house with an extremely affable and cosy ambience, which isn't surprising considering the tininess of its saloon bar. Holstein lager on draught, for those so inclined. Hot snacks and main courses lunchtimes. Piped music.

THE CROWN 24 Aberdeen Place. Not far from Lord's, this rambling building has a strong cricketing atmosphere with photos of stars past and present on the walls and a diversity of fixture lists. Beautiful marble columns and unusual wooden carvings highlight the decor and there's a rather spartan poolroom with *four* tables. Free house with draught Fuller's, Smith's and Bass. Hot meals lunchtime. Theatre bar has poetry and music in evenings.

WARRINGTON HOTEL 93 Warrington Cres. Large building was once a hotel and retains the fortunate legacy of splendid marble columns and art nouveau tiling. Seats outside beneath the trees. Courage house with draught Director's and Guinness. Grills lunchtime, hot snacks in evening. Comfortable and usually quite busy, the Warrington attracts the best-lookers of bedsitterland as well as a healthy smattering of locals, many of them Irish. Pool table.

THE PRINCE ALFRED Formosa St. Best drop of draught Guinness to be found in North West London, and the unusual cut-glass windows would attract even the tee-totaller. Unpretentious place with good jukebox, darts, etc., and cold lunchtime snacks to complement the Ind Coope ales.

WHERE TO SHOP

Clusters of small rows of shops, mainly food, dotted throughout; no real centre apart from Edgware Rd, renowned for hi-fi and audio equipment.

Edgware Rd: LASKYS, Nos 33, 346, 382. T 262 0387, 723 4453, 723 4194. Established 1917, now thirty-four-store chain. Equipment stocked by all branches – the newest and largest is

No. 346 – includes hi-fi separates, music centres, digital watches, record and tape accessories, portables (includes TVs) video and pre-recorded and blank cassettes.

BIRDS & BLOKES, No. 448. T 723 9385. Boots and men's shoes handmade to measure on the premises in two weeks.

CURIOS, No. 453. T 262 3598. Shack on edge of Grand Union Canal selling bric-à-brac, all types of old records and old books.

CLIFTON NURSERIES 6 Clifton Villas, Warwick Ave. T 286 9888. Set back from road, large garden centre selling plants and shrubs of all types, great selection pot plants, good pots, garden furniture. (See Where to Shop.)

VALE ANTIQUES 245 Elgin Ave. T 328 4796. Curiosity-type antique shop with a bit of everything: lamps, brass, silver, jewellery and furniture.

Clifton Rd: TRUDI, No. 32. T 289 0866. Casual and sophisticated Italian French and English dresses and separates to suit all ages. Some handbags and jewellery.

ROSIE NICE, No. 12. T 286 6500. Own fashion knitwear in natural cottons and Shetland; attractive and reasonably priced separates; accessories and unusual jewellery, also a small range of haberdashery. Colourful, functional children's French and Finnish clothes for babies to 8-year-olds.

BUYING FOOD

MARKOVITCH 371–373 Edgware Rd. T 723 4633. Kosher food specialist: butcher, cold meats, delicatessen, groceries, hot beef sandwiches. Good Sun night takeaway run by Mrs Markovitch.

PAUL TREGESER 125 Shirland Rd. T 286 4314. Run by Mrs Over and her two sons, employs craftsmen bakers. Breads and buns, cakes and Danish pastries, baked at Harlesden branch.

WALTON HASSELL & PORT 3 Lauderdale Parade. T 286 1682. One of old-established small chain of high-class grocers. Freshly ground coffee, range of delicatessen including English and Continental cheeses, ham on the bone and specialist groceries.

PRIBIK AND STERMAN LTD 207 Sutherland Ave. T 286 1343. See Clifton Rd.

MAIDA DELICATESSEN 310 Elgin Ave. T 286 6716. Small range of salamis and cold meat, salads and groceries.

Clifton Rd: PAUL TREGESER, No. 29. T 286 3523. See Shirland Rd.

GOURMET & GOBLET, No. 27. T 286 3133. Part of Cullens. Specialist groceries, freshly ground coffee, cold meats and Polish and French sausage, Continental cheeses, Greek bread and pastries, delicatessen. Wide range of wines, spa waters and fruit juices.

PRIBIK & STERMAN, No. 21. T 286 1668. Wide range of Continental salamis, English and Continental cheeses, freshly ground coffee, Greek rye and French bread, croissants; international canned foods, pasta and smoked salmon.

VANDERSLUIS, No. 6. T 286 6127. All round fishmonger with fresh fish on the slab and frozen cabinets for a range of Young's frozen shellfish.

CLIFTON FRUITERERS, No. 14. T 286 6228. Specialists in English and Continental fruit and vegetables. Anything unusual in season.

KEEPING AMUSED

PADDINGTON RECREATION GROUND. T 624 1688. Open during daylight hours. This twenty-seven acre site has seventeen tennis courts, a 400-metre running track with outside cycle circuit, a bowling green, a snack bar and rest gardens with deckchairs provided. Cricket played on the main field in summer, football in winter. Band concerts held every Sun throughout summer 4–6pm. Primarily military and local bands.

BBC STUDIOS 117 Delaware Rd. T 580

4468 (ask for Maida Vale Studios). No live television broadcasts originate from here, but a few radio shows are open to the general public. Mainly orchestral concerts, 'Old Time Dancing' programme and 'Jazz Club' (120 seats) at 7.45pm most Tue. Book a month in advance, send sae, stating name of show and how many people attending to: Ticket Unit, BBC, London w1A 4ww. (Anyone showing up without ticket will be squeezed in if space allows.)

CLARENDON COURT SAUNA CENTRE Edgware Rd, Maida Vale. T 286 7227/8080. In Clarendon Court Hotel sophisticated health centre has facilities for sauna, massage, steam baths, ultra-violet and infra-red heat treatments and exercise programmes. Men: Tue–Fri 2pm–9pm (last appointment); Sat 10.30am–4pm (last appointment). Women: Tue–Fri 9.30am–1pm (last appointment); Mon 4–10pm. Bar service and refreshments available.

LORD'S CRICKET GROUND St John's Wood. T 289 1615 for ticket enquiries; T 286 8011 for prospects of play (May–Sept only). Normal cricket match tickets are £1 for adults, 50p for children, prices rising for Test Matches and Cup Finals. Restaurant serves a medium-priced set lunch or teatime snacks. At least two hockey matches during winter, open to the public.

Boat trips along canal: JASON'S TRIP. T 286 3428. *Jason* built 1906 to carry cargo, then first pleasure boat on London's canals. Offices opposite 60 Blomfield Rd have displays of canal crafts and pottery. Round trip journey to Camden Lock and back 1½ hours; £1 for adults, 55p for children. Informal commentary. Easter to end-May, Sat & Sun 2 & 4pm; June–Sept 11am, 2 & 4pm daily. Salad lunch available June–Sept.

LEISURE TYME. T 402 9994/7524. 2½-hour dinner cruise every evening throughout year. Arrive 7.30pm, sail 8pm; enjoy five-course meal, stereo music and well-stocked bar for £6·95 per person (drinks extra). Must book.

BRITISH WATERWAYS BOARD. T 286 6101. Waterbus service from Little Venice to inside London Zoo, Regent's Park. Mon–Sat every hour from 10am to 5pm from Little Venice; on the half-hour from London Zoo; Sun and Bank Holidays evening boat departs one hour later. Single fare including ZOO admission £1·90, children and pensioners 95p. Season ends Oct.

FISHING Permissible in certain parts of Grand Union Canal with a Thames Waterways Authority rod licence (T 837 3300) and a permit from the London Anglers' Association (T 520 7477). With the exception of private property, the area west of Delamere Terrace in Little Venice itself has free fishing rights.

GOOD FOR KIDS

MEMORIAL GALLERY Lord's Cricket Ground, St John's Wood. Fascinating collection for cricket enthusiasts – 'the Ashes', the oldest bat in existence, many mementos of W. G. Grace, Jack Hobbs and all the other cricketing giants. Open when matches are being played 10.30am–5pm, closed Sun, can also be visited out of season by appointment. (T 289 1611).

CANOEING The Beauchamp Lodge Youth Club, 2 Warwick Crescent. T 289 3389. Specializes in canoeing on the canal. Join for 25p, 15p weekly – lots of other activities too.

Marylebone

Snuggled serenely between the twin madnesses of Oxford Street and the A40 extension called Marylebone Road, is an in-scale model of what life in an urban village can be. Marylebone somehow survives, true to its Georgian pleasure-garden origins, in the teeth of gale-force redevelopment and avalanches of tourists scrambling after Wimpole Street's Ms Barrett and Sherlock Holmes of the non-existent 221b Baker Street. For, though near the roaring commercial heart of London (including the rag, medical and broadcasting trades), we Maryleboners are not quite of it.

Maybe life in the capital's centre attracts a special type of person. More tolerant, less shockable, perhaps even a trifle addicted to the constant wail of public service sirens spiking the atmosphere of genteel bohemia. I work at home, and for weeks on end my psychic geography extends no farther westwards than Manchester Square, with its giraffe-tall gold-painted Victorian lampstands and the Wallace Collection, and eastwards to Harley Street, where only last week at my dentist's I stumbled across an Arab kneeling in prayer.

My personal playpen is Cavendish Square – scandalously, sole public square of Marylebone's six. There, lazing on a grassy knoll with lunchtimers from John Lewis and D. H. Evans stores, I can let my eyes feast on Epstein's majestic Madonna and Child.

The High Street, with its cosy, charming little tributary, Marylebone Lane (the delicatessen, Paul Rothe's, has been there seventy-seven years), is the best antidote to depression I know. If a quick visit to Sagne's venerable coffee house and patisserie doesn't lift your droopy morning spirit, one astonished look at the dotty hat emporium run by David Shilling – his mum wears those extravaganzas at Ascot – surely will. The three grocery stores that stay open till 9pm and on weekdays ensure a bustling and mixed domestic scene until past sundown.

After that, a truly catholic choice of pubs, including Finch's Wine Bar where some of the great names of English variety theatre hold court, and the Prince Regent where the most beautiful china cheese dishes in the world are hung, like Old Masters, on the wall.

The old palace gardens, once rival to Ranelagh and Vauxhall, are gone now. But the spirit of pure amusement lingers on, in the convenience of a place which, less expensive than Mayfair and less 'arty' than Chelsea, combines the best of both.

Clancy Sigal

WHAT TO SEE

MADAME TUSSAUD'S Marylebone Rd. Museum of wax, first came to England 1802, Mme T's own works – including severed aristocratic French heads of very different quality from some recent portraits; Royal family models almost treasonable. Extremely crowded in high summer. Daily 10am–6pm Oct–March 5·30pm, £1·20, (65p under 16 and pensioners) or combined ticket for Planetarium (see Keeping Amused). £1·60 (90p kids).

WALLACE COLLECTION, Manchester Sq. One of the richest collections of eighteenth- and early nineteenth-century French paintings and furniture in the world; also Italian maiolica, Sèvres porcelain, Limoges enamel and a magnificent display of armour. Mon–Sat 10am–5pm, Sun 2–5pm. Free.

HEINZ GALLERY 21 Portman Sq. (entrance Gloucester Place). Houses drawings collection of the Royal Institute of British Architects and organizes frequent architectural exhibitions. Mon–Fri 11am–5pm, Sat 10am–1pm. Closed between exhibitions. Free. Drawings collection can be seen by appointment only.

MADONNA AND CHILD Cavendish Sq. Widely accepted as Epstein's finest monumental work, this 13½-foot-high bronze was commissioned by the Convent of the Holy Child in 1950.

ALL SOULS Langham Place. Built to complement his Regent St development, by 'an obscure individual called Nash' (*Observer*, 1824). Spire and portico unique and delightful; interior elegant and simple.

ALL SAINTS Margaret St. The ultimate example of Victorian high church architecture. MARYLEBONE PARISH CHURCH Marylebone Rd. Dignified, spacious church in which the poets Robert Browning and Elizabeth Barrett were secretly married.

WHERE TO EAT

Indian restaurants are particularly good here, but perhaps the most remarkable feature is the number of places which do really good breakfasts. Service is good at the other end of the working day, too, with lots of places offering early dinners. Sample prices are for average three-course meal for two with house wine. Open lunch and dinner seven days a week unless otherwise indicated.

INDIRA 62 Seymour St. T 402 6733/723 4740. Indians eat here; those who are less certain about what to have should seek assistance from helpful proprietor or his wife. Food is delicious, place pretty. Take away, too. £10, drinking lager.

PETRA 9 Seymour Place. T 402 9930. Tiny Arab restaurant in the basement, restaurant and snack bar on ground floor. Downstairs recommended to Arabs who can afford both waiting time and £3 for main dishes, which are beautifully cooked; upstairs quick middle eastern meze-type snacks can be had for about 80p. £12. Upstairs open noon–midnight, downstairs 5pm–midnight.

BANGLADESH 52 Dorset St. T 486 1135. Been here twenty-five years and considered one of the best. Briefest information on menu to help uninitiated. Note spiced Bengal tea. No licence. £5.

SUSHI RESTAURANT (DEFUNE) 61 Blandford St. T 935 8311. Minute sushi bar and restaurant serving totally authentic Japanese snacks and meals plus Kirin beer. £10 with beer. Closed Sun.

OCHO RIOS ROOM 22 Harcourt St. T 262 3369. Ruled by Jamaican anti-smoking Bertie Greene for the past eleven years with benign bullying. Not a caff although it may look like one outside; he cooks real Jamaican food. £8. Offering Sun lunches at moment.

RUMAH MAKAN 82 Lisson Grove. T 723 0653. Malayan restaurant patronized by their Prime Minister during Jubilee celebrations. Snack bar upstairs for quick food £3 with tea. Smart restaurant downstairs for more elaborate Malay food. £7. Closed Sun.

SEA SHELL FISH BAR 35 Lisson Grove, T 723 8703. Fish and chips equalled by no other in London, well under £1. Spotless and cheerful. Also gateaux, apple pie and ice-cream. Take away, too. No licence. Closed Sun and Mon.

RAW DEAL 65 York St. T 262 4841. Well-established vegetarian bistro, favourite with slimmers. Imaginative dishes, clean, bright and friendly, with tables on the pavement. No licence. Live music in the evenings. £3·50. Closed Sun.

DOUBLE DUTCH 77 York St. T 262 8164. Very pretty, with theatrical connections. Anglo-French menu. £14. Closed Sat lunch, all Sun.

WHOLEFOOD FARM BAR 110 Baker St. T 486 8444. Open 7.30am for organically grown breakfasts and continuing until 8pm, except Sat when close 3pm, and Sun closed all day. Main dishes hot and cold; counter service. Wines by the glass. Lunch £5.

MAISON SAGNE 105 Marylebone High St. T 935 6240. Lovely old-fashioned Swiss patisserie, unaltered since 1921. Irresistible cakes and confectionery; lunch dishes all 75p–£1; delicious desserts 25p–35p. No licence and smoking discouraged. Breakfasts from 9am, open till 5 Mon–Fri, till 12.30 Sat, closed Sun.

LA CAMPANA 31 Marylebone High St. T 935 5307/9334. Italian restaurant recommended by the manager of Sagne – can't say better than that. Lovely seafood salad, tagliatelle and veal. £12. Closed Sun.

HELLENIC 30 Thayer St. T 935 1257. Exceptionally popular Greek restaurant specializing in sucking pig, duck stifado and halibut kebabs as well as the more usual Greek dishes. £9. Closed Sun.

LANGAN'S BISTRO 26 Devonshire St. T 935 4531. Easy going and cheerful, nice French menu offering plainly cooked food at reasonable prices. £12. Closed Sat lunch, all Sun.

ODIN'S 27 Devonshire St. T 935 7296. The dearest of Peter Langan's restaurants. Really pretty, with paintings covering every inch of the walls. Lovely waiters, but there are gaps between courses and some of the dishes ought to be better for the price; £8–£9·50 per head for dinner, £5·75 for set menu lunch, cheapest wines over £3. Closed Sat lunch, all Sun.

DOCTOR'S RESTAURANT 19 New Cavendish St. T 935 4251. Could be nowhere but England, is in fact owned and run by a Greek family. Menu mostly safe English, and cheap. Continuous meals noon–8.30pm. All main courses £1, puds 25p. No licence. Closed 3pm Sat, all day Sun. (Currently applying for licence, plans to expand with restaurant staying open later.)

Best Sandwich Bars

2 BAYS 32 Paddington St. T 935 7031 for orders before noon. Salt beef and fifty-four other varieties, plus salads to eat there or take away.

PAUL ROTHE 35 Marylebone Lane. T 935 6783. Sandwiches made from any of the delicatessen in the shop. Can eat there if you like.

NANI'S SNACK BAR 8 Wigmore St. T 580 7936. Been here forty years but you could walk right past it because they aren't allowed to hang a sign out. Excellent toasted sandwiches, breakfasts and snacks, lasagne 75p, escalope of veal with spag £1·10. Queues of course at lunch because it's so small.

Mon–Fri open to 7·30am (or earlier)–6pm, Sat 7·30–10am, closed Sun.

Picnics

Not blessed with many free seats, but does have an attractive small park (former cemetery) in Paddington St with a charming sculpture of a young street sweeper. A pleasant, shady Garden of Rest has been built on the site of the former parish church at the top of Marylebone High St. Or Regent's Park, of course.

WHERE TO DRINK

ROYAL OAK York St. Taped music and pin-table for the younger clientele, home-cooked bar snacks at lunchtime and outdoor tables are main attractions of this easy-going Ind Coope pub.

DUKE OF WELLINGTON 94a Crawford St. Sit outside this small Charrington's house and consider impressive portals of St Mary's Church opposite. Clientele is usually quiet, polite and definitely local.

HARCOURT ARMS 32 Harcourt St. Small pub frequented by advertising types offering a selection of lunchtime snacks and outdoor seating. Cheerful.

THE OLIVE BRANCH Homer St. Only pub we know of with a grand piano in the bar, this Courage house also has a pool table and bar snacks. Pavement seating on sunny days, too.

CRAWFORD'S WINE BAR 10–12 Crawford St. Cool cellar bar has usual selection of cold table and regularly offers a Wine-of-the-Month at a bargain price.

BARLEY MOW 8 Dorset St. Real Ind Coope Burton draught and hot and cold snacks served amidst wooden settles, stools and boxes. Live music Fri sometimes. Outdoor tables.

PRINCE ALFRED 118 Marylebone Lane. Small and eager-to-please; Schlitz beer and good fresh hot food. Pool table.

GOLDEN EAGLE 59 Marylebone Lane.

Bustling little Charrington's pub boasts lovely cut-mirrors and woodwork, great sandwiches and a pianist every night.

ANGEL TAVERN 37 Thayer St. Henekey's 'all-purpose' boozerama – wines and doubles bar upstairs, real Shepherd Neame draught and Ruddles Country on the ground floor. Jukebox and outdoor seating.

PONTEFRACT CASTLE 71 Wigmore St. Pop in to this modern, though cheerful, free house to recover from the shock of your Harley St specialist's bill. Real ale on tap, cocktail bar upstairs, wine bar in basement.

PRINCE REGENT 71 Marylebone High St. Fantastic woodwork and decorated windows plus a sense of tradition that's reflected in the service as well as the menus of the two small restaurants. Well worth the walk to the north end of the High St.

THE CONSTITUTION 91 Bell St. There's not much in the way of comfortable hostelries for those who've missed their train at Marylebone Station, but this airy Watney's house rewards a short stroll. Outdoor seating in summer, two pool tables and bar snacks at lunchtimes.

BAKER & OVEN 10 Paddington St, Nottingham Place. A long, thin free house serving draught Bass and a goodly choice of, you guessed it, pies. Outdoor benches and the odd bottle of carefully selected wine.

WHERE TO SHOP

Baker St: ALL CHANGE RECORDS, No. 231. T 487 5027. New but cheap and secondhand popular and classical records and cassettes.

CHRISTOPHER FOSS, No. 120. T 935 9364. General bookshop, some board games, maps and stationery.

ARTS AND CRAFTS OF CHINA, No. 89. T 935 4576. Jade, porcelain, ivories, basketware, decorative items and kimonos.

FINE DRESS FABRICS, No. 87. T 935 5876. Very good selection of difficult-to-find fabrics; silks, cottons and cotton jersey from Switzerland and Italy.

YOUNG MOTHERHOOD, No. 22. T 935 4549. Attractive and casual maternity clothes.

JAEGER, No. 6. T 935 0827. Contemporary classics, everything colour co-ordinated. Knitwear and accessories.

ALL CHANGE RECORDS, No. 20. T 487 5027. Cut-price new and secondhand jazz.

MARY FAIR, No. 18. T 935 8618. Range of Mary Fair evening dresses and instant French fashion copies of the collections.

Bell St: GREER BOOKS, No. 87. T 262 7661. Canopied secondhand and antiquarian bookshop, cheaper bargains can be selected outside the shop.

FARGAM ANTIQUES, No. 95. T 724 0876. Unusual period furniture and an excellent range of small out of the ordinary objects; nineteenth-century Staffordshire figures, porcelain, clocks and pictures.

MONTY MILES, No. 105. T 723 8455. Established 1934, general secondhand bookshop specializing in industrial history.

E. BURNS BOOKS, No. 83. T 723 6136. General secondhand and antiquarian bookshop.

BELL STREET BIKES, No. 73. T 724 0456. New and secondhand bikes; also hire them out by the day – an ideal way of seeing the area.

York St Antique centre, mainly dealing with the trade and for export.

SMALL AND TALL SHOE SHOP, No. 71. T 723 5321. Ladies' casual, walking and fashion shoes for small feet – 13–3 – and large – 8½–11 (English). Most are handmade and can be produced in any colour. Also made to measure boots.

Crawford St: MARYLEBONE ANTIQUE MARKET, No. 43. T 723 2727. Small covered market, many stalls sell small items: jewellery, silver, glass, Victoriana, furniture and general bric-à-brac.

BRIGLIN STUDIO, No. 23. T 935 0605. Functional decorated earthenware and engraved glass by craftsmen working in open studio. Commissions accepted.

CHESS CENTRE 3 Harcourt St. T 402 5393. Enormous range of chess sets from early reproductions to very modern sets. Also chess clocks, boards, score sheets and books.

MAG MELL GALLERY 31 Paddington St. T 935 4076. Functional stoneware pottery by Gérard Lennuyeux Comnène; handspun and woven rugs, belts, cushion covers and ponchos; silk and cotton batik squares; silver jewellery and sculptures.

Marylebone High St: MARISA MARTIN, No. 39. T 486 7870. Everything designed by Marisa Martin. Unusual evening and wedding dresses; combinations of antique fabrics and trimmings, Chinese embroidered panels, rare lace and buttons characteristic.

DAVID SHILLING, No. 36. T 487 3179. Extraordinary and fabulous occasion hats. Simple hats made to measure in a few hours, special hats take longer.

BEAUTY WITHOUT CRUELTY, No. 40. T 486 2845. Downstairs cheap and casual clothes in MARTHA HILL; upstairs cosmetics, lotions and creams made from pure oils, extracts from herbs, vegetables and flowers; also wide range of simulated fur coats and jackets. Clients include many leading models.

FRANCIS EDWARDS, No. 83. T 935 9221. Enormous antiquarian bookshop; old travel books, maps, cookery books, military books, incunabula and private press books.

CROCODILE, No. 90. T 935 7834. Classic knitwear by Rosilind Joffe, also Hardware Clothing – classic style jackets, suits and trousers, some accessories. Some very cheap items, most very expensive.

George St: ORIGINELLE CLOTHES, No. 1. T 935 5991. Well-cut French and Italian classic fashions in day and evening wear; silk shirts and trousers and pretty feminine Liberty-print style dresses.

JEANNE MARCUS. No. 2. T 935 0158. Exclusive gifts for men and women and christening gifts. Brass, leather and high class novelty items.

GANDOLPHI 150 Marylebone Rd. T 935 6049. Long-established theatrical clothier: ballet shoes, leotards in several colours and so on.

Chiltern St: EARLY MUSIC SHOP, No. 47. T 935 1242. Wide range of pre-1800 reproduction musical instruments. Lots of keyboard instruments.

GREY FLANNEL, No. 7. T 935 4067. Elegant English-look men's fashions. Classic fabrics and up to the minute styling. Fully co-ordinated colours.

LONG TALL SALLY, No. 40. T 487 3370. Fashion clothes for women 5ft 8in. or taller. Day and evening wear and co-ordinated blouses. Brochure available.

WARDROBE, No. 17. T 935 4086. Top designer collections from France and Italy and range of clothes made from hand-printed fabrics. Bags and other accessories.

LE TROUSSEAU Accurist House, 64 Blandford St. T 935 9776. Swimwear, bras, floaty flouncy lingerie.

Wigmore St: MALCOLM HALL, No. 128. T 486 1307. Casual men's fashions, slightly unusual and reasonably priced.

OLOF DAUGHTERS, No. 63. T 486 4772. Excellent Swedish leather clogs and shoes; Finnish and Italian boots that lace up the front, practical crepe soles.

Duke St: WAREHOUSE, No. 27. T 487 5909. Lively colourful shop that buys women's high fashion clothes in bulk. Jeans, shirts, T-shirts, skirts, dresses and separates from France, Italy and Hong Kong.

IRISH SHOP, No. 11. T 935 1366. Beautiful knitwear clothes and craft from Ireland including Waterford glass and Belleek china.

Barrett St Large covered antique market with beautiful coloured glass arcaded roofing, selling Victoriana, bric-à-brac, jewellery, furniture and so on. Stalls outside most days.

BUTTON QUEEN, 19 Marylebone Ln. T 935 1505. Most wonderful collection of old and antique buttons in London. Mrs Toni Frith always has a selection of horn, wood, metal, mother-of-pearl and ivory and most shapes and sizes.

St Christopher's Place Charming little paved-over street.

CASA ANDES, No. 1. T 935 2857. Clothes, knitwear and arts and crafts and homeware from Peru.

UNDER TWO FLAGS, No. 4. T 935 6934. Model soldiers, books and military prints.

TURAK, No. 5. T 486 5380. Handmade jewellery from Afghanistan, Ethiopia, India, Morocco and Yemen. Specialists in rare antique ethnic jewellery.

BUYING FOOD

JAWS 220 Baker St. T 486 3367. English and Continental cheeses, cold meats, small range of condiments and good selection of salads.

GLORIETTE PATISSERIE 3a Melcombe St. T 935 2179. Austrian patisserie, croissants, Danish pastries and cream cakes baked at the bakery in Montpelier Mews, Knightsbridge. Also Austrian chocolates, sweets and Floris breads.

WHOLEFOOD 112 Baker St. T 935 3924. Salads, fruit and vegetables grown with natural fertilizers, bread from wholemeal and stoneground flour, free range eggs, potted herbs and unpasteurized Jersey cream. Next door in restaurant, wholefood charcuterie.

Bell St Excellent fruit and vegetable market coming into its own Sat. Half day Thur.

Paddington St: WHOLEFOOD, No. 24. T 486 1390. The meat and poultry in this shop has been naturally reared and fed.

BLAGDENS, No. 65. T 935 8321. Fishmongers has been here for 100 years and Mr Blagden has been running it for twenty-five. Much of their fish comes daily from Aberdeen. Scotch salmon, also a range of fresh seasonal fish and smoked fish including Arbroath Smokies.

MAISON SAGNE 105 Marylebone High St. T 935 6240. Established 1921 as Swiss patisserie and bakery, still serving wide range of pastries, gateaux and cakes baked on the premises. Specialities include croissants and brioches, Black Forest Gateau and meringues.

BONNE BOUCHE PATISSERIE 2 Thayer St. T 935 3502. Swiss patisserie: breads, brioches, croissants, cream cakes and specialize in birthday cakes of all types.

BENDICKS CHOCOLATES 53 Wigmore St. T 935 7272. Handmade chocolates, thirty-two different types but their best known include Bittermints, Mint Crisps and Sporting and Military Chocolate.

KEEPING AMUSED

THE LONDON PLANETARIUM Marylebone Rd. T 486 1121. Different programmes regularly throughout the day, 11am–4.30pm. Laserium and laser rock 5.15pm and every evening except Mon (Laserium Thur, Fri, Sat; laser rock Sun, Tue, Wed.) For further information on laser programmes ring 486 2242. Planetarium 65p, under 16 40p; Laserium £1·75.

ROYAL ACADEMY OF MUSIC Marylebone Rd. Symphony, choral and operatic concerts performed for general public at end of each term. Admission by ticket free (apply in writing with sae). During terms informal student presentations and lunchtime concerts on Tue, Wed and Thur listed on notice board in the main foyer.

SEEN GALLERY 39 Paddington St. T 486 4292. Young, friendly gallery showing mostly up-and-coming British artists. Original paintings and drawings on sale from £25. SEEN TWO downstairs, limited edition prints of all types. Mon–Fri 10am–6.30pm, Sat 5pm.

WIGMORE HALL Wigmore St. T 935 2141. Recitals by artists of international standing, as well as lesser known musicians. String ensembles, cello–piano duets, flamenco guitar, even medieval bands. Programme of verse with guest actors. Excellent acoustics.

SEYMOUR HALL Seymour Pl. T 723 8018. Main swimming pool 132ft by 42ft by 12ft deep. Mon–Fri 9am–7.30 pm, Sat to 6.30pm. Adults 25p, children 10p, spectators 8p. Main pool covered in Sept for exhibitions of boxing, fencing and trade fairs, many open to public.

COCKPIT Gateforth St. T 262 7907. Very fully equipped theatre and arts workshop conceived, built and financed by ILEA.

PHILLIPS, Marylebone Auction Rooms Hayes Place, Lisson Grove. T 723 1118. General household goods, furniture and knick-knacks. Sales Fri 10am, viewing Thur 9am–5pm. Specialist sales include pot-lids, Baxter prints and Stevengraphs, antique cameras, dolls, phonographs, lead soldiers, models. Paintings every fortnight. Fri 12.30pm.

GOOD FOR KIDS

HAMLEYS MODEL CENTRE/SPORTS & LEISURE SHOP Welbeck St/Wigmore St. T 580 4444. Model centre is largest in Europe, selling vast range of models and model kits for beginners and mini-Brunels. New sports shop sells equipment and clothing for almost every conceivable sport and pastime, for children and adults.

WALLACE COLLECTION Manchester Sq. Anybody moderately bloodthirsty would love the curving scimitars, the wily Pathans' knives, the jousting helmets and suits of mail. (See What to See.)

HOW TO GET THERE

BR Marylebone.

UNDERGROUND Baker St, Marylebone, Regent's Park, Great Portland St, Oxford Circus, Bond St, Marble Arch, Edgware Rd.

BUSES 1, 2, 2B, 3, 6, 7, 8, 12, 13, 15, 18, 25, 26, 27, 30, 39, 53, 59, 73, 74, 74B, 88, 113, 137, 159, 176, 500, 616.

Notting Hill

Like Hong Kong, we have the rich people perched on top and the poor down at the bottom among the debris from the market, the broken crates and the take-away kebabs that are no more than pieces of sizzling fat on a skewer. The area was going to have been grand: a racecourse was planned before the land was found to be uncertain; and the crescents and gardens, where a growing number of the middle class are painting in sorbet colours and thrusting weeping willows into the scruffy ground, show signs of high fees and surprisingly high hopes for the future. At the far end of Ladbroke Grove, every year the carnival hangs like a frown over the brows of the police and the organizers. It's difficult to enjoy a party atmosphere when scrutinized by what seems to be the entire police force, but if they do insist in turning out in such numbers at the occasion of a party, then they should be less discriminating: there's a famous society beauty who entertains regularly in Elgin Crescent – ambassadors, financiers, all the most interesting people go there, and they might even get the opportunity of arresting one of them.

If you come into the area from Westbourne Grove, past the shop that sells the terrible twenties lamps ex-hippies don't read by, you skirt Powis Square where James Fox and Mick Jagger acted out the fantasies of 'Performance'. After going through the market – cabbages, cheap rings and old babies' stiff white dresses – you begin to realize you are reaching Ladbroke Grove, and that should be enough to stop you in your tracks. Science fiction writers live here! They always have, their king is Michael Moorcock, they wander dazed through streets he has transformed, in search of their separate reality. Watch out or you may be spirited away by them – but should they carry you as far as the bottom end of Kensington Park Road, then eat at Thompsons, by far the best restaurant for miles around. The homemade soup and fine *frites* will soon restore confidence in the sanity of the world we live in today.

Emma Tennant

WHAT TO SEE

PORTOBELLO RD On Sat, which is the main market day, it becomes the most entertaining street in London. Innumerable stalls selling antiques, fruit, fakes, clothes and all sorts of incredible junk, plus wild mixture of people wandering along in search of bargains – sixties-style hippies, visiting film stars, Rasta men with dreadlocks and woolly hats, old ladies poking among the discarded veg. Lots of buskers, too – shaven-headed sitar players, steel bands, a blind organ grinder with a parrot on his head. Whole drab street transformed into something almost as outrageously picturesque as Prince Gypsy Lee who tells fortunes in a Romany caravan just beyond the flyover. (See Where to Shop.)

ST PETER'S Kensington Park Rd. Pleasant Victorian classical building of the 1850s with rich interior designed by Charles Barry Junior.

HOUSES Holland Park Ave north towards Westway has many handsome houses: e.g. Addison Ave – prim early nineteenth-century semi-detached; Nos 9–12 Lansdowne Crescent, overgrown early Victorian gothic; Nos 21–35 Ladbroke Grove, classical terrace painted sugared-almond colours. You can also get tantalizing glimpses of some of London's prettiest locked communal gardens, e.g. the one between Lansdowne Walk and St John's Gdns.

HOLLAND PARK AVE The traffic roars by, but it's green and shady and there are more houses worth seeing – Nos 54 and 56 have a seaside look with iron balconies, No. 25 slightly pompous grandeur and the strange inside-out group towards Addison Rd that turn their handsome backs to the road, revealing conservatories and iron spiral staircases. HOLLAND PARK MEWS Long and sloping with stucco entrance arch, cottages with outside staircases – one of London's most impressive mews.

CAMPDEN HILL SQ. Steep, leafy, very pretty and prosperous – one of the most desirable addresses in London. Laid out in 1826, the houses are all different. Nearby roads, like Aubrey Walk, are well worth exploring with flowery cottages and Edwardian studios. Peer through the railings at Aubrey House, a survivor of many eighteenth-century mansions that once clustered round Holland House and gave this area the nickname 'The Dukeries'.

HOLLAND PARK Great seventeenth-century mansion of Holland House badly damaged during WWII. The grounds – now Holland Park – retain much sophisticated charm. Formal Dutch garden laid out in 1912 by the Hollands' librarian, scores of peacocks strutting about, avenues of lime trees and open lawns. Next to the smart Belvedere Restaurant is nineteenth-century orangery with white iron chairs, plants and statues – often deserted, a good place for romantic meetings. (See Keeping Amused, Good for Kids.)

8 ADDISON RD An extraordinary early twentieth-century house by Halsey Ricardo covered with brilliant green, blue and white glazed tiles – long colonnade with more tiles, some by de Morgan.

WHERE TO EAT

The restaurants of Notting Hill Gate might be of more interest to sociologists than they are to gourmets; they all reflect the different life-styles of this area with quite remarkable accuracy, but few of them are that good to eat at. The best are in the Hillgate St and Kensington Park Rd area, bang in the middle. Sample prices are for average three-course meal for two with house wine. Open for lunch and dinner seven days unless otherwise indicated.

ARK 122 Palace Gdns Ter. T 229 4024.

Same chef for eleven years, this place keeps up high standards of plain 'English bistro' food. Nice waitresses and value for money. £9. Closed Sun lunch.

GEALE'S 2–4 Farmer St. T 727 7969. A favourite fish restaurant, here since 1939, serving the most superior fish and chips at tables with service. Licensed. £7. Basic take-away branch in Hillgate St. £1·20. Closed Sun and Mon.

COSTA'S GRILL 14 Hillgate St. T 229 3794. Another old establishment, Greek with English trimmings, and the waiters getting brusquer every year. £5·50. Open noon–10.30pm, closed Sun.

IL CARRETTO 20 Hillgate St. T 229 9988/5040. Most popular Italian restaurant of many around, one or two Sicilian specialities on a very long menu. Family-run, friendly and pretty. Music at night. £11–£12. Closed Sun.

VERBANELLA 145 Notting Hill Gate. T 229 9882/727 7282. Italian again, but more Alpine in decor and character. Good homely food £12. Closed Sun.

A TASTE OF HONEY 2 Kensington Park Rd. T 727 4146/229 6731. Wholesome but not cranky food, exotic combinations like pieces of pork wrapped round slices of fresh nectarine cooked with chopped mushroom and bacon in a brandied demiglaze. No licence, but applying for one; at the moment bring your own drink – 25p corkage. Friendly, pretty, and possible to eat there for very little. £5 lunch. £10 dinner. Closed Sun.

NATURALLY 22 All Saints Rd. T 221 7342. Totally vegetarian. Unusually inventive cook, Maria, thinks up things like cheese parcels and nut and olive balls and is not averse to slinging Grand Marnier into the orange pudding. £7–£8. Evenings only, closed Mon.

OBELIX 429 Westbourne Grove. T 229 1759. Crêperie plus steaks for tourists visiting Portobello Market; newspapers on poles. Cider 90p a litre; £5. Noon–11.30pm. Sun from 9pm, live music.

THOMPSONS 29 Kensington Park Rd. T 727 9957/9372. New, and a very welcome addition to this part of W11, pretty check cloths and a superb display of food on the cold table, all made on the premises by the English chef (Thompson is the cat). Anglo-French provincial with French owner. Menu changes weekly, smaller choice at lunch – £7, dinner £11. Closed Sat night and all Sun.

JULIE'S 135 Portland Rd. T 229 8331. Almost a club for the regulars, a warren of cosy alcoves in a variety of styles ranging from the Moorish to the Gothic. Small French menu. Dinner £16. Evenings only, except Sun when set lunch available £4·50 a head excluding drink; children half-price. Upstairs wine bar doubles as tea room and coffee room when drinking ceases in mid-afternoon. Cakes are delicious, especially at weekends.

LA POMME D'AMOUR 128 Holland Park Ave. T 229 8532. Small but 100 per cent French menu, which is far from run of the mill. Appreciated for its professional service and pretty decor, with dining outside under a vine in summer or by an open fire indoors in winter. £15. Closed Sat lunch, all Sun.

LA JARDINIERE 148 Holland Park Ave. T 221 6090. Is also owned by Alain de Froberville, patron of la Pomme d'Amour, and aimed at a lower price range. Smaller, less sophisticated menu with all starters at 65p and most main courses at £1·65 (blanquettes and fricassées for example). Good place for family Sun lunch, adults £2·75, children £1·80, per head. Other days evenings only.

LEITH'S 92 Kensington Park Rd. T 229 4481. The sort of place most people can only hope to visit with the aid of a fairy godmother or an expense account, Leith's has to be included on any list of good restaurants because it does serve good food. *Prix fixe* menu at £8·50 includes three courses and coffee but not wine, VAT, service, etc. Dinners only, last orders midnight, Sun 11.30pm.

Picnics

Anywhere in Holland Park but otherwise difficult. There is an unexpected oasis at the end of Portland Road – a paved area with a long bench. All the pleasant squares are closed; tatty ones round Westway not recommended.

WHERE TO DRINK

WINDSOR CASTLE 114 Campden Hill Rd. Dimly-lit, unspoilt nineteenth-century Charrington's house serving draught Director's Bitter and good food at all times. Near enough to Holland Park to slake a jogger's thirst.

THE HOOP Notting Hill Gate. Large Finch's pub useful for patrons of nearby Gate and Coronet cinemas. Upstairs bar is more comfortable and serves a good selection of strong lagers.

LADBROKE ARMS 54 Ladbroke Rd. Quaint old-fashioned Watney's house with a flower-decked exterior and plenty of outdoor tables for imbibing on sunny days. Only drawback – it's bang opposite Notting Hill Police Station.

EARL OF LONSDALE Westbourne Grove/Portobello Rd. Popular with tourists and junktique dealers on Sat, this cavernous Henekey's establishment is less crowded in the evenings when you'll find a young and essentially local clientele.

THE ELGIN Ladbroke Grove/Elgin Ave. Beautiful windows, mirrors and woodwork largely unappreciated by the locals who tend to be young and/or Irish. Pool table, jukebox and occasional live Irish and rock music.

FINCH'S WINEBAR 120 Kensington Park Rd. Cool cellar bar with a wide range of cold food attractively laid out and several dark little alcoves for discreet wooing.

DUKE OF NORFOLK 202 Westbourne Grove. Sandwiched between antique shops, this is an attractively unkempt Watney's tavern with a jukebox, pool table and, perhaps with an eye to the tourist trade, American beer.

PRINCE OF WALES 14 Princedale Rd. Large Victorian pub with decorated glass screens dividing the two bars. Bar skittles, darts and some of the most erudite regulars one could wish to meet in London. Large 'beer yard' at the rear.

WHERE TO SHOP

There are many different characters to the shopping in Notting Hill. The High St has some interesting shops among the ordinary, Pembridge Rd is a mini hip clothes centre while all roads around Portobello Rd are full of antique shops.

FLOWER POWER 94 Holland Park Ave. T 229 8788. Excellent range of the less usual plants and cut flowers. Interflora service.

CUCINA 4 Ladbroke Grove. T 229 1496. Basketware, Portuguese pottery, cast iron kitchenware, bamboo furniture, novelty and gifty items.

Notting Hill Gate: THE SKI SHOP, No. 158. T 221 6042. Ski clothes for children and adults, swimwear and sporty French knitwear.

HOUSE AND BARGAIN, No. 142 T 229 9797. Reckon to undercut other homeware shops by 20 per cent. Discontinued lines and seconds: china, basketware, lamps, kitchenware, bamboo furniture and gifts.

VIRGIN RECORDS, No. 130. T 221 6177. Own label and all albums on British catalogue at discount prices. Also imports from America, Japan, Ireland, Jamaica, France, Germany and Holland. Punk labels and tapes.

DRESS POUND, No. 125. T 229 3311.

Designer label and good condition, newish secondhand clothes for women, a few for children and men. Also accessories and a few new clothes.

HUNDRED AND ONE, No. 101. T 727 2326. Silver and plate spoons, photograph frames, pepper-mills, watches and a range of modern silver jewellery.

LAMPARD & SON, No. 32. T 229 5457. Good quality secondhand and antique jewellery, secondhand silver. Old-fashioned shop trading for over fifty years.

BLAND & SON, No. 24b. T 229 6711. 102 years old, until recently made umbrellas, now sell wide range of umbrellas, handbags, suitcases and other travel accessories. Handbag, suitcase, umbrella and shoe repairs.

MANDARIN BOOKS, No. 22. T 229 0327. Good general bookshop.

QUADRANT STATIONERS, No. 65. T 727 2221. Despite name, essentially a gift shop with a range of cards. Snoopy goods, mugs, aprons, etc.

Pembridge Rd: MITSUKIKU, No. 4. Kimonos of all lengths in a choice of plain or flowered fabric, jackets and Japanese sandals, toys, mobiles, rice bowls and, of course, chopsticks.

JOHN BURKE & PARTNERS, No. 20. T 229 0862. Antiquarian books of no particular period or subject and range of antique objects and furniture.

BRASS SHOP, No. 23. T 727 8643. Antique metalware, wide range of antique brass and copper. Candlesticks, chestnut roasters, bed warmers, kettles, etc.

JOHN OLIVER, No. 33. T 727 3735. Distinctive matching fabrics and wallpapers, many designed by ex-Sanderson's John Oliver. All his designs hand-printed.

RETRO, No. 21. T 229 0616. Nostalgic thirties and forties clothes, mostly American. Day and evening wear, accessories. Alterations done.

YAK, No. 41. T 727 9193. Leather bags, wallets, sandals, boots and clogs; embroideries, kelims, patchwork covers and clothes from Afghanistan, Asian antiques and ethnic jewellery.

MOMTAZ GALLERY, No. 42. T 229 5579. Eighth- to fourteenth-century Islamic and Persian pottery, glass and metalwork, also pre-Islamic bronze from 500 BC. Delightful window shopping.

CHARLES & CO., No. 45. T 727 6306. Range of artists' materials, also general framers.

Ladbroke Rd: MERCURY ANTIQUES, No. 1. T 727 5106. Eighteenth- and early nineteenth-century English porcelain.

WARWICK, No. 5. T 229 1637. International collection of furnishing fabrics wallpapers and make curtains; also collection of original graphics: etchings, lithographs and screenprints by local artists.

Portobello Rd Famous road of antique shops, smart at top and becoming progressively tatty towards motorway. Many shops close during the week but whole street comes alive on Sat when open air market sells bric-à-brac, old clothes, jewellery, antiques and all sorts of oddities. Real feeling of vitality to market, but bargains few and far between. Further down the road another market takes place under the Westway; more craft and home industry orientated with fewer 'real' dealers.

CENTAUR GALLERY, No. 82b. T 727 8851. Long narrow room crowded with paintings, small antiques, Polish wooden toys and various primitive carvings.

JANS, No. 69. T 727 7229. Copper and brass domestic articles: kettles, etc. Also old nautical instruments and pub signs.

JACK DONOVAN, No. 93. Mechanical music machines and colourful old-fashioned toys and dolls.

ANTIQUE ARCADE, No. 109. One of many arcades with many stalls selling a variety of antiques and bric-à-brac. Carol Ann Stanton's old English dolls can be bought here.

DAEDALUS, No. 197. T 727 4151. Handmade leather bags and shoes, chamois leather dresses, tops, skirts and jackets. Also modern jewellery and dresses from Afghanistan.

SOUTH AMERICAN SHOP, No. 212. Clothes for adults and children, rugs and leather sandals from South America.

HINDUKUSH, No. 231. T 727 4865. Old and new Eastern clothing, jewellery and furniture. The entrance to the shop is decorated like an Islamic mosque.

SUNFLOWER, No. 305. Alternative books, joss sticks, cards, herbs, perfume oils, New Wave records.

Westbourne Grove Many antique shops. CATHERINE BUCKLEY, No. 302. T 229 8786. Clothes made from old lace, exclusive hand-painted and/or hand-printed fabrics. Also old shawls, dresses and beaded bags.

QUIP, No. 243. T 727 5377. Interior designers and lighting specialists; very modern and unusually shaped mirrors.

CARPET BAZAAR, No. 220. T 229 8907. New, old and some antique Persian carpets and rugs. All prices.

DODO, No. 185. T 229 8241. Old advertisement signs, labels, posters, tins and pub mirrors. Also clothes made from beautiful old fabrics, lace and appliqué.

IGOR TOCIAPSKI 39 Ledbury Rd. T 229 8317. Old scientific instruments and antique clocks.

Elgin Crescent: GRAHAM & GREEN, No. 7. T 727 4594. Delightful jumble of bamboo furniture, kitchenware, basketware and plants. Much imported from China. Lots of pretty cheap present items.

H. PASH, No. 5. T 727 5227. Acoustic guitar specialists. Also sheet music.

LONDON POSTCARD CENTRE 21 Kensington Park Rd. T 229 1888. Thousands of postcards of all ages, some used others not. Displayed under subjects.

ATTAR 282 Westbourne Park Rd. T 229 9932. Clothes, baskets, jewellery from Mexico, Guatemala and Afghanistan.

BUYING FOOD

Notting Hill Gate: GARNERS, No. 164. T 727 2454. Fancy breads, wide range of cakes and pastries cooked at Greenford branch and delivered daily. MOORE BROS, No. 66. T 229 5347. Tea and coffee merchants selling own teas and fifteen types coffee beans. Also high-class groceries and off-licence.

N. H. G. PANZER, No. 24. T 229 0822. Excellent delicatessen; high-class confectionery, salads, olives, fresh coffee. Next door croissants, cream cakes, tarts and pastries, tinned groceries.

Portobello Rd Past antique shops and market an excellent fresh fruit and vegetable market takes place; also eggs, chickens and tinned produce.

THE NORMANDY, No. 243. T 727 4790. Masses of garlic hang from ceiling at Continental and English delicatessen. Loseley dairy products, breads free-range eggs, cheeses and cold meats. Chilled wine and beer.

MARTINS, No. 202. T 727 9843. SMITHS, No. 208. T 727 6223. Run by the same management. Foreign fish like cuttle fish; sell forty different varieties of fish in season; live and cooked crabs and smoked fish.

CERES BAKERY AND HEALTH FOODS, Nos 269 and 269a. T 229 0817/5571. Wholemeal breads and pastries baked locally, but pies baked on premises. Natural foods and organically grown vegetables, fruit juices, etc.

MR CHRISTIAN'S 11 Elgin Crescent. T 229 0501. Continental delicatessen, wide range salamis, cold meats, own pâté, salads, lasagnes and so on. Justin de Blank breads, Loseley ice-creams. Licensed for wine and cider. Fresh coffee.

KEEPING AMUSED

HOLLAND PARK COURT THEATRE In beautiful grounds of Holland House, open-air theatre presents summer series of plays, operas and musical concerts both classical and modern. Sun concerts 7.30pm 18 June–31 July, reserved tickets from Booking Office, GLC Parks Department, Room 89, County Hall, SE1 7PB, T 633 1707. Tickets at box office for other performances Tue–Sat 7.30pm, Sat 2.30pm. Wine bar inside gates.

COMMONWEALTH INSTITUTE Kensington High St. T 602 3252. Sprawling modern complex built as information centre to promote better understanding of 36 independent states comprising Commonwealth. Permanent exhibitions mammoth and magnificent, nearer to Disneyland than documentation. Cinema/theatre presents daytime films, with evening performances by guest artists. Monthly pamphlet of details from publicity officer, Art gallery, library, resource centre and restaurant. Admission free except theatre events. Mon–Sat 10am–5.30pm, Sun 2.30–6 pm. (See Good for Kids.)

WESTWAY EXHIBITION CENTRE Under Westway/Ladbroke Grove tube. Details Kensington Town Hall Information Office. T 937 5464. Spacious premises holding non-commercial art and information exhibitions. Varying professional calibre, some on community level, some by prestigious local artists like Bridget Riley.

ACKLAM HALL Acklam Rd. T 960 4590. Dances every Fri–Sat 8pm–2am, prices vary. Frequent live music. At times taken over by theatre group shows. Large hall holds 300 people (350 dancing), smaller hall up to forty people.

GATE CINEMA Notting Hill Gate. T 727 5750. Independent company distributing and presenting own films. Generally European directors previewing in London, recurring themes have vague political air. Typed biography/filmography accompany most presentations. Double bill of excellent feature films every night at 11.15pm. First show of the day £1, others £1·50, late-night double bill £1·30.

ELECTRIC CINEMA CLUB 191 Portobello Rd. T 727 4992. Films you've missed – Electric people actually listen to patrons' requests. Cinema was second built in Britain, now shows frequently changing programme throughout day and evening and every night at 11.15pm. Fresh homemade food and juice on sale. Occasionally show 'Portobello' films, so one day you might see yourself on the screen. £1.

GOOD FOR KIDS

HOLLAND PARK Adventure playground in wood on Abbotsbury Rd side – great for Tarzan-like swinging about. Nearby toddlers' play area and 'One O'clock Club'. Don't miss the peacocks.

TIGERMOTH, No. 166. T 727 7564. Excellent selection of functional but jolly and attractive children's clothes: dungarees, knitwear, tights, dresses, etc. Also tiny toys – clockwork models, dolls' house stuff. Send sae for mailorder catalogue.

COMMONWEALTH INSTITUTE Fascinating for even the youngest children. Look out for transparent cow in New Zealand section – press a button and watch grass being turned into milk. Stuffed duck-billed platypus, stunning costumes, intricate panoramas, films, atmospheric background noises, surprises everywhere. Check with Public Relations department for special events, T 602 3252. (See Keeping Amused.)

HOW TO GET THERE
BR Westbourne Park.
UNDERGROUND Notting Hill Gate, Holland Park, Latimer Rd, Ladbroke Grove.
BUSES 12, 15, 27, 28, 31, 49, 52, 88, 295.

Pimlico

One of the best things about Pimlico is that it offers almost nothing
to the usual tourist. Visitors rush from their Bed and Breakfasts of
a morning, in headlong flight down the Wilton Road, towards the
tubes, trains, buses and coaches which will transport them to the
sights cruelly denied them here. Which gives us locals plenty of
breathing space.

The Tachbrook Market: centre of the Universe. It took me a
while to get into the market. ('Get into', that's the way we talked
in the late sixties.) First I had to kick the supermarket habit. It took
a while but I finally accepted that your British supermarket lacked
the surrealistic scope of its American counterpart. Was mean-
spirited. Was always out of the obscure items I needed, like Flash
and Dot. 'Try the market', a native advised. Wow – what was this?
To start with, the cut-price odds and end shop in a space the size
of a cupboard managed to stock all the detergents and cleansers a
guy could want. But more important: stalls. And here the lettuce
tasted lettuce-like, the chickens looked as if they died happy, the
Italian greengrocer, formerly of Venice, stocked fennel, for God's
sake, and the fishmonger had spent seven years in Show Business

before joining the family business. From him I learned all about cooking trout and what really goes on behind the scenes at Ipswich Rep.

The market's grown over the years, and with it my affection for Pimlico. Traffic is now banned on Saturdays and thousands of Pimliconians descend: Hooray Henrys from the squares (I live in Eccleston), Italian, Indian and Cypriot families, middle-class bohemians stained with paint from renovating that little Georgian house on Cambridge Street, and ex-East Enders, many from the miraculously beautiful Lillington Gardens Council Estate (which I hope is as good to live in as it is to look at).

I've also learned that after an exhilarating hour in the market, I can pick up brilliant spare ribs around the corner at the take-away Chinese, get an honest assessment of the brie from my Polish grandmother substitute employed by the Denbigh Delicatessen, and wind up with an earful of rock gossip from John and Harry at Recordsville. Then a stroll home via quiet back streets. Quiet because the council instituted a marvellously complicated one-way system which has successfully defeated non-village motorists by bringing them to the brink of nervous breakdowns. Yes, Pimlico has a message to the world and that message is Keep Out.

It's a minute from Victoria Station, it's alive and it's *all mine*.

Howard Schuman

WHAT TO SEE

EBURY ST has some early Georgian houses, including No. 180 where Mozart, aged eight, composed his first symphony. Nearby Bloomfield Terrace is an elegant little Regency street, and Ranelagh Grove a row of same period workmen's cottages.

WARWICK SQ. is one of the grander bits of Thomas Cubitt's mid-nineteenth-century development that still covers most of the centre of Pimlico. Some of his sedate stucco terraces are now divided up and decaying, others gentrified, sub-Belgravia.

ST JAMES-THE-LESS Moreton St. Splendidly eccentric Victorian church. Interior dark and richly patterned with gleaming tiles, font with a cover like a witch's hat, iron railings outside gloriously elaborate. Lillington Gardens, very imaginative modern estate in dark red brick, makes perfect setting.

LITTLE ST PAUL'S ON THE WATER. Name given by Thames watermen to the miniature St Paul's Cathedral held in the outsize paw of one of the large ladies decorating Vauxhall Bridge. To see it lean over the up-river parapet; the faint-hearted can catch a glimpse from the bank.

TATE GALLERY Millbank. T 828 1212. On site of 'English Bastille' where in the nineteenth century thousands waited to be transported. Two distinct collections, modern painting and sculpture, and British art from sixteenth century – room after room of Turners. Tate has 7000 works in permanent collection but can show only 20 per cent at a time. New extension due to open soon will give 50 per cent more space. Open Mon–Sat 10am–6pm, Sun 2–6pm, free except for excellent temporary exhibitions. Frequent lectures and film shows, shop with reproductions and books. (See Keeping Amused.)

ST JOHN'S, Smith Sq. An urbane baroque building with four towers. Dickens didn't like it: 'a very hideous church . . . generally resembling some petrified monster on its back with its legs in the air'. Well-restored interior now used for concerts (see Keeping Amused). Streets to the north are Georgian, quietly dignified, harbouring many MPs.

WESTMINSTER ABBEY. T 222 5152. Fight your way in if you can. Abbey Treasures Museum (see Good for Kids) and Chapter House less packed than Royal Chapels, Little Cloister just beyond museum is a tiny oasis. Open daily 8am–6pm, Wed 8pm. College Garden under cultivation since AD 1000 and said to be oldest in England, is open to the public Thur 10am–6pm April–Oct, 10am–4pm Nov–March. (See Keeping Amused.)

HOUSES OF PARLIAMENT. T 219 3000. Conducted tours on Sat 10am–4.30pm, also open Easter Mon & Tue, Spring Holiday Mon & Tue, Mon, Tue & Thur in Aug, Thur in Sept. Or you can queue for Strangers' Gallery in Commons or Lords on sitting days while Parliament is in session.

WESTMINSTER HALL Crowds may spoil atmosphere of this vast hall where Charles I, Sir Thomas More and William Wallace stood trial, but the hammerbeam roof really is worth seeing. Check opening times, T 219 3100, closed Fri.

WESTMINSTER CATHEDRAL Victoria St. An exotic sight, striped like a tiger in red brick and pale stone with saucer domes and a tall spindly tower – very Byzantine. The cavernous interior is still slowly being covered with marble and mosaic, not necessarily an improvement on the barebrick vaults that now arch sombrely up into the darkness. Open daily 7am–8pm. (See Keeping Amused.)

GREY COAT SCHOOL Rochester Row. Founded in 1698, part of the building is original, most rebuilt. Painted wooden figures of charity boy and girl are original.

QUEEN'S GALLERY Buckingham Gate. Hushed atmosphere and impressive attendants in royal livery. Pictures always from fine royal collections, and changed regularly. Tue–Sat 11am – 5pm, Sun 2–5pm. Adults 40p, children 20p.

WHERE TO EAT

Unlike 'a Chelsea restaurant' or 'a City restaurant', 'a Pimlico restaurant' is not a phrase that instantly calls to mind any particular sort of place. Some places seem to be rather full of what might be vaguely described as Chelseaites or Sloane Rangers, because Pimlico merges into Chelsea and Belgravia. Sample prices are for average three-course meal for two with house wine. Open seven days a week for lunch and dinner, unless otherwise indicated.

EBURY COURT HOTEL RESTAURANT 26 Ebury St. T 730 8147. Nice English hotel (no riff-raff) serves nice English lunches and dinners in small, but clean and pretty downstairs room. Very good value, best to book. Note Sun lunch of English roast lamb and spiced apple pie for about £3·75 a head. Wine extra. Dinner £11.

THE TENT 15 Eccleston St. T 730 6922. A small, pretty place. Swiss chef, German owner, French manager, Continental menu, rather serious at lunch time (mostly business men), much more fun in the evening. Set two-course lunch £2·50; set three-course dinner £3·65. Note cream cheese and cucumber mousse, pot-roast lamb with celery and apricot sauce. Closed Sat.

LA POULE AU POT 231 Ebury St. T 730 7763. Old favourite, 100 per cent French menu, staff and decor, which puts you in mind of a French country farmhouse. Set lunch starts at £3·30 a head, with some extras; dinner £16 for two. Closed Sun.

WESTMINSTER HOTEL SCHOOL RESTAURANT 76 Vincent Sq. T 828 1222. Essential to book ten days ahead, open for lunches only noon to 2pm. Meals booked, cooked and served by students who are about to be released into the catering trade. Heavily subsidized; a first-class three-course meal costs only £1·10 a head, with wine available at more real prices. Closed weekends and school holidays.

MOTHER'S UNION (MARY SUMNER HOUSE PUBLIC RESTAURANT) 74 Tufton St. Three floors up in a small lift, clean and homely, good canteen style cooking, most main dishes (salads, hotpots, roasts) 75p, pud 15p. Menu in shop window below. Lunch Mon–Fri, tea Mon–Thur, closed weekends.

VILLA DEI CESARI 135 Grosvenor Rd. T 828 7453. View over Thames. Done up like a Roman villa, with Italian waiters in tunics and the menu on a scroll in Latin. Evenings only with dining and dancing till 2.30am. Food said to be good, £25 at least. Popular with sheiks and their entourages. Closed Mon.

POMEGRANATES 94 Grosvenor Rd. T 828 6560. Much loved by Establishment and entertainment industry, ably run by a food fanatic who really likes to see people enjoy their dinners. Truly international cuisine, ranging from gravad laks to hung yen kai and rice. Comfortable, dark and smart decor, good wines. Set lunch £4 a head, dinner £17 for two. Closed Sat lunch, all Sun.

TATE GALLERY RESTAURANT Tate Gallery, Millbank. T 834 6754. The only restaurant in any of our museums or galleries capable of providing a first-class meal with excellent wines (but Whistler murals are badly in need of a clean and better lighting). Some remarkable Old English dishes have been added to the more usual menu, really praiseworthy. £14. Mon–Sat, lunches only.

COFFEE SHOP AT THE TATE. Canteen style meals (quiches, salads, sandwiches) 75p–£1. Choice of real coffee at 27p or instant at 16p. Same enterprising management as the restaurant. Open Mon–Sat 10.30am–5.30pm, Sun 2–5.30pm.

LOCKETS, Marsham Court, Marsham St. T 834 9552. English menu, but not quite as serious as the Tate. Establishment dinner in grandiose surroundings. £18–£20. Closed weekends.

GRUMBLES 35 Churton St. T 834 0149. Real neighbourhood sixties-style restaurant of great charm and friendliness. Chaotic at times but loved for it. All food freshly cooked on the premises and locally bought. Lunch £6, dinner £12, unlimited coffee 40p. Closed lunch Sat, all day Sun.

OPSARAS 46 Churton St. T 834 7311/828 6295. Wine bar at street level. Greek restaurant in basement. Really jolly of an evening. Not a kebab house (though there is one kebab on the menu), more like real eastern Mediterranean food with particularly unusual desserts £11. Closed Sun, restaurant also closed Sat lunch.

LE STEAK NICOLE 72–73 Wilton Rd. T 834 7301. Used to serve nothing but excellent steaks in the simplest French ways with pommes allumettes and salads or veg. Menus now expanded to include lamb, fish, calves' liver, tripe. Sit outside under giant red parasols, but cooler in the air-conditioned basement. New cocktail bar. £12–£14. Closed Sat lunch, all day Sun.

GRAN PARADISO 52 Wilton Rd. T 828 5818. Italian hunting lodge. Busy, cheerful and friendly. £14. Closed Sat lunch, all day Sun.

JULIUS 2, No. 15 Sussex St (corner Winchester St). T 828 3366. Related by marriage to Julius 1 in Islington (2 is 1's wife), therefore a similar professional chef's menu. Very pretty,

intimate decor. £12. Dinners only, closed Sun.

PIMLICO BISTRO 131 Tachbrook St. Small, slightly cramped place with small but varied menu offering excellent value. £7. Closed Sun, lunch.

PETER'S 59 Pimlico Rd. 7am–10pm (10am–10pm Sun). Pete's is one of the best traditional caffs in London. Delicacies like chicken vol au vent; generous portions of bacon, egg & chips. Value is good, regular haunt of cabbies, which in itself is a recommendation. £1–£3.

CAPRI 51 Pimlico Rd. Smaller menu but slightly cheaper prices than nearby Pete's. Good plate of steak pie with veg, pudding and tea for less than £1. 8am–6pm. Closed Sun.

Picnics

Pimlico not rich in parks and open spaces. Only square open to public is St George's, unappetizing. On the other side of Grosvenor Rd, Pimlico Gdns offer plenty of bench space and you can gaze at the toga-clad figure of William Huskisson, a Tory statesman run over by Stepehenson's Rocket (first victim of the Railway Age). Further along the Embankment beside the Houses of Parliament, Victoria Tower Gardens pleasant; or try new piazza in front of Westmister Cathedral.

WHERE TO DRINK

THE SURPRISE 110 Vauxhall Bridge Rd. Two-piece band Tue–Sat. Spartan, but drinks good value.

GREYCOAT BOY Greycoat Place. Extensive hot and cold buffet and wide selection of beers and spirits. Cellar disco Tue–Sat and affable though dimly lit ambience popular with off-duty office workers and locals.

MORPETH ARMS Millbank/Vauxhall Bridge Rd. Drag Show Tue & Wed, Pearly King of Hammersmith entertains Thur, drum/organ due every other night. Pleasant atmosphere.

PIMLICO TRAM 66 Tachbrook St.

Drum/organ duo every night. Large bar emulates tram decor, clientele mixed locals and tourists.

WHITE SWAN 12 Vauxhall Bridge Rd. Large buffet, nice, intimate alcoves, jukebox. Disco every Sat and Sun.

PLUMBERS ARMS 14 Lower Belgrave St. Georgian pub with excellent hot and cold buffet and real ale. Best bet for those looking for a comfortable drink near Victoria station.

T. A. LAYTON WINE BAR 12 Esterbrooke St. Open 12 noon–3pm only. Run by 'Tommy' Layton, wit, eccentric and author of many books on wine. Limited but thrifty menu which offers space for customers' 'personal adverts' or comments.

EBURY WINE BAR 139 Ebury St. Comprehensively stocked but slightly fussy wine bar with well-prepared food and regular special offers. Extensive wine list, many vintages available by the glass. Classical guitarist entertains most evenings.

ST GEORGE'S TAVERN 14 Belgrave Rd. Best pub in increasingly seedy vicinity of Victoria station, this Charrington's house has real ale, hot meals and comfortably unassuming decor.

THE ORANGE Pimlico Rd. Un-tarted Watney's house with lovely atmosphere: hot snacks, pool table and darts.

WHERE TO SHOP

Pimlico Rd On the edge of Belgravia and close to Chelsea, the street has become a fashionable and pricey antiques centre. Bargains tend to change hands between dealers only. There are also several places specializing in home decoration and soft furnishings.

ANTIQUUS, No. 90. T 730 8681. Life-size icons and early medieval objects and works of art.

LOOT, No. 76. T 730 8096. Fine array of bizarre things of no particular period or style.

ROBIN GAGE, No. 50. T 730 2878.

Has two shops – the more colourful deals in reproductions, particularly Victorian style chests of drawers painted with naval scenes; carved and painted figureheads; pub signs; ships models. Also a good source of old copper. Next door sells seventeenth-, eighteenth- and nineteenth-century antiques, mostly English furniture, and always has a fine collection of old dressing boxes converted into humidors.

J. ANTHONY REDMILE, No. 73. T 730 0557. The most exotic natural materials – elephant's tusk, horn, ivory, mother of pearl and giant tortoises – are incorporated into Mr Redmile's designs for ornaments, objects and bizarre furnishings. Prices are pretty bizarre, too.

GEOFFREY BENNISON, No. 91. T 730 8076. Seventeenth–nineteenth-century furniture, pictures and carpets. Prices and sources vary enormously, everything unusual, exotic, amusing. Lots of French and Oriental objects.

THE CONSTANCE SPRY FLOWER SHOP, No. 88. T 730 0342. Known for extravagant displays, the shop sports a fine show of flowers usually unavailable elsewhere. Specializes in country flowers, blossoms and sprays from unusual flowering trees; will deliver anywhere in London and make up bouquets for all occasions.

NINA CAMPBELL, No. 64. T 730 9136. With partner Mark Birley sells pretty accessories for the home. Fabrics designed by Nina Campbell, and their bed linen, matching cushions, lamps and china are exclusive. Also sell French porcelain and lots of pretty and frivolous knick-knacks for the home.

W.H.I. TAPESTRY SHOP, No. 85. T 730 5366. Full range of tapestry wools and canvas for novice and expert alike. Staff will design to order as well as selling designs from stock. A note for perfectionists: everything is hand-painted.

CASA PUPO, No. 56. T 730 7111.

Distinctive ceramic bowls, plates, dishes, plant pots, animals and fruits, lamp stands and containers from Spain, Portugal and Italy are displayed in colour themes in the large airy white-painted rooms. With a sister branch in Chelsea, this shop keeps to cheaper lines and has a large reject section. Small range of colourful Spanish rugs. Large lighting section. The latest addition is the 'Black Room', a gift shop with a more international flavour: English Crabtree and Evelyn jams and preserves, cane baskets, French candles shaped like fans, bangles and other small gifty items.

THE UPSTAIRS SHOP, No. 22. T 730 7502. Specializes in giving the bedroom a pretty, co-ordinated look. Will do it all for you, or you can choose one or more items from the range of bedspreads with matching valences, over-pillow cases, scatter cushions, curtains, lampshade and base, and even fabric-covered tissue-box, pretty, small pattern cotton fabrics.

ELIZABETH DAVID SHOP Bourne St. T 730 3132. Small unattended ground floor is a bit off-putting but basement shop is crammed with beautiful French kitchen equipment and every culinary device imaginable: earthenware, stoneware, terrines, baking dishes, special designs for pot au feu, marmites and poelons for use on direct heat. Also carbon steel French cutlery and a complete range of French cooking tins.

COLEFAX & FOWLER 149 Ebury St. T 730 2173. Smart and formidable looking, they keep a wide range of chintz and matching wallpapers.

INCA 45 Elizabeth St. T 730 7941. Peruvian multi-coloured knitwear, ponchos, hats, scarves, gloves, ribbons and some jewellery are displayed on the ground floor. Coloured woven shopping baskets, rugs, domestic ware, framed mirrors, jolly toys upstairs.

Ebury St: JUSTIN DE BLANK, No. 114. T 730 2375. Range of plants, flowers and seeds as well as freshly cut herbs herb plants and naturally dried herbs and spices sold by the ounce.

ZAIRE, No. 143. T 730 1808. African ivory sculptures and jewellery, woodcarvings, paintings, kaftans, khangas and soapstone carvings.

Buckingham Palace Rd: GIRL GUIDES ASSOCIATION, No. 17; SCOUT ASSOCIATION next door. All the bits and bobs of Scout and Guide uniform as well as comprehensive range of camping equipment.

BENARDOUT, No. 31a. T 834 8241. Antique and old Persian rugs and carpets – nothing younger than fifty years. Also undertake repairs and cleaning.

KEMP & CO., No. 28. T 834 1610. Artists' materials shop established 1870. Brushes, watercolours, oils, papers, etc.; also specialize in framing. Stationery section has unusual postcards and cards.

Victoria St: ARMY AND NAVY STORES. T 834 1234. Founded in 1871 by officers wanting to buy wine at a cheaper rate: they soon had a thriving import business on their hands. By 1930 the store went public and soon it will expand into four more floors. Provides a little of everything but is particularly noted for its food hall (see Buying Food) and wine section.

MITSUKIKU, No. 157. T 828 2058. Splendid new large branch. Kimonos of all lengths in a choice of flowered or plain fabric, jackets and Japanese sandals, toys, mobiles, rice bowls and, of course, chopsticks.

STAMPS, No. 77. T 799 2925. A must for fanatics. Run by George Korel who buys and sells stamps from all over the world. Shop always crowded.

PIKLIK, No. 199. T 828 1070. Women's clothes from Thailand and China. Crammed with colourful cotton and satin blouses, skirts, jackets and dresses loose enough to double as unusual maternity clothes.

FOUR CORNERS 201 Vauxhall Bridge Rd. Small shop impossible to miss with its bright red and yellow exterior. Clothes, basketware and jewellery from Peru, China, Guatemala and India sold very cheaply. Everything handmade from natural items including colourful jerseys, socks, hats, gloves, and cotton batik T-shirts, khangas, belts and jewellery and baskets.

CORNUCOPIA 12 Tachbrook St. T 828 5752. Like an Aladdin's cave of clothes and accessories from 1900 to 1960. No particular style but most clothes are for women; odd things like top hats and dancing shoes for men.

THE DELIGHTFUL MUDDLE opposite Cornucopia. A junk hoarder's delight, it certainly lives up to its name, crammed with china, glass, lace, fabrics, clothes – 'stage and screen supplied'. If Gertrude Lee the proprietor isn't in, you are invited to call at Herbert's Drugstore opposite.

The Unexpected

AXFORD 306 Vauxhall Bridge Rd. Sells secondhand men's clothes and flashy, sexy women's underwear. They've been going since 1880, so the combination obviously works well.

ASHTON BOSTOCK INTERIOR DECORATIONS 21 Charlwood St. T 828 3656. If you break a valuable wine glass, they will repair it for you.

J. A. ALLEN & CO. 1 Lower Grosvenor Pl. T 828 8855. *The* place for browsing through books on horse breeding, management, showing, riding, racing, hunting, driving and polo.

BUYING FOOD

There are not many specialist and high quality food shops around here.

Strutton Ground Just off Victoria St is one of areas oldest markets. It happens every weekday, is particularly busy Fri–Sat lunchtimes. Fruit, veg and flowers.

ARMY & NAVY STORES Victoria St. T 834 1234. Excellent grocery, cheese counter and delicatessen serving range of cold meats, pâtés and even haggis. Grind coffee of several blends. Large Gloriette patisserie sells delicious cream cakes and pastries and bread baked on premises. Large wine counter.

WOOLWORTH 19 Wilton Rd. T 834 3465. Excellent and large range of groceries, surprisingly up-market with a choice of Jackson's teas. Bread counter and delicatessen.

OVERTON'S 4 Victoria Buildings. T 834 3774. Opposite the station, been selling fish for 104 years and pride themselves on providing the very best quality. All fish comes daily from Billingsgate, regular supply of lobsters and salmon from Scotland and oysters from Devon.

WESTMINSTER HEALTH FOODS Rochester Row. T 834 2711. All usual health foods, can be relied on for excellent Allinson's stoneground bread and other delicious breads from Ceres and Justin de Blank. Biggest turnover is in vitamins and Kevin Smith, the manager, is doing a grand and increasing trade in bran!

SQUARE ORANGE 41 Pimlico Rd. T 730 2365. Everything free of preservatives. Apart from standard health foods, they sell fresh yeast, 100 per cent wholemeal flour and breads, health food cheeses made from goat's and skimmed milk, extensive range of pulses, brown rice, aduki and mung beans, homemade jams and pickles and seaweed.

THE CORNER GROCERY Warwick Way and Belgrave Rd. Mini-supermarket but has a small delicatessen counter selling pâtés, cold meats and Continental breads.

CULLENS 4 Lupus St. T 834 7401, 25 Eccleston St. T 730 8946. Traditional grocers with wide range of brands. Delicatessen is good for pâtés, has a small range of cold meats and English cheeses.

JUSTIN DE BLANK 40 Elizabeth St.
T 730 0605. Excellent range of delicatessen, cheeses, own pâtés, etc.,
good bread, wines.
Tachbrook St Market essentially for
fruit, veg and flowers, but on Sat there
is a wonderful seafood stall where a
charming straw-hatted gentleman sells
crabs, winkles, whelks and prawns.

KEEPING AMUSED

TATE GALLERY Millbank. T 828 1212.
Lectures every day and films Mon–Fri,
programme from information desk,
main foyer. Also occasional poetry
reading. All free. (See What to See
and Good for Kids.)
BIOGRAPH CINEMA 47 Wilton Rd.
T 834 1624. Best value for movies in
town if not too choosy about surroundings. Two first feature films every
programme, little-shown or good
classics, changing frequently. 50p and
60p. Open from noon.
NEW VICTORIA THEATRE Wilton Rd.
T 834 0671. Comfortable and reasonably small music venue (capacity:
2574). Several attractions every month,
primarily top rock groups. £1·50–£4.
Good acoustics, one large bar and
two smaller ones.
WESTMINSTER CATHEDRAL Victoria
St. July to mid Oct international organ
recital series 4.45pm every Sat. July to
mid-Oct (not 27 Aug). Sept–Oct evening orchestral and choral concerts, 60p
per recital or £1·80 for any four.
Details: T 834 7452. Tickets at door,
Cathedral Bookshop, or by post from
Advance Booking Office, 42 Francis
St, SW1P 1QW. (See What to See.)
VICTORIA PALACE 191 Victoria St.
T 834 1317/8. Showcase for lavish
floor shows, sequinned and feathered
middle-of-the-road productions. Beautiful domed interior, Royal Command
Performances used to be held here.
Wide range of ticket prices, including
a choice of twelve boxes. Capacity
approx 1500. Five bars to booze from.

ST MARGARET'S Parliament Sq. Dean
of Westminster holding dialogues with
notable personalities Thur throughout
July; 1–1.40pm, free. Music concerts
various evenings throughout July.
Dates on posters outside church. (See
Good for Kids.)
WESTMINSTER ABBEY Morris dancing
in Broad Sanctuary every Wed at
8pm during summer. Band concerts in
College Garden Aug–Sept Thur 12.30–
2pm. Organ recitals July–Sept alter-
nate Thur 6.30–7.30pm. Admission
60p from Chapter Office, 20 Dean's
Yard or at door. (See What to See
and Good for Kids.)
STREET ARTIST West side of Victoria
station, has been there for years.
Chalk drawings on pavement and
upturned hat for coinage. All proceeds
he says, go to support of his dog.
KARATE Westminster Cathedral Hall,
Ambrosden Ave. T 352 7716. London
Karate Club allows casual participants
in regular classes every Tue. Visitor's
fee £1. Karate 6.45pm, Kung-Fu
7.45pm.
DOLPHIN SQUARE T 834 3800. Large
complex furnished flats with facilities
open to public. Sauna £2 including
swim. Massage £3 per half-hour.
Swimming pool (surrounded by plate
glass bar with 'gold' dolphin hovering
above pool) £1 per session; Mon–Fri
noon–9pm, Sat–Sun 9am–6pm. Squash
Courts £1 per 30 min; Mon–Fri
7.30am–9pm, Sat–Sun 9.30–6pm.
ST JOHN'S Smith Sq. T 799 2168.
Former church produces unusual
cultural entertainments, including
poetry readings in the Crypt and very
extended dance recitals. Throughout
summer until July, resuming Sept.
Most choral, orchestral and dance
programmes Sat 7.30pm. Lunchtime
performances (refreshments in Crypt)
1 and 1.15pm. Tickets at door.
METROPOLE CINEMA 160 Victoria St.
T 834 4673. Former movie house now
has laser/light show, projecting intri-

cate patterns and swirls of colour to accompanying recorded sound. Extended run. No need to book.

GOOD FOR KIDS

BRASS RUBBING CENTRES Facsimile brasses of knights, skeletons and grand medieval ladies in Westminster Abbey cloisters, Mon–Sat 10am–5.30pm, and St Margaret's, Mon–Sat 9.30 am–6pm. Paper and materials provided, about 50p to £3 depending on size.

ABBEY TREASURES EXHIBITION (5p, adults 11p). Fascinating wax funeral effigies with real hair and staring eyes (Charles II looking alarmingly spivvy) and superb medieval effigies, two actual death masks. Oddest exhibit is a jemmy used by Scots Nats in 1950 to remove Stone of Scone from Coronation Chair. April–Sept daily 9.30am–5.30pm, Oct–March Mon–Sat 9.30am–3.30pm, closed some holidays. T 222 5152.

TATE GALLERY organizes children's activities most holidays, sometimes special exhibitions. Don't miss Beatrix Potter's minutely detailed illustrations for *The Tailor of Gloucester*, hung at child height. (See What to See and Keeping Amused.)

ROYAL MEWS Buckingham Palace Rd. Marvellous fairy-tale state coaches, immaculate horses and harnesses. Open Wed & Thur, 2–4pm (5p, adults 15p).

CARTOON CINEMA Buckingham Palace Rd. T 834 7641. All U-films, mainly cartoons, occasional family comedy, always newsreels. Open Mon–Sat 10.45am, Sun 12.30pm.

HOW TO GET THERE

UNDERGROUND Pimlico, Victoria, Westminster, St James's Park.

BUSES to Pimlico – 2, 2B, 24, 36, 36A, 36B, 77, 88, 181, 185; to Victoria – 2, 2B, 10A, 11, 16, 24, 25, 26, 36, 36A, 36B, 38, 39, 52, 149, 181, 185, 500, 503, 506, 507; to Westminster – 3, 11, 12, 24, 29, 39, 53, 59, 76, 77, 77A, 77C, 88, 109, 155, 159, 168, 170, 172, 184, 503, 507.

Richmond

Where can you walk eight miles in one direction, two in the other, perfectly smooth and level underfoot, in unbroken countryside, without ever stepping on to a road or seeing a car, and yet without being once obstructed by barbed wire or bull? Nowhere, as far as I know, except Richmond – on the tow-path along the river, eight miles upstream to Hampton Court, two miles down to Kew. For walking in half a daze, pretending to be at work on the next chapter, there is nowhere to match it.

The Riverside is my Richmond, but for others it's the Park (for those who prefer to be disturbed by the raucous sex lives of deer rather than ducks), and River and Park are joined by the Hill. The Hill is the place for shopping – and, considerately, it stays open for Sunday strollers. Here within a stretch of 200 yards are an excellent range of little antique shops (all unpompous, but few now cheap), a secondhand bookshop bulging with unexpected items, a shop that specializes in coffee beans, a good delicatessen, and some splendid male boutiques (that decadent-sounding hybrid) which have some-how provided almost every suit I've needed in the past ten years and never for more than £40. Down the hill and into King Street (which contains a tiny shop, Frails, with the most consistently pretty dresses that I've ever seen in any shop window to gladden my eye on the way to the morning paper), and King Street leads to the best Green in London, surrounded on two sides by eighteenth century houses with little pedestrian alleyways running off . . . the list of such pleasures could be endless.

For those who want the feel of a country town within fifteen minutes of Waterloo, and countryside to walk in, Hampstead and Richmond are the obvious rivals. For me it's to Richmond's advantage that Hampstead has for so long been the winner. Everyone knows Hampstead. There is even supposed to be a Hampstead Person, of a loosely intellectual sort. But amazingly few Londoners have ever been to Richmond, and Richmond Person has yet to be identified. There's a peculiar pleasure in giving detailed instructions on how to get here to people who then marvel that they've never been before.

Bamber Gascoigne

WHAT TO SEE

RICHMOND GREEN Narrow alleys lead from main shopping street, George St, into the unexpectedly wide expanse of the green – once a medieval jousting place. Little more than a gatehouse remains of Henry VII's great palace at Richmond, said to be haunted by a phantom horseman. Maids of Honour Row, four very elegant flat-fronted houses, built by George I for the ladies of his court. Houses between Cricketers pub and Duke St are Queen Anne and early Georgian – most have fine carved doorways. Richmond Theatre, a red brick and green domed late Victorian building, makes a brash, jolly contrast; inside panelled mahogany vestibules, stained glass windows, marbled floors, rich plush and gilt. (See Keeping Amused.)

RICHMOND HILL The famous view – an excuse for a day out for Londoners since the eighteenth century – still looks good. The Thames curves and sparkles beautifully and surrounding suburbs seem to vanish in haze.

RICHMOND PARK Charles I high-handedly enclosed these six square miles for hunting in 1637. There are still gnarled oak trees that date from before the enclosure and herds of red and fallow deer. Set in the beautiful rolling landscape are White Lodge, birthplace of Edward VIII, and Pembroke Lodge, a nice rambling house, now a rather dreary tearooms, where Bertrand Russell lived as a child. (See Keeping Amused and Good for Kids.)

MARBLE HILL HOUSE Richmond Rd. Twickenham side of river is elegant Palladian mansion built in 1728, well restored by the GLC – fine pictures and furniture. Open daily except Fri, 10am–5pm. Free.

ORLEANS HOUSE GALLERY. T 892 0221. Nearby interesting early eighteenth-century octagonal building houses the Ionides Collection of pictures, mostly local views and changing exhibitions. Tue–Sat, 1–5.30pm; Sun 2–5.30pm, 4.30pm in winter.

HAM HOUSE Ham St. T 940 1950. Early seventeenth-century mansion, one of very few houses of this period with almost unchanged interior. April–Sept Tue–Sun 2–6pm; Oct–March Tue–Sun noon–4pm. Adults 30p, children 10p.

KEW GREEN Surrounded mostly by Georgian and early nineteenth-century houses with Decimus Burton's grand entrance gates to Kew Gardens in one corner. A good place to lie about watching urban village cricket on summer weekends. St Anne's, eccentric red brick domed parish church, sits on the green. It has a rather sinister mausoleum and graves of Zoffany and Gainsborough.

KEW GARDENS. T 940 1171. Wonderfully refreshing after city sight-seeing. Entrance charge of 1p to Royal Botanical Gardens is unbeatable bargain. Princess Augusta, the mother of George III, began the botanical collection and employed Sir William Chambers to decorate the grounds with temples and follies. You can't miss the pagoda, now sadly without its original bells and eighty dragons, but look out for ruined Roman arch and the thatched cottage where Queen Charlotte had picnics à la Marie Antoinette. Palm House is magnificent, all sweeping curves of glass and iron, built 1844–8. Rare and beautiful plants all clearly labelled. Open daily 10am, closing from 4pm–8pm. No dogs. (See Keeping Amused.)

RIVERSIDE WALK Go down a road called Ferry Lane at the corner of Kew Green and you find yourself on the river bank at the beginning of a most beautiful walk. Soon all is completely rural with huge willow trees bending over the water, then on the opposite bank urns and roses appear under the trees in the grounds of

Syon House and there is an elegant little domed pavilion, painted pale pink on the edge of the river.

Next comes Isleworth with its church, pretty houses and pub. Then boatyards, fishermen and bridges, and as you near Richmond fine houses like Asgill House, a honey-coloured formal villa and the splendid sight of 200-year-old Richmond Bridge, its five stone arches spanning the river.

Further on people sit in the riverside gardens snoozing in deckchairs, handkerchiefs knotted over their heads as if they were at the seaside. If you're energetic go on across cow and buttercup-filled meadows to Petersham – little church has box pews and Elizabethan monuments and there are grand Georgian houses with big gardens. Finish the walk with a restful trip across the river on Hammerton's Ferry and a delicious surprise – in York House Gardens lots of hilarious and charming stone nymphs, larger than life and completely naked, clamber about on an overgrown fountain.

WHERE TO EAT

There are dozens of places to choose from – maybe the proximity of the parks, river and Botanical Gardens, plus acres of playing fields, encourages healthy appetites. Sample prices are for average three-course meal for two with house wine. Open lunch and dinner seven days a week unless otherwise indicated.

VALCHERA'S 30 The Quadrant. T 940 0648. Family-run Swiss-Italian restaurant here since 1874 and, to judge by its appearance completely, unchanged. Three-course set lunch at £1·85 a head must be the best bet in Richmond; special list includes seasonal items like salmon, lobster or game, bringing à la carte meals up to more like £12·50 for two. Closed Sun.

BISTRO VILLAGE 27f The Quadrant.

T 948 2786. Popular with people who like informality. Menu written on blackboards and windows as part of the decor; bare boards and simplicity matched by the food which aims to be French and includes coq au vin as well as steaks. £8·50.

MRS BEETON IN THE 21st CENTURY 58 Hill Rise. No booking. Approached through a remarkably undivering craft shop, this enterprise is run by a group of seven or eight local ladies who take turns to cook own menus each day. Try to keep standards and prices level. Success marked by signs in the craft shop saying 'no queues beyond this point'. Homemade pâtés, flans, soups, cakes, scones and pies almost always sold out by closing time (5.15), open 10am including Sun. Not licensed. Lunch £1·50 for one.

FRANCO'S RISTORANTE 5 Petersham Rd. T 940 9051. Popular little Italian restaurant with view towards river and a few unusual specialities like homemade pasta, snails, rabbit, cheese pancakes. £10.

RED LION 18 Red Lion St, Richmond. T 940 2371/948 1961. Held by many to be the best Chinese restaurant for miles around, noteworthy for prawn with sesame seeds £1·65, sweet and sour fish £1·45 and Peking duck. Set menu at £8 for four. More adventurous à la carte £8–£10 without wine.

RICHMOND RENDEZVOUS 1 Paradise Rd/1 Wakefield Rd. T 940 5114/6869/0579. Also contestant for title of best Chinese restaurant in area. This one is the original Rendezvous Restaurant of W. T. H. Young, the amazing Chinese waiter made good who now owns eleven other places. Famous for the spareribs. £7–10 without wine. Dinners only in Paradise Rd; Wakefield Rd open all day.

KEW RENDEZVOUS 110 Kew Rd. T 948 4343/940 1334. Exactly the same menu as at the other Rendezvous, but slightly dearer, perhaps to help pay for smart new modern decor, which is very soothing, with plenty of space.

PITAGORA 106 Kew Rd. T 940 0278. Also very smart and soothing in appearance, Italian with a front that slides fully open, rather like a car showroom's, so that people sitting at the tables outside still feel that they are part of the restaurant. Homemade pasta, trout cooked in a paper bag and Apicella pictures on the walls. £10–£12. Closed Mon.

LA VERANDA 102 Kew Rd. T 940 9044/8938. Another Italian restaurant, with a more old-fashioned approach to the business. Latin American trio play every night. Specials include home-made pasta, wood pigeon, sea bream, and sometimes gnocchi. £10. Closed Sat lunch and all day Sun.

OSCAR'S 149 Kew Rd. T 940 8298. Determinedly English menu with a careful pub-like decor, named after Oscar Wilde. Boiled beef and carrots, with special Sunday roasts for families, £3 for three courses and half price for half portions. £12. Closed Sun evenings.

FANNY'S BISTRO 100 Kew Rd. T 940 9966. Under same management as Oscar's and catering for an evening trade with a French menu and bistro-like atmosphere (i.e. menu chalked on blackboard). £10. Dinners only, closed Sun.

GEORGE'S 94 Kew Rd. T 940 1693. Wildly popular Sun, with menu covering specialities from most European countries, and a tempting offer of T-bone steak with strawberries and cream to follow for a little over £3. Dinners only.

NEWENS 288–290 Kew Rd. T 940 2752. Appears to be HQ of the blue-rinse brigade, but only goes to show how well they know when they're on to a good thing, the cakes and luncheons (a hot roast every day) being quite outstanding and so near Kew Gardens. Maids of Honour, cooked to a secret and original recipe served warm, and pastries, all at 20p and full of fresh cream, are the main attractions here. Set lunch £1·85 per head, fully licensed. Closes 5.30pm, no lunch Mon, closed Sun.

JASPER'S BUN IN THE OVEN 11 Kew Green. T 940 3987/948 2049. Most ambitious and expensive restaurant hereabouts, amusingly furnished with bric-à-brac and three macaws in the garden, which is very nice for dining out in. French menu, food richly garnished. Set lunch £3·40 per head, dinner £14 for two. Closed Sun.

Picnics

Perfection – Kew Gardens for highly civilized lunch on the grass (the lack of dogs an asset) and Richmond Park for more basic, jolly family outings. Or you could choose the Terrace Gardens on the slopes of Richmond Hill – very Victorian atmosphere, pretty formal flowerbeds and lawns.

WHERE TO DRINK

CRICKETERS Richmond Green. How idyllic to lie on the grass outside this pretty Victorian pub and watch a leisurely game of Britain's great summer sport on the tree-lined green. Real ale, of course, and an à la carte menu in the excellent restaurant.

ORANGE TREE 45 Kew Rd. Young's house with some of the best kept special bitter yet tasted. Other attractions include a well-patronized upstairs theatre, full meal service in the cellar bar and an interesting brick and marble façade.

ROEBUCK Richmond Hill. Popular with summer tourists, the Roebuck is a fairly modern building trying to look older, but has breathtaking views across the Thames. Younger's ales and extensive bar snacks as well as full meals in the first floor restaurant.

WHITE SWAN Old Palace Lane. Dating back to the sixteenth century, this cosy Courage house is close to the Thames and has a delightful little garden and a separate restaurant. WHITE CROSS Water Lane. Old pub with superb views of river and Richmond Bridge. Large forecourt between pub and river where children can be taken. Young's ales.

CHRISTIE'S BARS Bridge St. A large, modern complex of bars and 'games rooms', which isn't as bad as it sounds as the prices are reasonable and the management enthusiastic. Popular with the under-twenty-fives as disco and coin-slot games.

WHERE TO SHOP

KEW BOOKS 9 Mortlake Ter. T 940 2512. Antiquarian and old books on botany, gardening and all natural history subjects, also Charles Darwin. Small general stock.

Kew Rd: OLD TYME, No. 58. T 940 7850. English 1700–1850 longcase clocks, also small bracket and dial clocks.

CROCKS, No. 2. T 940 0466. Over eighty tons of china in stock at any one time! 75 per cent of their stock is reject so prices are low. Also glassware and casseroles.

CRAFTSMITH 18 George St. T 940 9987. Wide range of fabrics from tweeds to Liberty prints and an enormous range of craft kits and lots for children.

King St: FRAILS, No. 6. T 940 1398. No trousers; clothes ultra-feminine. Fid is the main designer and she uses Liberty cottons and silks, chiffons and rayon jersey to create interesting designs that are a little bit special, from £30. Also dresses, tops and skirts made from old fabrics and a cheap range of Indian imported dresses; Deco-style jewellery.

QUELQUE CHOSE, No. 9. T 948 3036. Handmade British products, natural skin and hair care, soft toys, children's clothes, crochet, pottery and other craft.

LION AND UNICORN BOOKSHOP, No. 19. T 940 0483. Lively children's bookshop with books for up to twelve years. Wide range of fiction and non-fiction, plenty of picture books and all the popular paperback publishers. Run Bookworms Club on Sat. (See Good for Kids.)

BAZAAR 6 Duke St. T 948 3626. Ethnic clothes for women selected with style: antique Chinese shawls, hand-stitched blouses from Hungary and Romania, full-skirted and colourful dresses from Afghanistan and matching outfits and dresses from India.

Hill Rise: DOLPHIN HOUSE, No. 3 and 5. T 940 5949. Wide range of sportswear and equipment for children and adults. Riding, bowls, ballet, football, judo, rugby, tennis, badminton, swimwear, training shoes, roller skates, ice skates, après ski wear.

BALDUR BOOKSHOP, No. 41. T 940 1214. General secondhand bookshop with selection of Victorian ephemera and children's books.

DOLL SHOP 18 Richmond Hill. T 940 6774. Antique dolls, some in original clothes and some dressed in careful reproductions of period costumes (many of the trimmings, including lace, are period). Also old wood and tin toys and old children's games in good condition.

BUYING FOOD

Kew Rd: NEWENS, No. 288. T 940 2752. Olde worlde tea shoppe selling original-recipe Maids of Honour and also homemade bread and cakes. Closed Mon pm.

MATTHIAS BAKERY, No. 84. T 940 1626. High-class groceries, crusty bread baked on premises, homemade cakes and locally made marmalade.

BERTORELLI'S, No. 131. T 940 4448. Delicatessen owned by Charlotte Street/ Queensway Bertorelli Italian restaurant. Frozen dishes from their menu, cold meats, salamis, vast variety of pâtés, cheeses, Italian bread and cakes. KRAMER 3 Duke St. T 940 1844. Austrian konditorei and patisserie, made on the premises. Specialities include Black Forest gateaux, strawberry flan, German apple strudel and fresh cream cakes. Breads made by another bakery.

RICHMOND TEA & COFFEE CO. 9 Hill Rise. T 940 0855. Coffee lounge and shop selling fourteen blends of coffee, thirteen China and Indian teas and all coffee-making equipment, Continental chocolates.

Richmond Hill: THE DELICATESSEN, No. 22. T 940 3952. Up to 100 varieties of fresh cheese available with about sixty-five whole cheeses in stock at a time. English and Continental range of homemade pâtés, salamis, olives, breads, range of homemade salads, frozen foods, cheesecakes, own desserts and gateaux. Off-licence.

KRAMER. T 940 1417. The building dates back to 1741 and decoration matches the period. (See Duke St.)

KEEPING AMUSED

RICHMOND THEATRE Richmond Green. T 940 0088. This 1899 building is more of an attraction than some of the performances (see What to See). Nightly shows include pre-West End runs on a changing weekly basis. Tickets £1·75–£2·50.

ORANGE TREE 45 Kew Rd. T 940 3633. Professional pub fringe theatre holds evening and occasional lunchtime performances with seats £1 or under. Playwright in residence during some productions. Large pool of actors known as Richmond Fringe Group has given frequent presentations abroad. Theatre capacity 80.

RICHMOND ICE RINK Richmond Bridge. T 892 3646/892 3957. Large rink 200 by 80ft, with smaller private ice surface open publicly three afternoons and evenings a week. Mon–Fri

adults 70p, children 45p per session; slightly more weekends. 10am–10pm (Sat 10.30am). Café, bars, car park, skate hire.

RICHMOND PIER Riverboats to Westminster and Hampton Court; rowing and motorboats for hire; all trips subject to river conditions.

FISHING Licence from the Thames Water Authority, T 892 1061. Good coarse fishing, some trout.

Richmond Park: GOLF COURSE. T 876 3205. Two eighteen-hole public courses (one hilly, one flat) open all year round 8am until one hour before sunset, seven days a week. Mon–Fri green fee £1 or £1·50 for day ticket; weekends £1·50 per round and booking a must. Club-hire £1. Par 69 on both courses.

FISHING Pen Ponds permit from Superintendent, T 948 3209. Adult season ticket £1, children 50p. Perch and roach most likely catch.

ROEHAMPTON GATE RIDING AND LIVERY STABLES Priory Lane. T 876 7089. One of the biggest stables in London, adjacent to park and those who hire its horses can roam throughout it freely. However, weekend rides must be escorted and Mon is four-legged day of rest. £3·50 an hour, must book.

HAM POLO CLUB Petersham Rd. T 948 2558. Ham Common every Sat at 3.15 and 4.15pm April–last Sun in Sept. Programmes at gate. £1 per car, free if on foot.

THE CASTLE Whittaker Ave (by Town Hall). T 948 4244. Large entertainment complex with several clubs and a terrace with lovely riverside view.

CHEEKEE PETE'S DISCO six nights 8pm–midnight, Sun 7.30–10.30pm. Approx age 18–23, prices 55p–£1·30. Admission fee covers entry to BROLLYS a Fri–Sat night disco across the corridor attracting slightly older crowd.

BIER KELLER employs a musician Mon

nights, dressed German-style, but will play anything going.

POOL ROOM 20p will get you a session, 5.30–10.30pm.

RICHMOND BATHS Old Deer Park, Twickenham Rd. T 940 8461. Open-air pool Mon–Fri 8.30am–8.30pm, till 7pm Sat, 5pm Sun. Adults 30p (45p weekends), juniors 20p (30p weekends). Indoor pools same charges as above to 25 Sept, winter charges slightly less. Summer opening 8.30 am; closing Mon 6.30pm, Tue, Thur, Fri 8.30pm, Wed 8pm, Sat–Sun 5pm. Winter, thirty minutes later in the morning, thirty minutes earlier in evening. Sun open until noon only.

RICHMOND ATHLETIC GROUNDS. T 940 0397. Golf driving range, T 940 5570. Sixty balls for 50p; 5p hire for woods, no charge for other clubs. 10am until dusk, Sat 9am–1pm during rugby season. Grounds HQ for London Scottish and Richmond Rugby Club, matches every Sat Sept–April.

ROYAL MID-SURREY GOLF CLUB Old Deer Park. T 940 1894. Although private, members of recognized golf clubs anywhere in the world can play on two eighteen-hole courses Mon–Fri upon payment of a green fee, £5 charge for one round £6·50 a day. Bar and dining room, club hire from the professional. Par on inner eighteen is 71, outer course 70. 8.30am until dusk.

THE NATIONAL MUSICAL MUSEUM 368 High St, Brentford. T 560 8108. Housed in undistinguished brick church next to a giant gasholder are some musical instruments, all in working order and including the only self-playing Wurlitzer in Europe, pianos with racehorses which gallop in tune, and a piano with two keyboards. 60p. Several evening demonstrations and performances during autumn. Sat–Sun 2–5pm April–Oct.

Kew Gardens: T 940 1171. (See What to See.) GENERAL MUSEUM South-east part, near pond. Exhibitions on history of Kew, botanical-related art, general botany.

WOOD MUSEUM Easternmost edge, near Director's Office. Part of Cambridge Cottage, presented by King Edward VII. Ancient and modern examples of timber craftsmanship, samples of indigenous and imported wood.

MARIANNE NORTH GALLERY Southern boundary, along Kew Rd. 848 paintings of flowers and landscapes by Marianne North, botanist and amateur artist, from travels throughout the world. The lovely collection presented to Kew in 1882.

ORANGERY North-east part, on Broad Walk. Built 1761 for Augusta, Dowager Princess of Wales, now houses a bookstall and space for permanent and changing exhibitions. The selection of botanical reproductions are good value for money.

KEW PALACE North-east section of Gardens, next Queen Elizabeth's Lawn car park. Also known as Dutch House due to architectural style, 1631 palace was main royal residence at Kew until death of Queen Charlotte in 1818. Museum since turn of the century, adults 20p, children 5p. Closed winter. Buildings open at 11am with varying closing hours, but never open later than 4.50pm Mon–Sat and 5.50pm Sun.

GOOD FOR KIDS

MILKING TIME If you walk along the river bank towards Petersham and go down River Lane you come to the Express Dairy's Farm. Between 3 and 4.30pm every day you can see their pedigree herd of Guernsey cows being milked and fed. Usually calves to stroke, too.

KEW BRIDGE ENGINES Kew Bridge Pumping Station, Kew Bridge Rd. T 568 4757. Huge Victorian water pumping engines working again – they thunder up and down dramatically, all gleaming brass and hissing steam. A marvellous sight. Open Sat, Sun and Bank Holidays, 11am–1pm, 2–5 pm. Adults 40p, children 20p.

LION AND UNICORN BOOKSHOP King St, Richmond. T 940 0483. Specialist children's bookshop – welcomes young browsers. Thriving Saturday Bookworm Club -- visits from famous writers for children, all sorts of related competitions. (See Where to Shop.)

TRIDIAS 6 Lichfield Ter., Sheen Rd. T 948 3459. Very good toyshop with stock ranging from funny things for a few pence – false moustaches, marbles – to expensive, beautifully made rocking horses and dolls' houses.

RICHMOND PARK Perfect place to run wild. Sail toy boats on the ponds – one near Ham Gate good for this; ride bikes round a special track; fish for tadpoles – proper fishing in Pen Ponds needs a permit (see Keeping Amused); play football or cricket, or if you fancy swings and roundabouts you can find them near the Petersham Gate. Deer are lovely to watch but can be dangerous. Look out for foxes, weasels and badgers. (See Keeping Amused).

HOW TO GET THERE
BR and UNDERGROUND Richmond, Kew Gardens.
BUSES 15, 27, 33, 65, 71, 90B, 202, 270.

Soho

In spite of the fact that Soho is steadily going downhill it remains London's best village. Strip clubs, dirty bookshops and amusement arcades have replaced the city's best bistros and cafés, but the area surrounded by Charing Cross Road, Shaftesbury Avenue, Oxford Street and Regent Street still has more character to the block than any other part of London. Its inhabitants represent the best and, sometimes, the worst of city life and so give it an utterly unique flavour. Where the likes of Dylan Thomas and Brendan Behan once cavorted, there are still people, pubs and restaurants who will never be forgotten even when the GLC tear the place down. And it seems that one day they'll do just that.

The quality of Soho may change but the interest of it never does. Mozart lived there and so did Hazlitt. Logie Baird invented television in the house that's now the restaurant Bianchi's, and if film-cutting rooms, afternoon drinking clubs and betting shops have replaced the studios where once harpsichord and quill made history, there is, in spite of inevitable modern change, an aura of a bonhomie not to be found anywhere else in London. The Yorkminster, more commonly known as the 'French' pub, haunt of writers, painters, actors and layabouts, remains one of the few London pubs that haven't been ruined by the big brewery obsession with modernization and muzak. The Swiss Tavern in Old Compton Street possesses an air of chaotic friendliness. The Coach and Horses in Greek Street boasts London's rudest publican plus the custom of the staff of *Private Eye*. Wheeler's fish restaurant, old, traditional English from the fourth floor to the pavement, has what's probably the friendliest staff of any eating house in town. The Terrazza and Paparazzi restaurants are the last lines of defence against the mediocrity of the big combine restaurants that have polluted catering in this country.

There are, of course, local inhabitants, too. There's Frank Blake – the Duke of Soho – a wrestling MC and a man with more tales to tell than Damon Runyon. There's the Embassy attaché who's been secretly writing pornography for twenty years, and there's Muriel Belcher presiding over the Colony Room Club who's been publicly drinking champagne for much longer.

The whole place is as nice a nut house as you could wish to be committed to.

Jeffrey Bernard

WHAT TO SEE

SOHO SQ. One of London's most chic addresses in eighteenth century. Originally laid out *c.* 1681 but none of the original houses survives; the Tudor folly in the middle is Victorian. Charles II's statue is the battered survivor of a huge monument on which he was surrounded by figures representing England's main rivers.

HOUSE OF ST BARNABAS-IN-SOHO 1 Greek St. Fine Georgian town house which has been a house of charity since 1862. Magnificent staircase and fine plasterwork, recently cleaned; rare crinoline staircase; 300-year-old mulberry tree in the garden and oddly attractive little Victorian chapel in thirteenth-century French Gothic style. Wed 2.30–4.15pm, Thur 11am–12.30 pm. Free, but donations gratefully received.

CARNABY ST. When London was Swinging, it swung most ostentatiously here. Now the street is filled with more ·ultimate in tourist-orientated tat.

LIBERTY'S CLOCK, Gt Marlborough St/Kingly St. As the hour strikes amid genuine ship's timbers in the amazing 1924 Tudor façade, St George takes a feeble stab at the dragon. Below him is a chastening message for the time-wasters who stop to view.

PICCADILLY CIRCUS 'Hub of the Empire' when there was one, garish, noisy, sinful and centre of gravity for all London's visitors. Statue of 'Eros' might seem very appropriate to Soho's most obvious obsession, but he's really the Angel of Christian Charity (or maybe a pun on Lord Shaftesbury's name: the statue was made in his honour).

NOTRE DAME DE FRANCE Leicester Pl. Interesting post-war French Catholic church with Aubusson tapestry over the altar, chapel mural by Cocteau and mosaic by Boris Anrep.

WHERE TO EAT

Although Soho has more restaurants to the area than any other part of London, the *cuisine* in none of them is outstandingly *haute*. Most of the favourites are liked – even loved – by their regular customers not primarily for the food but more for the ambience. Conveniently central, full of old waiters and familiar faces, the best Soho restaurants, particularly if they are Continental, are like clubs or meeting places for various groups of people, film folk, actors, writers, etc., rather than places in which to find perfectly cooked scaloppine or coqs au vin. The southern half of Soho is virtually Chinese. Their restaurants offer fantastic value for money and many stay open into the early hours. Sample prices are for an average three-course meal for two with house wine. Open for lunch and dinner seven days a week unless otherwise indicated.

These are nine of the best **Continental** restaurants in Soho; all, bar one, are old-established, are still run by the original families, managers, or owners and have masses of devoted customers.

RISTORANTE VENEZIA 21 Great Chapel St. T 437 6506. Here thirty-one years, Italian to the core, somewhat off the beaten track but worth finding. Specials change daily. Venetian dishes recommended, also their sole dieppoise, zuppa di pesce and scaloppa alla finanziera. £13. No lunch Sat, closed Sun.

BIANCHI'S 21a Frith St. T 437 5194. Italian, loved especially by media folk for its manageress Elena, who is found only upstairs; although the food on the ground floor is exactly the same none of them will eat down there. Pasta, fritto misto and calves' brains recommended here. £12. Downstairs closed Sat lunch, upstairs closed Sun.

PETER MARIO 47 Gerrard St. T 437 4170. Here since 1933, now run by son and daughter of original owner, who is also famous as the uncle of Henry Cooper's wife. Restaurant is almost swamped by its Chinese neighbours, but is well known to theatrical and boxing pros and is a pillar of the Italian community in London. Daily specials might include lobster, crab, suckling pig, or game if in season. Lasagne, calamare and involtini also recommended. £10–£12. Closed Sun.

CHEZ VICTOR 45 Wardour St. T 437 6523/734 3123. Founded 1902, and this 'Victor's' since 1955. A perfect example of 'le style Français en Soho', a writer's restaurant complete with wax-encrusted candles, brusque waiters, darkness, Gauloises and garlic. Rely on the raie au beurre noir, foie de veau, and steak au poivre. £14. Closed Sun.

L'ESCARGOT BIENVENUE 48 Greek St. T 437 4460. French, and the snails are good here (their shells decorate the lampshades). Possibly the oldest and nicest waiters in the business. Have Chambery as an aperitif, house wine is good, Alsace wines are strongly recommended. Try the saucisses de Toulouse for lunch. £13–£14. Closed lunch Sat and all day Sun.

MYKONOS 17 Frith St. T 437 3603. Very successful, popular with ad-men with a Greek cookery book by the patronne coming out soon. (She knows her dolmades). Kleftiko, garides, moussaka and veal cooked in avego-lemononi sauce favourite dishes. £8. Closed lunch Sat and all day Sun.

JIMMY'S 23 Frith St. T 437 9521. Generations of students have eaten either here or in the mirror-image of the present basement which Jimmy moved from a few years ago. Enormous portions of Jimmy-version Greek food, all with chips and veg served for about £1 a plateful, with doorsteps of bread and rough wine at 35p a glass. Lunches and dinners Mon–Fri, continuous meals 12.30–10.30pm, weekends.

DONER KEBAB HOUSE 134 Wardour St. T 437 3027. A comparative new-comer, here only seven years, but at once a firm favourite with local film folk and the natives, Robert Arif's doner kebab is the real thing (he disposes of two swordfuls a day). Take-away upstairs, proper restaurant downstairs, with night-time live music and a wide choice of Turkish specialities. £8–£10. Closed Sun.

GAY HUSSAR 2 Greek St. T 437 0973. Hungarian, strictly for treats in the evening as not cheap, but the food – from menu which lists fifty-five regular items – is lavishly served and rich. But there is a special lunchtime menu of three courses – and plenty of choice – at £4 a head; with carafe of excellent wine and cover charge, just under £10 for two. Dinner £15. Closed Sun.

The next batch of restaurants is more **English**, listing places which serve cheaper and homelier food. No coincidence that three of them do fish and chips albeit on a rather higher scale than usual; Jewish influences are at work here.

GRAHAME'S SEA FARE 38 Poland St. T 437 3788. Kosher fish and dairy menu. Near the rag-trade in Oxford St and covered in testimonials from the theatre world. Marvellous fish, fried or grilled, and simply served. Air-conditioning £7–£8. Last orders 9.30pm, Fri 8pm. Closed all Sun and Mon evening.

MANZI'S 1–2 Leicester St. T 437 4864. Fish again, ranging from jellied eels and calamares to oysters or lobster, cooked plain or fancy. Steaks, too, but why bother with them here? The bustle, noise and variety of customer is as much a reason for liking the place as the food is. Round midnight a man comes in with the morning *Mirror* and *Express*. Must book, chance callers have to wait ages. £8–£10. Closed Sun lunch.

NEPTUNE 37 Frith St. T 437 3281. Tiny, friendly, fish place run here by Mr and Mrs Abrahams for thirty years. Small menu, no frills but it's *the best* fish. No licence, bring your own drink. Open noon–8pm so avoid busy lunchtime and relax. Very soothing talking to the Abrahams. £4, unless you have sole at £2·20 a go. Closed weekends.

STAR CAFÉ 22 Great Chapel St. T 437 8778. Run with great enthusiasm by a Mario Forte (absolutely no relation to the one who runs the catering empire) who believes in trying to give his customers good meals at lowest cost possible. Casseroles, pies, grills, at incredible prices. Open for breakfast, lunch and tea, 7am till 6pm. Licensed. Meal for two with glass of wine £2·75–£3. Closed weekends.

TRACKS 17a Soho Sq. T 439 2318. New café-wine bar, is chic, smart and serving commendably fresh and unusual salads, quiches and cakes. Wines during licensing hours, tea and coffee (fresh filtre at 40p with cream) between times. Tables outside too. Breakfast 9–11am, closes midnight. Lunch possible under £1 a head, just. Closed Sat morning and all day Sun.

Now four **Chinese** places and one **Indian** restaurant which are outstandingly good of their kind.

POONS & CO., 27 Lisle St. T 437 1528. The original Poons, run mostly by women; beautiful cooking seen in process in the front window. Half the price and twice as good as the new one in Covent Garden, but tiny, hot, cramped and uncomfortable as hell. Not licensed. £6. Closed Christmas Day.

CHIU CHOW INN 21 Lisle St. T 437 8919. Pekinese cooking, chef here makes dumplings and noodles in the window. More comfortable and spacious than Poons. Part of the empire of Mr Young of Richmond Rendezvous fame. Sliced sole in wine sauce, smoked chicken in yellow bean sauce,

etc. Licensed. Meals from £2 to £5 a head.

CHUEN CHENG KU 22 Lisle St. T 437 6332. Open 4pm–5am. 17–23 Wardour St/20 Rupert St. T 437 1398, 374 3281/3509. Open 11am till midnight. The latter a vast warren of happy families, both Eastern and Western, trying every sort of Chinese culinary delight. Steamed dumplings (tim sum) till 6pm, one of the best places for them, otherwise find a good waiter (there are some here) for help with the menu. Set meals at £2·10 a head. Licensed.

FUNG SHING 15 Lisle St. T 437 1539. Cantonese cooking, open midday till 2am. Spacious and comfortable, the best place (seriously) to try funny things like 'tripe, rope and melt' or 'chicken with pig's liver' or 'duck's palm (web) in oyster sauce'. Specialities are dishes stewed in the pot and seafood. Set meal £2·20 a head. Licensed.

THE GANGES 40 Gerrard St. T 437 0284/8705. Most sympathetic Indian restaurant run with great care and concern by Mr and Mrs Ahmed. The menu a model of helpfulness and the food adventurous and imaginative. An ideal place for newcomers to Indian food, and not ignored by Indians either. Complete kebab meal £1·95, other set meals from £3 a head, à la carte, too. Licensed. Closed Sun.

The **Charlotte St** area, a few minutes' walk from Soho, is excellent for reasonably priced eating places.

L'ETOILE 30 Charlotte St. T 636 7189. Great French restaurant of consistently high standard, unchanged for years. First courses so delicious that some people have two and skip entrée. Closed Sat and Sun. £14–£16.

BERTORELLI'S 19 Charlotte St. T 636 4174. Run by genial family with Peter Bertorelli presiding. Since pre-war days a meeting place for artists and writers. Basic cuisine Italian but marvellous English touches like roast rabbit. Closed Sun. £8–9.

LITTLE AKROPOLIS 10 Charlotte St. T 636 8198. Comfortable Greek Cypriot restaurant with marvellous cooking by chef who has been there for fifteen years. Niki Ktori has constructed arbour of vines around doorway and tiny terrace. Taramasalata is among best in London. For entrées try lamb chops which must be biggest and most succulent in London. Closed Sat lunch, all day Sun. £12.

THE WHITE TOWER 1 Percy St. T 636 8141. Greek family-run place famous for moussaka. Closed Sat and Sun. £18.

GREEK VILLAGE 17a Percy St. T 636 4140. Extraordinarily high standard of cooking, meat especially good. Live bouzouki music in basement Fri, Sat, Sun night. £8–£10.

AGRA 137 Whitfield St. T 387 883. Friendly old Indian favourite; curries are authentic, very hot and very good. Are they the best in London? £7.

Picnics

Attractive churchyard of the bombed St Anne's (of which only Cockerell's incredible steeple remains) has lots of bench space, meths-drinkers permitting. Soho Sq. has much charm, and a half-timbered summerhouse to boot. Golden Sq. is a little rigid, but the roses were a gift from the city of Sofia as a gesture of civic goodwill, a fact which might give you a warm glow. Leicester Sq. had a Jubilee revamp and most of it is now a pedestrian precinct.

WHERE TO DRINK

DUKE OF WELLINGTON Wardour St. Wide range of bright beers from Scottish and Newcastle breweries. Bar walls have panels showing famous (or infamous) family tartans and windows have inset coloured glass clan crests. Imposing stag head overlooks large, comfortable bar.

INTREPID FOX Wardour St. Spacious, bright pub with friendly, efficient barmaids. Large selection of beers including Burton Ale dispensed by handpump. Busy food bar open for lunch only. Unusual name derives from eighteenth-century aristocrat Whig statesman, Charles James Fox, who was much admired by the then landlord, Sam House.

RED LION Windmill St. Bass Charrington pub serving traditional ale in the heart of Soho. Popular with young visitors escaping bustle of nearby Shaftesbury Ave. Basic bar snacks.

THE GLASSHOUSE Brewer St. Ind Coope house with warm, welcoming decor. Mirrors of all shapes and sizes adorn one wall giving the narrow bar a spacious dimension. Hotplate snacks. Pool, bar billiards and darts available in upstairs room.

KING CHARLES II (alias Blue Posts) Kingly St. Popular with Carnaby St visitors so not the place for a quiet lunchtime drink. If you can get to the bar Thomas Wethered's real ale is the recommended brew. Service is cheerful and the friendly Scouse barman is eager to please ('no rip-offs here'). Excellent salads to order.

THE AVENUE Shaftesbury Ave. Included here mainly because of its full range of Ruddles bitter and country beers which are well kept and very strong. Otherwise it's a large rather anonymous place.

SPICE OF LIFE Romilly St/Moor St. Nice name for a well-run Watney's pub with a glittering array of shorts, fined bitter and a rather plush upstairs lounge. There's also a cellar bar with a dart board and jukebox.

WINDSOR CASTLE Dean St. Small bar with cheapish spirits, amusing photos and caricatures on the walls and a clientele that spills out on to the streets most summer lunchtimes.

THE ROUNDHOUSE Wardour St. Upstairs there's a pukka sit-down restaurant serving unusually good pub fare; down below it's a fairly typical West End saloon selling Charrington's ales.

COACH AND HORSES 1 Gt Marlborough St. Small congenial Whitbread pub which has stood since 1739.

BLUE POSTS Berwick St. Not to be confused with Blue Posts in Kingly St and Rupert St. Market pub used by chatty street traders and local theatrical celebrities. Unpretentious, with down-to-earth charm. Watney's ales.

KING OF CORSICA Berwick St. Bass Charrington house serving traditional ale. Unsophisticated, with a raucous market atmosphere at lunchtime. Appetizing homemade pizzas served day and night.

STAR AND GARTER Poland St. Deservedly popular Courage pub serving the powerful director's bitter (not to be trifled with). Combines the intimacy of a village pub with the atmosphere of a famous rendezvous. Food prepared for regulars morning and evening. Daily newspapers to hand for those anxious to keep abreast of events. Others can admire the display of coloured glass and antique daggers.

DOG & DUCK Bateman St/Frith St. Tiny pub notable for its decorated tiles and a good drop of Ind Coope's draught Burton ale. Cold bar snacks.

CROWN & TWO CHAIRMEN Bateman St/Dean St. Another Ind Coope house a few yards from Dog & Duck, but this is a larger place with hot and cold fork meals and a small selection of wines and sherries. Popular with film biz execs and their secs.

LYRIC TAVERN Gt Windmill St. An oasis of calm, excellent cold cuts and salads in the heart of strip city. Exterior woodwork and etched glass is original and interior decor is Victorian without being twee. Sherry available from the wood.

BLUE POSTS Rupert St. Yet another pub of this name and unusual in its selection of topical cocktails (e.g. Jubilee Special at 69p) and liqueur coffees. Rather boring modern interior, but good bar food.

POLAR BEAR Lisle St/Newport Pl. Recently subject to a Finch's 'up-rate', this is now a very comfortable, spacious saloon with thick carpets and cosy alcoves. Charrington's draught and a good hot and cold food bar. Jukebox.

WHERE TO SHOP

Such a tiny area is packed with interesting and many old-established shops.

Z. KOPELOVITCH LTD 84 Berwick St. T 437 6194. Shop been going for seventy years. Mrs Gilbert presides over *the* shop for lace and broderies. Most of her best laces come from France, many are hand-finished. Closed Sat.

ANYTHING LEFTHANDED 65 Beak St. T 437 3910. As its name suggests, commonplace items specially adapted for the lefthanded. Can openers, scissors, pen, wristwatch, potato peelers.

CARNABY ST Now paved over so that visitors can freely browse amongst the many young, trendy (and often tatty) fashion clothes shops.

Charing Cross Rd One of London's leading centres for bookshops.

FOYLES, No. 119–125. T 437 5660. Probably the largest bookshop in London and perhaps Britain. Titles on most subjects but best for academic text books, philosophy, fiction, biography and social sciences.

A. ZWEMMER, No. 76–80. T 836 4710. Small crammed bookshop specializing in art and architecture with an excellent coverage of cinema and craft.

ASCROFT & DAW, No. 83. T 734 0950. Large selection of paperbacks and London guide books.

COLLET'S LONDON BOOKSHOP, No. 64. T 836 6306. Wide range of left-wing political and social books.

COLLET'S PENGUIN BOOKSHOP, No. 52. T 836 2315. Attempt to stock every Penguin in print but because Penguin's list gets bigger all the time and their shop doesn't, they average 90 per cent. Also secondhand and out-of-print Penguins.

JOSEPH POOLE, No. 86. T 836 2608. One of better secondhand bookshops in the road.

GAMBA 46 Dean St. T 437 0704. Theatrical shoemakers: famed for their ballet shoes, one-bars, tap shoes. Also smart ready-to-wear men's fashion shoes. Theatrical shoes, leotards and tights also made to measure.

THEA PORTER DECORATIONS 8 Greek St. T 437 6224. Exciting and extravagant evening clothes with a theatrical bias. There is a small selection to browse through in the shop or Thea Porter will make for you. Shoppers and browsers are likely to encounter Lauren Bacall and other celebrities. Gowns cost from £22–£800.

HONG KONG CULTURE SERVICES 46 Gerrard St. T 734 5037. Probably Chinatown's largest art and craft shop with a room devoted to Chinese records and cassettes. Caters almost exclusively for Chinese with a range of curious comics and periodicals.

HOUSE BROS 85 Brewer St. T 437 3857. Established 1864 and a family concern, House Bros can supply virtually any hand tool, many of which can't be found elsewhere.

EATONS SHELL SHOP 16 Manette St. T 437 9391. Beautiful shells, many are rarities, and rocks. Cane roller blinds made to any measurement. Upstairs raffia work and matting. They operate a mail order service and are a charming tiny old-fashioned shop.

CRAFTSMEN POTTERS ASSOCIATION OF GREAT BRITAIN William Blake House, Marshall St. T 437 7605. Located on the site of William Blake's birthplace, Craftsmen Potters sells the pots of its over 150 members, all of whom have been scrupulously chosen. Special orders can be taken.

Old Compton St: LIBRAIRE PARISIENNE, No. 48. T 437 2479. Wide range of English and foreign newspapers and magazines.

MORONI & SONS, No. 68. T 437 2847. Virtually every foreign newspaper and magazine can be found here.

SANGORSKI AND SUTCLIFFE 1–5 Poland St. T 437 2252. By appointment only at this well-known and long-established book binders. Everything done by hand and to the highest standards.

Shaftesbury Ave The home of many of London's theatres and on the edge of Chinatown.

THE CHINESE SHOP, No. 110. T 437 8789. Clothes for men, women and children imported mostly from China, with some from Hong Kong and Taiwan. Also soft toys, fabrics, and jewellery.

Wardour St: S. & S. MOSS (WOOLLENS), No. 122. T 437 3402. Quality English suiting by the metre. They do a special: three metres of fabric (enough for a gent's suit said Mr Moss) for £8. They don't make up garments but know all the tailors in the area.

BLUNDELLS, No. 199. T 437 4746. A trade counter where queues form to buy silver in the form of wire, chain, tubing, rod and sheet in a variety of gauges. Also gold if you have a licence. They do a full range of findings (clasps for necklaces, earrings, etc.) and are very helpful to learners, although try to have worked out what you want by the time your turn comes.

S. FERRARI & SONS LTD, No. 60. T 437 6515. Founded in 1901 and holding a Royal Warrant Ferrari's stock an excellent range of catering equipment. They are famed for cutlery, notably their Sabatier and other knives.

BUYING FOOD

Some of London's finest food shops are to be found in Soho.

Berwick St Every weekday a wonderful fruit and vegetable market takes place. Traders vie with each other for shoppers' attention and it's a very jolly affair. Great food bargains can be had but like all markets watch out for duff goods sold from *under* the barrow.

Brewer St: RICHARDS, No. 11. T 437 1358. A large range of fresh fish, live and boiled crabs and lobsters, Smoked fish and other shellfish in season.

RANDALL & AUBIN, No. 16. T 437 3507. French butcher (all nerves and most fat is cut off the meat) with an enormous and excellent delicatessen counter. They were the first to import quiche lorraine (in 1906), cook all their own cold meats, make up pâtés and sell various salamis. Also forty French, Italian and Dutch cheeses, wine and bread.

HAMBURGER PRODUCTS, No. 1. T 437 7119. No dye or artificial ingredients used in smoking of salmon, sturgeon, cod roe, buckling, trout and mackerel sold at Hamburger. Smoking done in their Holborn factory. The name is nothing to do with food, but originates from a trip the owner made to Hamburg!

PARMIGIANI FIGLIO 43 Frith St. T 437 4728. Largest selection of Italian cheese in London, with weekly deliveries from Italy. Also specialities include olive oil, parma ham, salami from Milan, wine and dried pastas.

MAISON BERTAUX 28 Greek St. T 437 6007. French patisserie where brioches, croissants, a range of pastries, fruit flans, tarts and slices, marzipan figs, eclairs and chestnut meringues are baked on the premises. They also serve tea and coffee. Closed Mon, open Sun am for pastries.

Gerrard St So many Chinese shops and restaurants that the area around is known as Chinatown.

DUGDALE & ADAMS, No. 3. T 437 3864. Reputed to sell London's best imitation of a French loaf. Apart from baguettes, all white English loaves. Everything baked downstairs.

LOON FUNG SUPERMARKET, No. 39. T 437 1922. Chinese grocery, mostly labels are written in Chinese which doesn't help. Fresh ginger, fresh beansprouts, dried mushrooms, bean curd, noodles, etc. Also woks (rounded frying pan used in Chinese cooking), chopsticks and bowls.

CRANKS SHOP 8 Marshall St. T 437 2915. Wide range of health foods, interesting salads, pies and 100 per cent wholewheat breads made round the corner in their bakery. Also have a restaurant where smoking is forbidden.

CLARKE'S OF SOHO 27 Peter St. T 437 6622. London's best dark rye bread baked on the premises. Also egg bread.

ARTHUR MYALL & SONS 23 Romilly St. T 437 4063. Essentially a wholesalers supplying many of Soho's Italian restaurants. Will only sell a whole fish which they clean and fillet for you.

Old Compton St: CAMISA & SON, No. 61. T 437 7610. *The* place for fresh pasta. Wide range of Italian and French salamis, cold meats, Parma ham, Parmesan and other Italian cheeses.

LOUIS ROCHE, No. 14. T 437 4588. The first shop in London to import produce direct from France, which they still do twice a week. Seventy-five French cheeses, including many goat cheeses, prepared snails, Breton pâté and frogs' legs. But – sadly – may be closing.

VINORIO, No. 8. T 437 1024. Italian grocer with cheap range of Italian wines.

GREAT WALL 31–37 Wardour St. T 437 7963/6313. Enormous supermarket with a good range of teas. Also Chinese bowls, chopsticks, etc.

KEEPING AMUSED

Shocking! Erotic! Xciting! enter-

tainment so dominates the Soho scene one could almost forget that three dozen West End theatres and cinemas crowd those grubby streets. Massage parlours and saunas proved too strenuous for us to research individually, so if it's hot air you're after – ask a taxi driver. Ditto any 'glamour palaces'. We've included the up-market range, and some places we found a laugh, the rest is down to you.
NELL GWYNNE/GARGOYLE CLUB 69–70 Dean St. T 437 3278/6455. Striptease with a smile! The girls are pretty and seem to enjoy their job. Three shows a night in the theatre upstairs (6, 8 and 10pm) and a midnight peel in the club Mon–Fri. Acts are often elaborate as the establishment employs its own choreographer and costumier. Fully licensed topless bar.
PAUL RAYMOND'S REVUEBAR Walker's Ct/Brewer St. T 734 1593. London's 'Nudie King' has a reputation for staging professional and well-produced shows.
WINDMILL THEATRE Gt Windmill St. T 437 6312. The theatre that 'never closed' during the WWII now brings us 'the erotic experience of the modern era' twice nightly. Tickets £4·50 and £3·50.
LONDON EXPERIENCE Piccadilly Circus Shopping Arcade. Bernard Delfont presents a seventy-foot screen, forty-two still projectors and 3600 sequences of the History of London. We'll 'see, hear, feel, live the life and times of the world's most exciting city'. All in quintaphonic sound. Adults £1·25, children 75p. Programme lasts fifty minutes.
TALK OF THE TOWN Hippodrome Corner. T 734 5051. Bernard Delfont presents dining, dancing, a floorshow and an international star six nights a week, evening's entertainment beginning at 8.15pm, celebrity cabaret 11pm. £8·50 Mon–Thur £10·45, Fri–Sat £11·55. Closed Sun.

PALLADIUM Argyll St. T 437 7373. Showcasing everything from Sinatra to ice-skating. Prices accordingly.
CHERRY'S DISCO Piccadilly Circus. T 734 1958. Situated right in the heart of the circus and catering to a mainly young passing trade. £1 most nights, £1·20 Fri, £1·50 Sat. Three DJs.
CAFÉ DE PARIS Coventry St. T 437 2036. Former socialite watering hole (Noël Coward, Marlene Dietrich appeared here), now best known as one of London's few remaining ballrooms. Two bands nightly, open 7.30pm–2am. Tea dancing 3–5.45 each afternoon. The fox trot and flouncy skirt brigade come on strong.
EMPIRE BALLROOM Leicester Sq. T 437 1446. More of an international youth club than a ballroom, with hardly an English face in sight. Enormous, sprawling and excellent for female fatties – the man/woman ratio is roughly 5:1. Live bands and disco, prices £1–£2 according to day and time.
CLASSIC Charing Cross Rd. T 930 6915. Snooze and sleaze at the same time. This cinema shows all-night movies of the 'Depraved! Divine!' variety each evening from 11pm onwards. £2·10 cover includes free refreshments.
MAXIMUS DISCO NIGHT CLUB Leicester Sq. T 734 4111. Licensed until 3am. Average age 21–22 years, with emphasis on the constantly passing trade. Live acts two or three times monthly, otherwise 'Mr Melody' spins primarily soul music. Capacity 250.
PHOENIX Charing Cross Rd. T 836 8611 box office, 836 8727 information. Indian films every Sun afternoon and evening. No sub-titles. £1·50 and £2.
ODEON Leicester Sq. T 930 6111. Chinese films every Mon, after the regular scheduled programme. Usually sub-titled. £1·80 and £2·20.
ROUND LONDON SIGHTSEEING TOUR T 222 5600. Starting point: Piccadilly

Circus. Two-hour circular trip covering twenty miles of the West End and City. Daily 10am–9pm (4pm in winter). Excellent value as introduction to Central London. No need to book. Tickets about £1·30 adults, 80p children.

HONG KONG CINEMA Gerrard St. T 439 3935. Difficult-to-find Chinese cinema in the heart of Chinatown. (It's next to the Hong Kong Cultural Services shop.) Tickets £1·80 or £1 for children. Most films screened with sub-titles.

ESSENTIAL CINEMA 76 Wardour St. T 439 3657. One of the swinging independent clubs, showing old classics or anything interesting. Small, informal and friendly, they hope soon to provide tables outside for leisurely loitering. 25p membership, no waiting period. Seats 99p.

TIFFANY'S Shaftesbury Ave. T 437 5012. Dancing in 'Aladdin's Cave' under rather ominous stalactites. Open 8pm–2am seven nights a week (Fri, Sat until 3am). Several bars in separate rooms, with a welcome check-in counter for handbags. The sort of place where you tell your friends in Rome to meet you in London. Young crowd.

ANTHEA'S Fouberts Pl. T 734 5003. Open seven nights a week, the dance floor of this establishment is lit with what appear to be picturesque tin cans. DJ and records. Entrance fee £2.

THUMB GALLERY D'Arbley St. T 439 4059. This red-floor and black-bricked gallery is intriguingly laid-out and exhibits drawings, watercolours and small paintings by young British artists. Moderate prices with most under the £50 bracket.

CRACKER'S 201 Wardour St. T 734 4916. Rock Wed, soul Thur and Sun, disco other evenings. Fri–Sat 8pm–3am, £1·25 until 10.30pm, £1·80 after 10.30pm, inc. meal. Sun 80p inc. meal.

ALMOST FREE THEATRE CLUB 9–19

Rupert St. T 485 6224. Fringe group presenting lunchtime and evening performances and the unusual (and idealistic) system of paying what you can afford.

LE KILT Greek St. T 734 9598. Long-established club catering to young Continentals. Tartan walls and moose heads add a friendly incongruous touch.

RONNIE SCOTT'S Frith St. T 439 0747. Founded over twenty years ago as London's premier jazz club; anybody worth a blow has at some point entertained here. Lush and plush downstairs, hot and steamy upstairs as entrance fee to the former allows free access to the smaller club above. Price £3–£6·50, or £1·50 for upstairs only.

GILLY'S 69 Dean St. T 734 2179 (night). No teeny-boppers here; this basically membership club allows a certain number of visitors, thus ensuring a more sophisticated clientele. Occasional live music, but mainly soul and reggae. Long bar and mirrored dancefloor. About £2 per head.

MARSHALL STREET BATHS. T 437 7665. Apart from the saunas, about the only athletic activity around. Glass windows let you see what you're diving in to. Adults 20p, children 7p. Open 9am–7pm (6pm Sat and 30 Sept–31 March).

MARQUEE 90 Wardour St. T 437 6603. Will have been going twenty-one years in spring 1979. The Rolling Stones, Jimi Hendrix, Stevie Wonder, Rod Stewart all sweated it out here in the sixties, but aim to reflect music trends of the moment so currently a lot of punk, though some bands are old favourites. Concert area with bar, also separate bar and snack bar. 7–11pm every night. Prices approx 75p–£1·30.

GOOD FOR KIDS

JAMES GALT & CO. 30 Gt Marlborough St. T 734 0829. Probably best known for their wooden toys, but do sell fluffy and frivolous items as well.

HAMLEY'S 200 Regent St. T 734 3161. A huge emporium in which many parents must have been bankrupted. Everything a child could wish for, in great abundance. Carnival and Magic Shop has a separate entrance in Kingly St, a treasure trove of masks, vampire nails and dehydrated worms.

HOW TO GET THERE

BR Charing Cross.

UNDERGROUND Piccadilly Circus, Oxford Circus, Tottenham Court Rd, Leicester Sq., Trafalgar Sq.

BUSES 1, 1A, 3, 6, 7, 8, 9, 9A, 12, 13, 14, 15, 19, 22, 24, 25, 29, 38, 39, 53, 59, 73, 88, 159, 176, 505, 506.

South Kensington

In other countries the Old Brompton Road would be called a boulevard. The route of constant heavy traffic and the inconstant No. 30 bus, it runs from South Kensington, past the bottom of Gloucester Road, to Earls Court: from, that is, the French colony, through the Arabs, to the Australians. It has patches of itchy red brick, but the main mode is cool stucco and plane trees. The district it draws together (which has no single and unambiguous name) is still residential and still, in its very cosmopolitanism, pure London.

Not that we live in the style for which our residences were designed. The 'family houses' no longer bear down on servants in the sub-basements but were long ago split into flats, where we evidently lead busy but untimetabled lives. Our shops cater for our convenience as well as our ethnically varied palates. You would be up late indeed if you couldn't find a supermarket or a chemist open. We go in for take-away meals, portable snacks (such as paper pyramid-fuls of Indian sweets) and instant gardens in the form of potted flowers for our window ledges.

Earls Court contains a famous gay pub, the most exhaustive ironmonger's in London – Carpenter's, and an Art Deco exhibition hall. South Kensington contains Lamley's bookshop, the Museums and, lest you thought the V & A unequalled for architectural monstrosity, the Institut Français. Halfway along the Old Brompton Road is the Star of India, my favourite restaurant and one of the few non-specialist ones where vegetarians like myself can exercise actual choice. The cooking is splendid, as the high proportion of French customers bears witness, and the genius who presides is a benign Burmese, U Kim, who looks like the Buddha.

Brigid Brophy

WHAT TO SEE

NATURAL HISTORY MUSEUM Cromwell Rd. T 589 6323. Romantic Victorian monster of a building designed by Waterhouse. Newly cleaned, stripey façade is covered with animal gargoyles and statues. Inside, grandeur of the central hall dwarfs even the stuffed elephants. Great cavernous galleries house an endearing mixture of slightly moth-eaten turn of the century taxidermy and very imaginative modern displays using all the latest techniques. They cover animal development from fossils and dinosaurs to Chi-Chi the giant panda – sadly now stuffed. The new 'Human Biology, an Exhibition of Ourselves' is most successful and stimulating, really involves the visitor. Open Mon–Sat 10am–6pm, Sun 2.30–6pm. Free. (All museums, see Keeping Amused and Good for Kids.)

GEOLOGICAL MUSEUM, Exhibition Rd. T 589 3444. Exciting displays, by no means just the endless lumps of rock in glass cases one might imagine. 'The Story of the Earth' exhibition traces its geological formation from solar beginnings with lots of interesting audio-visual effects including an earthquake simulator; 'Black Gold' exhibition demonstrates how Britain's oil, coal and gas resources produce power and energy. Also interesting temporary exhibitions and one of the finest gem-stone collections in the world. Open Mon–Sat 10am–6pm, Sun 2.30–6pm.

SCIENCE MUSEUM, Exhibition Rd. T 589 6371. Hours of bliss for the mechanically minded, an enormous collection including pioneer aeroplanes, Stephenson's 'Rocket', splendid early cars, trams and buses, the oldest working clock in the world, agricultural machinery – endless buttons to press and working models. Open Mon–Sat 10am–6pm, Sun 2.30–6pm. ST AUGUSTINE'S Queen's Gate. Designed by Butterfield, gaunt brick façade of this church contrasts with neighbouring stucco houses. Colours and patterns of the interior recently restored to their original startling brilliance.

INSTITUT FRANÇAIS, Queensbury Rd. Maybe you won't share Brigid Brophy's dislike (see her introduction) – worth a look anyway. An extremely odd thirties art nouveauish building.

THE BOLTONS Big, plushy, gleaming white villas set round an oval garden with a pleasant church, St Mary Boltons, in the middle. At the Old Brompton Rd end, a piquant contrast, is Bousfield Primary School – much admired when it was built in the fifties – it's a little tatty now, but still communicates gaiety and enthusiasm.

KENWAY RD, WALLGRAVE RD, REDFIELD LANE A stone's throw from the multi-national hubbub of Earl's Court Rd is this triangle of pretty, intimate little streets – early nineteenth-century terraces with flowery front gardens, small shops. All very villagey, worth exploring.

BROMPTON CEMETERY Long grass, cow parsley and thousands of cramped Victorian graves – many pretty chipped angels and interesting inscriptions. Look out for the tombs of Robert Coombs – champion sculler of the Thames, with an overturned skiff on top of the monument – and the boxer Gentleman Jackson – commemorated by a very cosy lion with a medallion.

WHERE TO EAT

In this part of London, some of the best people live at some of the best addresses, so it comes as a bit of a shock that many of the local restaurants are not only unwilling to accept credit cards, but are even likely to refuse banker's cards. These are the dozens of busy establishments clustering round South Ken tube station and along the Earls Court Rd whose trade is mainly passing through – visitors to the museums, guests at local hotels, travellers from the Air Terminal. As well as mistrusting their clients' credit-worthiness, many of them couldn't care less whether they give satisfaction or not, but the following places come into a different category. Sample prices are for average three-course meal for two with house wine. Open for lunch and dinner seven days a week, unless otherwise indicated.

BANGKOK 9 Bute St. T 584 8529. Thai restaurant, newly moved from across the road where it established itself as one of the best Oriental restaurants in London eleven years ago. Family-run, kitchen on view, freshly cooked food. £10. Must book evenings, closed Mon.

KHYBER PASS 21 Bute St. T 589 7311. As so often, the best restaurants in a cosmopolitan area are Indian. This is a prime example. Here eleven years, clean, soothing, good food. Try the murgh mussalam £2·75 for two, chicken dhansak £1·35, prawn patia £1·35. £10–£11. Must book evenings.

IL GIORNO E LA NOTTE 60 Old Brompton Rd. T 584 4028/7609. If best restaurants in a cosmopolitan area are not Indian, they're Italian, like this one. Pretty, airy, spacious with attentive waiters and a few less common items on the menu like zuppa biancaneve, filetto con salsa castagne, linguine alla genovese. Patronne comes from Genoa, is married to Indian restaurateur Bill Naraine (q.v.). £11–£12, closed Sun.

STAR OF INDIA 154 Old Brompton Rd. T 373 2901. Deaf to the proprietor's pleadings not to mention his restaurant ('we cannot cope with any more customers') since Brigid Brophy has already sung its praises in her introduction, we can only say try it at lunchtime, when there is plenty of room. If you do book a table in the evening, don't be late or it will be gone

in a flash. £8. Closed only Christmas and Boxing Day.

L'ARTISTE AFFAME 243 Old Brompton Rd. T 373 1659. Describes itself as 'a quaint embodiment of the nineteenth century', but the food seems fairly up to date English/French/Italian. Folk guitarist saunters about most evenings. £14. No lunch Sat, closed Sun.

PONTEVECCHIO 256 Old Brompton Rd. T 373 9082/370 1984. Large, bustling, modern bourgeois Italian restaurant serving first-class food with maximum efficiency. Walls hung with paintings by friends of the patron who thus reveals himself as a tennis fan. Specials on menu change three times a week 'depending on the weather and what's interesting'. Tables outside. £10–£12.

LOTUS GARDEN 257 Old Brompton Rd. T 370 4450/6939. Small and popular Chinese restaurant and take-away; prettily furnished, clean. Set meals as little as £9·50 for four.

NARAINE 10 Kenway Rd. T 370 3853. Indian haven in a side street off murderous and unenticing Earls Court Rd. Here fifteen years with the same chef for fourteen of them, and run by Mr Naraine with immense care and pride in his work. Menu made invaluable with glossary of Indian cooking terms. £8. Closed Mon.

IL GIRASOLE 126 Fulham Rd. T 370 6656. Italian, with plenty of tables, outside and six-yard-long hors d'oeuvres table inside from which you can have anything you like for £1·20. Popular with smart couples lunching à deux. £12, Closed Mon.

SAN FREDIANO 62 Fulham Rd. T 584 8375. Italian, eleven-year favourite with the smart young from Chelsea and round about. Best for lunch when professional people eat there; too many Hooray Henrys in the evening. Good food and excellent house wine.

AL BEN ACCOLTO 58 Fulham Rd.

T 589 0876. Italian again, but quieter than San Fred and more for serious eaters. Chef has very high standards, mostly Italian menu except for the ever popular Agnello Shrewsbury (£2·05). Thoughtful management provide crudités with very good sauces to toy with while you wait for your order. £10–£12. Closed Sun, wise to book evenings.

DAQUISE 20 Thurloe St. T 589 6117. Polish–Russian restaurant full of expatriates meeting each other and eating the specialities of the house (zrazy, kasza and kolduny, for example). Set lunches £1·20 and £1·40 a head. A la carte more like £3 a head. Licensed. Open all day until midnight.

PAPER TIGER 10 Exhibition Rd. T 584 3737. 'London's first Szechuan Chinese restaurant'. Like Chinese only spicier, in other words. Pretty place in a basement which has housed an ever-changing string of different restaurants. Let's hope this one is here to stay, even if it *is* staffed by Chinese male chauvinist pigs who appear not to take orders from women. £14–£16.

Picnics

Not easy: a patch of grass and some seats beside Natural History Museum; Redcliffe Sq. gardens a possibility; couple of seats beside herbaceous border in garden of St Mary Boltons. Much the best place, if it doesn't worry you, is the Brompton Cemetery – graves make good tea tables.

WHERE TO DRINK

CORKS 3 Harrington Rd. The older established of two wine bars within spitting distance of South Kensington tube: its pavement tables and rugged wooden furnishings allied to a fair selection of vino seems to attract a loyal clientele.

SWIFT'S Pelham St. Also close by the tube, Swift's wine bar is a neatly contrived facsimile of, one supposes, a Victorian inn. Wood-panelled alcoves, dim lighting and an unusual choice of seafoods, but rather pricey wines. Cold buffet.

PRINCESS OF WALES Dovehouse St. Popular with the young, many of whom pop over from the hospital across the road for a quick one between ops. Don't take your dog – they are warned off by large notices. Director's draught, sandwiches and outdoor tables.

THE CROWN 153 Dovehouse St. Tiny bar is more comfortable, congenial and better value than the mass of slicked-up frozen lager dispensaries that seem to proliferate in this area. Real ale and the well-stuffed sandwiches are recommended.

THE DENMARK 102 Old Brompton Rd. Well patronized by bedsitter folk, this large Courage pub stocks several good, strong lagers and a goodish choice of bar snacks.

ANGLESEA ARMS 15 Selwood Ter. Heaven-on-earth for real ale freaks, this inevitably crowded free house supplies a variety of regional draughts including the legendary Theakston's Olde Peculiar. Lunchtime food usually includes a hot speciality. Outdoor spillage area!

HEREFORD ARMS 127 Gloucester Rd. Pleasant old pub serving Watney's fined bitter as well as a selection of cold dishes at all times. Jukebox, video game and darts tend to attract a predominately young crowd.

DRAYTON ARMS Drayton Gdns/Old Brompton Rd. Impressive edifice with quirky exterior and mirrored interior, but imitation art nouveau lamps are an eyesore. Charrington's on draught and bar snacks.

THE BOLTONS Old Brompton Rd/ Earls Court Rd. Cavernous saloon bar at the back serving food and a somewhat more convivial bar at the front. Known for its trad jazz presentations, but these are now restricted to Sun lunchtimes.

WHERE TO SHOP

Earls Court Rd: RASSELL'S, No. 80. T 937 0481. Very pretty garden centre with large garden behind, helpful staff. Sells trees, shrubs, house plants and cut flowers in season; sundries, including a wide range of tools, soils, containers, especially terracotta pots. BOTTOM PRICE/WAREHOUSE, No. 127. Lively colourful shop that buys women's high-fashion clothes in bulk. Jeans, shirts, T-shirts, skirts, dresses and separates from France, Italy and Hong Kong.

ABC MOTOR-CYCLE CLOTHING CENTRE No. 231. T 373 4737. Latest fashions in motor-bike clothing plus helmets, boots, gloves, scarves and accessories. **Kenway Rd** Tucked behind Earls Court Rd, quite different in atmosphere with a village feel.

LIVING ART, No. 35. T 370 2766. English country craft plus changing monthly exhibitions. Framing service. ORBIS BOOKS, No. 66. T 370 2210. Books in Polish, English translations of Polish works and books about Poland and East Europe. Also some Polish craft objects.

KENWAY ANTIQUES, No. 70. T 373 1631. Early Chinese porcelain, Chinese furniture and Victoriana.

Old Brompton Rd: DAVID BAGOTT DESIGN, No. 266. T 370 2267. New pine furniture but several homeware gift items: lampshades, macramé hanging baskets, handmade pottery, bamboo and basketware.

UNIQUITY, No. 170. T 373 8956. Collection of clothes made by young freelance designers and art students. Very wide range of styles; prices £10–£200.

MERCURIUS BOOKSHOP, No. 80. T 589 7967. Books on astrology, psychology, Eastern and Western mysticism, ecology and related subjects.

MIDNIGHT BLUE, No. 76. T 584 7161. One of many denim shops but this one stays open until midnight Mon–Sat. Jeans, knitwear and pretty range of separates.

MITSUKIKU, No. 15. T 589 1725. Japanese kimonos of all lengths in a choice of flowered, plain or embroidered fabrics, range of Japanese sandals, mobiles, kites, a few toys, rice bowls and of course chopsticks.

BAG END, No. 6. T 581 0299. Leather bags, travel goods, trunks, handbags and handbag repairs. Also gold and silver jewellery, ear piercing, custom-made jewellery. Small range of second-hand jewellery bought and sold.

Harrington Rd: TABICAT FABRICS, No. 25. T 584 4167. Cheap and unusual dressmaking fabrics; end of rolls and remnants a speciality.

MOME, No. 27. T 589 8306. Chic boutique for children up to the age of ten. Mostly own designs or clothes imported from France and Italy. Pricey but attractive.

ALLISON'S WONDERLAND, No. 7a. T 589 8429. Permanent sale of dressmaking fabrics, broderie anglaise, treviras, cheesecloth and sari materials at half normal price. Linings 40p yard. Also cheap towels and tea towels.

Gloucester Rd: ORIGINELLE, No. 107. T 373 4833. Mixture of well-cut French and Italian classic fashions for day and evening wear, silk shirts and well cut trousers and range of pretty feminine Liberty-print dresses and co-ordinates.

WAREHOUSE, No. 101. T 373 5712. (See Earls Court Rd.)

EARL'S COURT exhibition centre, Lillie Rd. Sun market 9am–2pm, clothes, souvenirs, antiques.

BUYING FOOD

Earls Court Rd: TIRANTI, No. 38. T 937 3895. Old-fashioned top-class grocery. Full range of delicatessen: smoked salmon, English and Continental cheeses, cold meats, salamis, range of unusual salads, fresh crusty bread, coffee beans and freshly ground

coffee. Wines and self-service groceries.
BEATONS, No. 151 T 370 1020. Very
best plain English crusty white bread
(supply Tiranti), cakes and pastries.
BESTWAY DELICATESSEN, No. 206.
T 370 1490. One of many Indian-run
delicatessen/supermarkets in Earls
Court Rd that stays open until 10pm
closed Sun. Sells a little of everything
at inflated prices.
KASHMIR STORE 16 Kenway Rd.
T 373 8722. Oriental grocery, excellent
range of spices sold by the ounce.
Old Brompton Rd: CONNOISSEUR,
No. 255. T 373 9131. Delicatessen,
English and Continental cheeses,
salads, cold meats and salamis, pâtés,
olives and a range of fruit and veg-
etables. Open Sun.
CHELSEA DELICATESSEN, No. 11.
T 584 3825. English and Continental
cheeses, salamis and cold meats,
homemade pâtés, olives, coffee beans,
French bread and wine. Also groceries
and provisions.
Bute St: ARTHUR, No. 24. T 584
0740. Continental delicatessen with a
wide range of salamis that hang in
the window, cold meats, smoked fish,
French bread, preserves, fresh coffee
and a range of groceries.
MAISON VERLON, No. 12. T 584 0485.
Croissants, brioches, French and
English loaves, Piece Monte – cakes
which tell a story – are their speciality
and stunningly intricate cakes with
fountains and waterfalls. Also Austrian cheesecake, Black Forest cake,
Verlon Tarte with fresh cream, white
wine and grapes. Use only pure wines
and liqueurs.
DAQUISE, 20 Thurloe St. T 589 6117.
Delicious cakes and pastries baked on
the premises. Especially good: strawberry or apple tart, doughnuts, cheesecakes and fresh cream cakes. Also
reasonably priced licensed restaurant
serving Polish and Russian specialities.
Open all day until midnight seven
days a week.

KEEPING AMUSED

PARIS PULLMAN 56 Drayton Gdns.
T 373 5898. First alternative cinema
to show late-night movies seven days
a week, Friendly, young atmosphere,
mainly foreign films. £1·20, student
reduction to 90p on Mon, Tue. 249
seats, late show 11.05pm.
BACKSTREET CLATTER (Horse-drawn
carriage tours). T 584 7387. Seven-mile
tour of London, relating history from
George II to World War I, and
viewed from the only private carriage
other than Her Majesty's, resplendent
with footman and liveried driver.
Commentary is folksy and factual,
perfect for tourists or local trivia
buffs. Examples: Queen Victoria was
4ft 9in on Coronation Day, and the
pointing out of Mr Crapper's residence,
the man who invented the flush toilet.
£8 per person for 1½ hour circular
journey.
NATURAL HISTORY MUSEUM Cromwell
Rd. T 589 6323. Talks on subjects
relating to natural history held most
Tue–Thur, plus Sat at 3pm in Lecture
Theatre (past the Giant Squid, down
the crocodile and snake hall). Admission free. All lectures illustrated by
colour slides or films. (All museums,
see What to See and Good for Kids.)
SCIENCE MUSEUM Exhibition Rd.
T 589 6371. Tue and Thur lectures at
1pm relate to particular collections,
Sat 3pm talks concern a specific
technological subject. All free, and
held in the Large Theatre (turn right
at 1896 diesel engine). Sept Sat lectures
only. Scientific films shown in the
basement Small Theatre at 1pm
Wed–Sat.
GEOLOGICAL MUSEUM Exhibition Rd.
T 589 3444. Current 2.30pm series of
demonstrations, lectures and films
ends 3 Sept. Autumn sessions resume
Tue 4 Oct. Programme available in
foyer.
CHRISTIE'S SOUTH KENSINGTON Old
Brompton Rd. T 581 2231 Approx

ten auctions a week, viewing two days prior to sale. 10.30am and 2pm. General schedule: Mon, silver and watercolours; Tue, jewellery; Wed, furniture and English, Continental pictures; Thur, Oriental works of art; Fri, photographs. Open Mon–Fri 9am–5pm; Mon until 7pm.

EARLS COURT EXHIBITION BUILDING Warwick Rd. T 371 8141. Largest seated arena in Europe, over one million square feet exhibition space. Regular venue for major rock concerts and showcase for most large trade fairs (Menswear Fashion, Motorcycle and Motorfair Shows, etc.). Public welcome to most trade fairs.

TROUBADOUR COFFEE-HOUSE 265 Old Brompton Rd. Twenty-five-year-old meeting place for the artistic or merely hungry. Music seven nights a week (jazz, folk) in the rather grubby basement, poetry Mon. Beginning around 9pm, 20p–£1. Ground floor eating area is cosy and cheap. Oddly, with all those coffee pots in the window serves only cappuccino, but it *is* tasty. Open noon to midnight.

NATIONAL POETRY CENTRE 21 Earl's Court Sq. T 373 7861. From mid-Sept Poets-in-Person readings on Fri 7.30 pm. 50p. Publish guidebook siting different poetry 'haunts'.

LONDON APPRECIATION SOCIETY 17 Manson Mews. T 370 1100. Visits to places of interest in capital and organized lecture tours. Concentrating on London's history, culture and modern attitudes. Open to any age group.

GOOD FOR KIDS

NATURAL HISTORY MUSEUM Children's centre for drawing and making models, materials provided, and there are two teachers to help with projects. Centre also produces Nature Trail leaflets for different age groups so you can follow a particular theme round the museum. Open Sat and school holidays 10.30am–12.30pm and 2–4pm. Models

– dinosaurs, etc. – leaflets, postcard and reproductions on sale at the bookstall. (All museums, see What to See and Keeping Amused.)

GEOLOGICAL MUSEUM 'Journey to the Planets' exhibition is great fun. You go into a room shaped like a spaceship and really get the feeling you're flying among the stars and planets. 'Pebbles' exhibition – explains how they are formed, how to identify them, ideas for painting and making things.

THE SCIENCE MUSEUM Children's gallery is full of fascinating gadgets and dioramas – test the speed of your reactions, look through a periscope, watch working models of wood and water-wheels, see if you're colour blind, etc. At the small theatre near children's gallery films every day at 12.30pm suitable for younger children and at 1pm Wed–Sat scientific films – slightly more technical. Shops sells cards, books, etc. and very good posters – excellent value.

BADEN-POWELL HOUSE Queen's Gate. Scouts and Guides might be interested in 'The Baden-Powell Story' a permanent, free exhibition on the ground floor (rest of the building a hostel for Scouts, etc. visiting London). Includes B-P's sketches, relics of the Relief of Mafeking, his collection of strange walking-sticks, etc. Outside the building is a slightly ludicrous statue of the Great Man, shorts and all.

ICE DREAM 212 Fulham Rd. Good place for a summer birthday treat. The walls are decorated with kids' paintings and smiling ice-cream cones. They sell huge, delicious sundaes, sorbets, etc. and first-course food.

HOW TO GET THERE

UNDERGROUND South Kensington, Gloucester Rd, Earls Court, West Brompton.

BUSES 14, 30B, 31, 39A, 45, 49, 74, 74B.

Wimbledon

In the eighteenth century, the Swedish botanist Linnaeus knelt down
and thanked God for 'the good and glorious sight' of the silver
birch and oaks of Wimbledon Common. In the nineteenth century,
the luckless poet Leigh Hunt, who used to drink in the Rose and
Crown with Swinburne, was ravished by the springtime gorse: 'a
veritable Field of Cloth of Gold'. Civil servants homing in on the
5.22 from Waterloo may well feel, as William Pitt used to do, that
they were coming out to the countryside. 'I will be with you before
curfew,' Pitt wrote to his great friend William Wilberforce, 'and
expect an early meal of peas and strawberries.'

The local harriers now use the stables of Wilberforce House as
their headquarters and the view across to the windmill remains
unchanged. Indeed my grandfather, who kept a dairy in the Ridgway
in the nineties, would not feel out of place if he were to return and
trot down the High Street in his burnished Ben Hur milk float.
The mansions on which he waited three times daily have been
converted into flats; Eagle House (1613) is now offices. But Ashford
House (1720) is still there and the eighteenth century cottages with
their Victorian and Edwardian shop fronts survive even though their

functions change with bewildering rapidity. Gone the milliners boot-makers, oilmen, saddlers, and cornchandlers. The shops now have cryptic names like Bojangles, Triad, Pennybee, Tootsies, One and a Half and Nutshell.

The chiming clock on the old Fire Station now tolls the knell of passing TIR juggernauts belching black smoke through the fan-lights of the Wong Pao and Rawalpindi restaurants. The horse trough at the top of the hill sprouts wallflowers, but there's still a smell of fresh bread from the baker's, and there are horses in the livery stables beside the Dog and Fox. The village still has its pond, its cattle pounds and its pubs. The highwaymen have gone from Putney Heath but footpad stoats still lie in wait for rabbits and the badgers tunnel still beneath the gorse.

Derek Cooper

WHAT TO SEE

LAWN TENNIS MUSEUM All England Club, Church Rd. Opened 1977 for Centenary Championships, claims to be unique. Interesting exhibition illustrates history of the game, with emphasis on Victorian, Edwardian and pre-war greats. Tue–Sat 11am–5pm, Sun 2–5pm. Restricted opening during Championships. 30p (pensioners and children 15p).

ST MARY'S St Mary's Rd. Flint-faced church by Sir Gilbert Scott, incorporating earlier buildings. Cecil Chapel has exquisite stained glass from fourteenth and sixteenth centuries, seventeenth century armour and black marble tomb of Viscount Wimbledon. Warrior Chapel has manuscript of the verse 'They shall grow not old . . .' given by the poet Laurence Binyon.

WINDMILL MUSEUM Windmill Rd, Wimbledon Common. Built 1817 by local carpenter, houses small permanent exhibition on use and history of windmills. Sat–Sun 2–5pm, 10p (5p children). Baden-Powell wrote part of 'Scouting for Boys' in the Mill House. (See Keeping Amused, Good for Kids.)

ROLLS-BENTLEY (1935 3½-litre) displayed as a fund-raiser for research into Parkinson's Disease, on Broadway pavement near Town Hall.

ST MARK'S St Mark's Place. Interesting modern church by Humphrys and Hurst, 1968–69. Pentagonal in shape with abstract windows by local artist on theme of Creation.

CAESAR'S CAMP. Wimbledon Common. Earthwork 300 yards in diameter has footpath running through the middle and golfers everywhere else. May have been stronghold of Cassivellaunus, scene of his last stand against the Roman legions in 54 BC, or possibly even older. Nearby Caesar's Well has even less to do with the noble Julius; has also been called Robin Hood's Well, now says 'H. W. Peek MP 1872'.

WHERE TO EAT

Even if the rest of the world associates Wimbledon with nothing but tennis and the Wombles, the restaurants here give scant attention to either of these phenomena; like everything else in Wimbledon Village the restaurants are steadfastly conservative; standards are what matter, not tricksy names and decors. The best eating-out is reliable and unadventurous, the locals naming among their favourite restaurants two which belong to Joe Lyons and one which belongs to the Pizza-Express chain. Sample prices are for average three-course meal for two with house wine. Open for lunch and dinner seven days a week unless otherwise indicated.

High St: FISHERMAN'S WHARF, No. 36. T 946 6773. Specializes in fish, as indicated by name and nautical decor (yards of expensive new rope swathed round central pillars, and many ship's lanterns). Expensive but reliable both for cooking and service, being one of J. Lyons chain. Jimmy Connors ate here. £15.

TOOTSIES, No. 48. T 946 4135. Wimbledon's hamburger and fast food place, good for families and the young, handy for the Common. Budweiser beer and Schlitz, special milk shakes. Breakfasts any time, continuous meals noon–midnight, Sun 12.30am–11.30 pm. £5.

CAFÉ ROYAL, No. 72. T 946 0238. Manageress Connie here for many years; an old fashioned friendly restaurant. Very good sauces and homemade soups, duck a speciality. £16. Closed Sun.

PIZZAEXPRESS, No. 84. T 946 6027. Same as all PizzaExpresses, good, clean, jolly, fast, pleasant service. £4.

LONDON STEAK HOUSE, No. 18. T 946 8377. Like all Steak Houses, belongs to Lyons; consistently good and reliable. This one, which is air-conditioned, has been here twenty years and so has one of the waiters (others have been here almost as long). £10–£13.

LEMON TREE, No. 8. T 947 6477. Opened in 1977, with pretty vernal colour scheme and a bright bistro-type menu listing unusuals like noisettes d' agneau village, poularde St Herbon. Special Sun lunch. £18. Closed Mon.

WIMBLEDON TANDOORI 26 The Ridgeway. T 946 1797. Not the only Indian restaurant hereabouts, but the favourite. Clean, friendly, courteous. Quiet at lunch but busy at night. Specializes in tandoori food, including king prawn. Also take-away. £6–£7.

SAN LORENZO FUORIPORTA 38 Worple Rd Mews. T 946 8463. A branch of the San Lorenzo in Knightsbridge. Nicest place to eat on a hot sunny day because half the tables are in a very pretty garden shaded by limes and sycamores. Excellent Italian food, and unchanged since opened in sixties. £12–£14. Very popular for family Sun lunch.

Picnics

Wimbledon Park is attractive and civilized, but wilder, scratchier land on the Common provides free blackberries.

WHERE TO DRINK

CROOKED BILLET On road also called Crooked Billet off West Side Common. Large neo-rustic Young's pub with jukebox, but also has intimate corners. Bar food, also Loose Barn restaurant open for lunch and dinner except all Sun and Mon night. Clientele mainly local.

HAND IN HAND Crooked Billet. Pretty, cottagey free house with country atmosphere, e.g. shove ha'penny in low-ceilinged bar with pine benches round walls. Young's and Ruddles ales. Also country wines including elderberry and damson. Tables outside; sandwiches, etc.

FOX & GRAPES Camp Rd. Large civilized Courage place with speedy service and mixed custom. Muzak.

KING OF DENMARK 83 Ridgway. A smallish Courage pub with a pleasant garden at the rear, giant filled rolls and real draught bitter.

THE SWAN 89 Ridgway. Like the Denmark next door, The Swan is but a short jaunt from Wimbledon Common. It's an uprated Watney's pub, cheekily decorated in Young's livery, with a games room tucked at the rear where younger clients brush up on their pool, video games and darts. Small but excellent choice of hot and cold meals.

ROSE & CROWN 55 High St. Voted 'Pub of the Year' in 1970, this 300-year-old Young's house has character oozing out of the walls and a beautifully kept drop of special bitter gushing from the taps. Ivy-enveloped yard at the rear for outdoor types.

DOG & FOX High St. Vast complex includes restaurant and two bars and there's live music with Terry Seymour's Big Band on Sun evenings. Like most of the better Wimbledon inns, it's a Young's house.

WARREN'S WINE BAR High St. Very pleasant little place with good food that's some 50 per cent cheaper than its Central London contemporaries and a very fair house wine.

WHERE TO SHOP

Wimbledon Village is perched on top of a hill. Shops are a mixture of long-established family-run concerns and smart new boutiques. More down-to-earth shopping is at the bottom of the hill around the station.

High St: WIMBLES, No. 39a. T 947 4899. A mixture of crafty made things: dried flower pictures, pottery, prints and lampshades and bamboo and cane furniture. Wide range of basketware. Specialize in made-to-measure cane furniture and lampshades.

TOM ALLEN INTERIORS, No. 38b. T 946 7404. Tom Allen specializes in wall coverings with an unusual finish – grasspapers, corks, silks, suede, hessians and linens. He also keeps an enormous range of English and imported fabrics. French visitors find it cheaper to buy French fabrics in his shop than in France.

SKIDS, No. 33a. T 946 2556. Colourful, sturdy, fun children's clothes. Brightly decorated window can't be missed.

LLOYDS, No. 64. T 946 6723. Large choice of secondhand and antiquarian books on most subjects. Room full of children's antiquarian books which can be viewed on request.

HILL BOOKSHOP, No. 87. T 946 0198. Small village bookshop with a reasonable selection on most subjects. Good children's section.

KITCHEN DRESSER, No. 14. T 946 4973. Wide range of cookware including the French Le Creuset range and French pottery. Also cane and basketware and decorative but functional items for the kitchen.

J. F. EWING, No. 11. T 946 4700. Comprehensive range of antique jewellery in the £3–£1000 price range. Also old and antique silver pieces.

TRIAD, No. 2. T 946 4559. Gifts and stationery: Scandinavian glass, English china, modern jewellery.

PANACHE, No. 70. T 947 4200. Every village seems to have one – a good quality dress agency where only the best in secondhand clothes and casserole dishes. Can also sit down to drink their coffee.

GALERIE AZIZA 7 Church Rd. T 946 4727. Large elegant gallery with international reputation. Carpets, paintings, objets d'art.

THINGUMMIES 32–34 Ridgway. T 947 5369. Owners run British Toymakers Guild. Handmade toys – for children and adults – and craft goods.

BUYING FOOD

High St: THE COFFEE SHOP, No. 38a. T 947 5341. Six blends of coffee freshly roasted on premises. Melita system and filter papers. Also a selection of exotic teas and handmade domestic pottery – jugs, mugs and casserole dishes. Can also sit down to drink their coffee.

EXPRESS DAIRY, No. 34. T 946 9421. Established in 1864 and retains original shop front. No external changes are allowed, so much so that when they modernized inside they had to knock a hole in a side wall to get in the new fridges! Range of dairy produce and groceries.

RUDMAN, No. 71. T 946 4251. All fresh fish in season displayed on the slab. Shellfish, game and poultry in season. Closed at lunchtimes.

VILLAGE STORE, No. 21. T 946 2383. Excellent small supermarket with large selection of delicatessen at the front of the shop. Salads, pâté, cheeses, salamis and cold meats. You'll recognize the shop by the enormous whole Swiss cheese in the window.

GOURMET & GOBLET, No. 93. T 946 1084. Cullens the grocers re-vamped shop. Range of specialist groceries, freshly ground coffee, comprehensive range of cold meats and Polish and French sausage, Continental cheeses, and delicatessen counter. Also wide range of wines, spa waters and fruit juices.

R. B. GRAVESTOCK, No. 9. T 946 3774. Mr Gravestock runs a family bakery where all breads are baked on the premises. Make French sticks, but specialize in English loaves – farmhouse bread and wheatmeal loaves. Small range of cakes and buns.

VILLAGE PANTRY, 4 Church Rd. T 946 7834. Cramped corner grocery with a good selection of preserves and herbs, also small selection of salamis and cold meats.

KEEPING AMUSED

TENNESSEE COUNTRY CLUB 267 The Broadway. T 542 4600. One of Britain's foremost country and western venues.

George Hamilton IV, Tammy Wynette played here, with their sequinned costumes on the wall to prove it. 250 seats face the 'Grand Ole Opry' stage, with immediate free membership, but no buying spirits until three days' clearance period. Live music Wed–Sun, entrance fee varies. Closed Mon.

WIMBLEDON THEATRE The Broadway. T 946 5211. One of the larger theatres (1800 seats), with four bars and facilities to present ballets and operas. Usual programme includes touring musicals and plays, with the occasional celebrity Sun concert. 90p–£2·25.

TIFFANY'S DISCO 111–115 The Broadway. T 542 3869. This (one of many) Tiffany's aims for a grotto effect with hanging fishnets and imitation seaweed Live music Tue, Fri, Sat; 18–30-year-old ravers asked to don 'smart casual wear'. Mon–Thur 8pm–midnight, Fri–Sat 8pm–2am. 80p–£1·70p, cheaper weekends before 10pm. Licensed bar, food. Capacity 550.

ANNEXE GALLERY 45 Wimbledon High St. T 946 0706. Unpretentious little gallery on one corner of the Common, holding monthly exhibitions ranging from art students to established painters. Proprietor with *Private Eye* connections offers running commentary of news, views and local gossip. Open daily 10am–6pm, Sun 11am–4pm.

Wimbledon Common:

WINDMILL MUSEUM Houses scale models and photos detailing how windmills work. Future plans include exhibitions of photos taken on the common and establishing a general museum of local interest. Admission 5p children, 10p adults. Sat and Sun 2–5pm. Closed Dec–March. (See What to See.)

GOLF COURSE Camp Rd. T 946 0294. Green fee for eighteen-hole par 72 course is £1·50 for the day. Bring your own clubs. Payment includes use of clubhouse for bar and snacks. No

women's changing room, so ladies – come prepared. Open 9am to 5pm on Mon, 9am until dusk Tue–Fri.

HILCOTE RIDING SCHOOL 24b High St (rear of Dog and Fox Hotel). Riding on Common, where there are sixteen miles of bridlepaths, Tue–Sun 8am–8.30pm, earlier return during winter. £3.50 per hour weekdays, £4·50 weekends. Placed in groups according to ability. Hilcote stables twenty-one horses. T 946 2520.

DENINA 9 Church Rd. T 946 3898. Ladies' salon. Beauty treatments include facials, manicures, pedicures, waxing. Cabin sauna £1·75, body massage £4. 9.30am–5.30pm.

JOHN EVELYN MUSEUM Lingfield Rd, Ridgway. T 946 7017. for details. 'History of Wimbledon' collection pre-historic to present, organized by John Evelyn Society. Sat only 2.30–5 pm, admission free.

FURNEAUX GALLERY 23 Church Rd. T 946 4114. Living British artists. Open Thur, Fri, Sat. 10am–6pm.

WIMBLEDON STADIUM Plough Lane. T 946 5361. Bars and restaurant overlooking events. Greyhound racing every Wed–Fri 7.45pm, plus occasional Mon. Speedway Thur 7.45pm March–Oct. Stockcar racing Sat 7pm March–Nov. Solarium men and women 10am–11pm, seven days a week. 90p per twenty-two minute session.

WIMBLEDON BATHS Latimer Rd. T 542 1330. Two pools (one covered in winter for badminton, archery) plus council-run sauna.

Swimming adults Mon–Fri 18p, weekends 22p; children Mon–Fri 9p, weekends 11p. Mon, Tue, Thur, Fri, Sat 9am–7.30pm; Wed closes 6pm for family bathing, Sat family bathing in teaching pool; Sun 8–10am summer, closed winter. Sauna 90p, sun-ray lamp treatment 50p. Mon 11am–7pm men only; Tue 11am–7pm women only; Wed 9am–2pm men, 2–8pm women; Thur, Fri 9am–2pm women, 2pm–7pm men; Sat 9am–7pm men only.

GOOD FOR KIDS

POLKA 240 The Broadway. T 542 4258. Toy exhibition and puppet museum (including famous Lanchester Collection), puppet-making can be seen in workshops, Mon–Fri 9.30am–5.30pm. Also Children's Theatre, ring for details.

WIMBLEDON COMMON. Famous for ponds, good for skating in the winter and model boats in the summer. 1000 acres of heather, bracken and silver birches are perfect for riding: ponies can be hired from Hilcote Stables, 24b High St (T 946 2520). (See What to See and Keeping Amused.)

STOCKCAR RACING Wimbledon Stadium, Plough Lane. T 946 5361. Sat 7pm, Mar–Nov. 75p or 50p, £1·50 or £1·20 for adults. (See Keeping Amused.)

BAGATELLE, No. 79. T 946 7981. Quality toys for children up to the age of twelve. A little bit of everything.

HOW TO GET THERE

BR Wimbledon from Waterloo or Holborn Viaduct.

UNDERGROUND Wimbledon, Southfields, Wimbledon Park.

BUSES 57, 77A, 77C, 93, 131, 155, 200, 293.

Acknowledgements

Village London was co-edited by Margaret Comport and designed by Leslie Jessup.

Research for What to See, Good for Kids and How to Get There by Sarah Howell and Liz Strauli; Where to Eat by Susan Campbell, co-author of *Cheap Eats in London*; Where to Drink by Mark Williams; Where to Shop and Buying Food by Lindsey Bareham, Sell Out and Food Editor of *Time Out* magazine; Keeping Amused by Martha Ellen Zenfell.

While every effort has been made to ensure the accuracy of the contents of this book at the time of going to press, the publishers cannot be held responsible for errors.